UNNATURAL RESOURCES

HISTORY OF THE URBAN ENVIRONMENT

Martin V. Melosi and Joel A. Tarr, Editors

UNNATURAL RESOURCES

ENERGY AND ENVIRONMENTAL POLITICS

IN APPALACHIA

AFTER THE 1973 OIL EMBARGO

MICHAEL CAMP

UNIVERSITY OF PITTSBURGH PRESS

Published by the University of Pittsburgh Press, Pittsburgh, Pa., 15260
Copyright © 2019, University of Pittsburgh Press
All rights reserved
Manufactured in the United States of America
Printed on acid-free paper
10 9 8 7 6 5 4 3 2 1

Cataloging-in-Publication data is available from the Library of Congress

ISBN 13: 978-0-8229-4571-0
ISBN 10: 0-8229-4571-1

Cover art: *Closeup of an Old Coal Company Mining Town of Red Ash Virginia, near Richards in the Southwestern Part of the State (1974)*, by Jack Corn. From DOCUMERICA: The Environmental Protection Agency's Program to Photographically Document Subjects of Environmental Concern, 1972–1977.
Cover design: Melissa Dias-Mandoly

CONTENTS

ACKNOWLEDGMENTS

As all historians know, published books are the result of the efforts of many.

I would first like to thank the members of my dissertation committee at Emory University—Joseph Crespino, Patrick Allitt, and Thomas Rogers—for their advice and input into the process of preparing the dissertation manuscript on which this book is based. I would also like to thank additional members of the Emory faculty—especially Jeffrey Lesser, James Roark, and Elena Conis—for help at other stages of the process. I am also grateful to graduate student colleagues, including Colin Reynolds, Scott Libson, Louis Fagnan, Danielle Wiggins, Andrea Scionti, Chris Brown, Carrie Crawford, Sean Byrnes, and Glen Goodman, who provided comments and suggestions on the manuscript as well as invaluable friendships. Thanks also to the staff in the Department of History for assistance in navigating the university environment; special thanks to Katie Wilson for her tireless efforts as well as for being a fantastic hiking partner.

Archivists at the Jimmy Carter and Gerald Ford presidential libraries, the National Archives at Atlanta, the University of Tennessee Special Collections Library, and the Howard H. Baker Jr. Center for Public Policy provided important research assistance. Thanks to the Gerald R. Ford Presidential Foundation and the Laney Graduate School for research funding. Thanks also to Cambridge University Press for permission to reprint portions of the introduction and chapter 2, which previously appeared in the *Journal of Policy History,* and to the Johns Hopkins University Press for permission to reprint portions of chapter 3, which previously appeared in *Technology and Culture.*

I am also grateful to Stephen V. Ash for sparking my interest in historical research at the University of Tennessee. I have pinpointed the satisfaction experienced while completing my undergraduate thesis under his direction as the moment when all of this really got started. Thanks are due also to Adam Green and James Sparrow for continuing the process at the University of Chicago, where they commented on my master's thesis on the 1982 World's Fair and energy exposition in Knoxville.

Thanks also to supportive colleagues at the University of West Georgia's Irvine Sullivan Ingram Library, including Blynne Olivieri, Shanee' Murrain, and Catherine Hendricks.

Sandy Crooms at the University of Pittsburgh Press guided this project to completion, and I am grateful for her help. Thanks also to the two anonymous reviewers for providing trenchant and insightful comments on the manuscript.

On a personal note, Beth, Greg, and Anna Jones provided a pleasant respite from the university atmosphere in Atlanta. I met Shari Wejsa near the end of completing my dissertation manuscript, and that changed everything.

This book is dedicated to my parents, who have been with the project since its beginning, and who have been a source of essential support much longer indeed than that.

All remaining errors in the manuscript are my own.

UNNATURAL RESOURCES

A JOKE TOLD TOO MANY TIMES

On a 16 June 2010 episode of *The Daily Show*, host Jon Stewart played a clip of President Barack Obama proclaiming the need for America to pursue a bold new plan to reduce dependence on foreign oil. Stewart followed the clip with scenes of all of Obama's predecessors back to Richard Nixon making similar statements about the need to make big changes in America's energy economy. The joke was clear: decades of doomsday warnings about US dependence on oil from unstable parts of the world had yielded no practical outcomes. Stewart's segment came within the context of a recent event that pointed to one possible reason for this frustrating continuity in presidential rhetoric—namely, the blowout on the Deepwater Horizon oil rig in in the Gulf of Mexico. While attempting to increase domestic production of oil, this disaster eventually released nearly five million barrels of oil into the gulf. Subsequent reports indicated that faulty equipment and inadequate testing had increased the possibility that danger might occur. Public protest in the Gulf region and across the nation decried the apparent recklessness of the BP oil company, which had played a large role in the blowout and subsequent poisoning of the gulf.[1]

As the Deepwater Horizon calamity indicated, the two goals of producing more energy and protecting the environment, both popular public policy goals on their own, can come into stark, and sometimes disastrous, conflict. Politicians attempting to address this tension must pay close attention. When energy supplies tighten, public concern for the environment can diminish, but when environmental catastrophe strikes, consumers often proclaim the need for increased protection. The hierarchy of these two priorities in public opinion has not always been clear; often, it has seemed that the more pressing of the two receives higher priority at any given moment.

The Deepwater Horizon explosion and oil spill was hardly the first time that the priorities of energy policy and environmental protection conflicted. This book explores a major turning point in the history of this tension. The story begins with Richard Nixon. After nascent debates about potential resource scarcity emerged in the 1960s, the 1970s brought full-blown crisis. When the United States supported Israel in the Yom Kippur War against Egypt in October 1973, OAPEC (the Organization of Arab Petroleum Exporting Countries), a subset of OPEC (the Organization of Petroleum Exporting Countries), began steady cutbacks in oil exports to the United States as punishment.[2] Decreasing supply, combined with domestic price controls that kept the price of domestic oil artificially low, led to shortages and lines of angry motorists waiting hours for the fuel needed to complete their daily routines. For most Americans, this was the first sign of the vulnerability of the nation's energy supply. It was also a key moment in the history of American consumption, American politics, and American culture.[3]

Nixon promised a bold response, yet the White House plan was diffuse. The oil crisis occurred just as Nixon was dealing with emerging revelations that eventually became the Watergate scandal. Though Nixon did announce an initiative called Project Independence to secure the nation's energy future, few of its components received serious legislative consideration. Nixon's successor Gerald Ford inherited the proposal. Ford pushed for and signed the Energy Policy and Conservation Act in December 1975, which created the Strategic Petroleum Reserve and established conservation standards for appliances and automobiles, but this initiative fell far short of the goal of achieving "energy independence."

Jimmy Carter, who believed that the United States was being both immoral and foolish by consuming too much energy and putting its security at risk, took the effort to formulate a national energy policy to a new level. Carter created the federal Energy Department to centralize the nation's energy policy. He mounted an extensive public relations campaign to convince Americans to use less energy in order to decrease the need for foreign sources. Many Americans, disillusioned by the Watergate cover-up and the controversial pardon of Nixon, embraced the Washington outsider's claims about the need for a new way forward. For a time it appeared that Carter might succeed in establishing a coherent national energy policy, thereby removing the threat of future 1973-style crises.

Yet by the end of Carter's term, his presidency was in shambles. In 1979 another oil price spike slowed commerce, and Carter seemed powerless to solve it. Though Carter proposed a few ideas to mitigate at least some of the economic suffering, it seemed that the nation had stopped listening. The Department of Energy spent the bulk of its time and money maintaining the nation's nuclear weapons stockpiles, not implementing a centralized national energy policy. Former California governor Ronald Reagan, who until that point had seemed like a right-wing extremist unfit for national office, defeated Carter in a landslide in 1980 to take back the White House for the GOP.[4] Reagan advocated much *less* government involvement in the energy sector. The private sector needed to take free rein of the nation's energy future, he declared. Furthermore, candidate Reagan expressed skepticism about the environmental regulations that had enjoyed broad bipartisan support during the environmentalist wave a few years before. Something had happened in the intervening years to transform American political thinking about the relationships among energy, the environment, government, and business. Just what that was is the focus of this book.

The Carter presidency was a time of dramatic reconfiguration of thought about the relationship between energy and the environment. Energy is a historical concept that involves numerous places, spaces, and power interests. The processes of production and consumption involve corporations, small businesses, laborers, consumers, environmentalists, and other interest groups. Policies also affect the landscapes from which energy supplies emerge and upon which they are used. Carter's energy policies affected all of these diverse components of energy systems in unexpected ways, as the policies had wide-ranging consequences beyond what he or his advisers could predict or manage. They intersected with a number of other public policy issues of the late 1970s, including the deregulation of American business, the increasing popularity of market-based thinking in economic and political discourse, the uncertain future of American organized labor, and the emergence of the American Sunbelt. The story of energy in the late 1970s both affected and was affected by these other major narratives about America in the 1970s. The result of the changes in these complex relationships was a more skeptical and ambivalent attitude toward both environmental protection and government intervention in the economy to secure energy supplies.

This book begins by revising our understanding of Jimmy Carter's political problems in the field of energy policy by broadening the scope of analysis. The current consensus about Carter and energy focuses on the 1977 bill creating the Department of Energy, zeroing in on Carter's troubles with Congress. In these accounts, an arrogant and tone-deaf Carter fights a losing battle with an assertive and independent legislature. William Chafe, in a survey of the post–World War II United States, claims, for example, that "instead of going to Congress, enlisting the expertise and ideas of relevant committee chairs, and drafting bills that reflected their views, Carter created an energy task force made up of *his* experts." Carter's energy bill "reflected the insights of wise men whom he, as steward of the country, had mobilized," Chafe writes sarcastically, and he attributes Carter's political failures to Congress's determination to be neither strong-armed nor condescended to.[5] Somewhat more charitably, Garland A. Haas portrays Carter as a tragic figure who faced circumstances and opponents beyond his control, but he still locates the roots of his energy policy problems in his relationship with the legislature. "[I]t is hard to imagine how any president facing the same issues and two Congresses as intractable as the Ninety-fifth and Ninety-sixth," says Haas, "could have succeeded."[6]

This is an unconvincing way to account for Carter's troubles in formulating energy policy. Many historians have indeed made the opposite argument about Lyndon Johnson, attributing LBJ's domestic political successes to his refusal to leave policy in the hands of a fractious and disagreeable Congress. Though LBJ may have simply been better at glad-handing and applying political pressure to get legislators to do what he wanted, Carter's comparatively less savvy capabilities still do not fully explain his challenges in governing. As John Dumbrell has pointed out, Carter's ability to get major government reorganization legislation creating the Department of Energy through Congress was a significant accomplishment in itself.[7] The striking decline in Carter's popularity and public image cannot be located in these congressional antagonisms alone.

Such arguments ignore broader political and economic contexts, which created challenges that were just as significant as those involved in working through the lawmaking process. Every particular source of energy involved a number of interest groups, each of which had a stake in preserving its place in the broader energy economy. Carter's initiatives affected each of these groups, which often expressed contradictory and irreconcilable positions. Carter's inability to align these conflicting interests provoked much opposition and protest on all sides. His problems were deeply rooted in the vast complexities of the American energy economy, especially the complicated local politics involved at myriad sites of energy production across the country.

As a close analysis of these interest groups, this book also portrays energy as a historical concept rooted in a particular time and place. Scholars have examined the history of energy from the vantage point of the highest levels of government, detailing the interactions between policymakers and businesses to secure reliable supplies of oil, formulate a workable nuclear policy, and mobilize hydroelectricity as a tool of regional planning and development.[8] These approaches have often paid little or no attention to how the constant daily processes of producing energy affected the politics and identity of localities, or how consumer expectations of cheap and reliable energy shaped policymaking and policymakers' rhetorical strategies. While some more recent works have more thoroughly examined how the installation of nuclear plants shaped local politics and landscapes, they have not gone far enough to investigate how energy can be broadly constitutive of local and regional identity.[9] Regions that contained coal mines, nuclear plants, or hydroelectric dams—and particularly a combination of these—saw their local politics and economics revolve around energy issues, especially after the OAPEC embargo.[10] National policies pursuing energy security affected the daily lives of those who resided and worked in these areas of intensive energy production.

This is a study, ultimately, of national politics and local impacts. The first chapter analyzes changes in national thinking about energy issues in the 1970s. The next four chapters use events that occurred in East Tennessee and the broader Appalachian region as examples to illustrate the interrelationships among policymakers, interest groups, and local identity as national policies played out on a local level. East Tennessee is home to the quasi-public Tennessee Valley Authority, the Oak Ridge National Laboratory, and the nationally controversial Tellico Dam. It also lies adjacent to major coal-producing regions of West Virginia and Kentucky where the United Mine Workers of America union was strong, regions highlighted in national discourse as recently as Donald Trump's 2016 presidential campaign. The relationship between East Tennessee and the federal government in the 1970s was especially reciprocal: East Tennessee played a major role in Jimmy Carter's energy agenda, and congressional representatives from the area emphasized East Tennessee's energy identity to gain national attention. Two Tennessee senators, Howard Baker and Bill Brock, ascended to powerful positions—Baker to the post of senate majority leader and Brock to the head of the Republican National Committee—that allowed them to shape policy and political rhetoric surrounding energy. The multiple interests within and outside the region competed for the benefits that could be derived from harvesting and mobilizing the region's energy resources, and Carter's inability to reconcile the goals of these clashing entities helped create the perception that his energy agenda had failed. Aligning all of these conflicting interests was impossible, yet Carter's failure to do so damaged not only his public image but also the very idea that government could play a constructive role in resolving the nation's energy challenges.

These failures were key to the surprising emergence of deregulatory, antigovernment politics at the end of the 1970s. At the beginning of the decade, the liberal regulatory state was at high tide in the United States. On the heels of Johnson's Great Society, Nixon presided over the creation of the Environmental Protection Agency and the Occupational Safety and Health Administration, along with the passage of the Clean Air Act, Clean Water Act, and Endangered Species Act. These laws invested power not just in centralized bureaucracies but also in citizen groups and localities that could bring their concerns before the judicial system. They therefore broadened the reach and power of government regulation of the economy. Furthermore, starting with the crippling inflation of the early 1970s and increasing with the oil embargo, Nixon instituted a schedule of price controls on wages, raw materials, and consumer goods throughout the

American economy. Adding these diverse measures to the existing regulatory structure of the Progressive Era and New Deal brought the regulation of private business in the United States to an all-time high.[11]

The 1973 oil crisis by itself was not enough to overturn this paradigm. The crisis, as many historians have noted, did indeed represent a significant blow to many ideas taken as self-evident since the end of World War II, including the reliability and security of key resources. Yet in the wake of the embargo and oil crisis, the idea that a deregulatory, private-sector approach would emerge predominant was far from obvious. As Meg Jacobs has noted, government had addressed and in many cases solved all major issues of the twentieth century thus far, including war, depression, civil rights, and labor unrest. Many people assumed it could do the same with the energy crisis.[12] Indeed, Nixon's immediate response to energy turmoil in the early 1970s took the form of complex, mandatory rationing schemes and price controls on domestically produced crude oil.

It appeared that government was primed to step in to fix this problem, too, and for a time it did. The price controls on oil continued—despite some executive opposition—through the Ford years and most of the Carter administration. Though Ford made a few forays into government subsidies for domestic energy production and conservation incentives, Carter took these ideas to a new level. Carter created a Department of Energy to encourage, incentivize, and even compel American consumers to use less energy in their daily lives. He also gave regular speeches emphasizing sacrifice and a reduction in standards of living for the sake of preventing another energy crisis from ever happening again.[13]

Carter told the nation that shared sacrifice, combined with a significant mobilization of state action, would prevent disasters like 1973. Though living with lower standards was inconvenient, he said, it was ultimately necessary for long-term sustainability. Yet only a few years later, the Iranian revolution and hostage crisis brought back the intense consumer pain suffered during the first oil crisis. In the minds of many casual observers, it appeared that Carter's agenda had failed and that the political space was open for an alternative, which the anti-regulatory right wing of the Republican Party provided. Ronald Reagan and the GOP Right rejected the idea that energy security required either government action or consumer sacrifice, and argued that these measures were in fact impeding the nation's ability to reduce its dependence on foreign oil. They claimed that removing price controls from oil and getting the government out of the business of managing energy resources would allow the mechanisms of the market to choose the best path forward. Allowing the market to determine energy prices would incentivize producers to increase production in a way that could not happen with controlled prices, and market primacy would ensure that consumer dollars naturally flowed to the energy sources produced most cheaply and efficiently.

Americans did not need to resign themselves to a future of reduced expectations, Reagan said, because these policies would generate an era of abundance. That Carter initiated price decontrol, and that Reagan merely spoke more forcefully about its benefits and sped up the decontrol schedule, were facts rarely mentioned by Carter's political foes. Some basic deregulatory ideas indeed had widespread consensus and seemed to be commonsense measures when paired with a broader strategy involving conservation, which is the agenda Carter pursued. Under Reagan, however, deregulation became not one piece of the puzzle, but rather a blunt instrument in a broader ideological attack on big government.

Though Reagan spoke of deregulating energy and allowing the private sector to pursue the alternatives that seemed most promising, there was another dimension to the deregulatory politics of these years. It had to do with the aforementioned slew of environmental legislation passed under Nixon. As Meg Jacobs notes, "the expansion of regulation on business between 1970 and 1976, when Republicans controlled the White House, was as great, if not greater, than what had occurred during previous periods like the Progressive Era or New Deal." The conservative appeal to get "government off our backs," which had been part of GOP rhetoric for decades, gained traction only in this this world of growing regulation.[14] Yet left out from Jacobs's analysis is exactly *how* conservatives proved successful in depicting regulation as an insidious force prone to overreach and abuse. The search for a cure for inflation in the 1970s helped build support for deregulation in the circles of academic economics, with economists writing about the virtue of marginal-cost pricing to allow the most efficient firm to triumph in the marketplace, and some policymakers pursued this agenda in the legislature.[15] However, the circulation of ideas in academia does not explain why the idea of regulation came to have such a negative connotation in everyday American discourse.

Part of the answer has to do with the conflict between environmental quality and energy production. As Patrick Allitt has pointed out, environmental protection is something that societies must choose to "buy"—in other words, choosing to forgo economic development and other possible priorities for the sake of the environment. Societies, especially the United States, generally tend to do so only when other basic needs are met and a decent standard of living has been achieved.[16] The environmental legislation of the early 1970s triumphed in a generally healthy macroeconomic climate, at least in terms of unemployment. When the oil embargo created a structural economic problem that imparted fear and uncertainty to American consumers, they became less likely to support environmental laws. When environmental statutes began preventing initiatives for increased energy security, many people began to reconsider the usefulness of these laws. Republicans began speaking of environmental protection as a goal achievable not by government mandate, but by making sure that businesses pursued a careful "balance" between industrial production and the quality of the surrounding environment. Though this rhetorical strategy had questionable intellectual coherence—what would be given up in order to maintain "balance" between energy and environment was often vague—the second oil crisis in 1979 guaranteed the demise of Carter's conservationist approach.

The visceral impact of energy crises, which hit American consumers squarely in their pocketbooks by increasing the cost of driving their cars and heating and cooling their homes, *does* explain the popularity of deregulation among Americans ill equipped to understand complex economic concepts, and also among those who cared little for the financial health of large corporations and industries. The backlash against environmental regulation accelerated this anti-government trend and gave it ideological coherence. The energy crises of the 1970s helped usher in an era of bipartisan support for deregulatory, anti-government politics.

Prior to the second crisis, Carter himself backed away from unqualified support for environmental regulation. For example, he signed amendments in 1978 that limited the power of the 1973 Endangered Species Act and proposed an Energy Mobilization Board authorized to override state and local regulations. Americans in the early 1970s had voiced support for the idea of protecting the environment, yet when applied to specific cases, environmental laws could yield outcomes that seemed to defy common sense. In this context, the very idea of the virtue of government action to maintain energy supply and protect the environment came under intense scrutiny and skepticism. Reagan accelerated and amplified the deregulatory agenda started under Carter, discarding the accompanying pleas for conservation and replacing them with promises of future abundance.

Like any major political shift, the weakening of environmentalism in the late 1970s was incomplete. Building on the achievements of the late 1960s and early 1970s, environmentalism did continue to enjoy some political successes during the Carter and Reagan years. The Clean Air Act and Clean Water Act remained especially popular in public opinion. Americans across the political spectrum credited these laws with improving the quality of American air and water over the course of the 1970s, and many Americans appreciated how they helped to clean up the spaces where they lived and worked on a daily basis.[17] Indeed, a Reagan White House attempt to weaken the Clean Air Act in late 1981 failed in the face of opposition from the majority Democrats in Congress, who believed that supporting the law would help them perform well in the 1982 midterm elections.[18] Nevertheless, despite some sporadic victories, the examples in this book demonstrate that the energy problems of the era also led to several major policy defeats for the environmentalist cause. The conventional wisdom favored erring on the side of having too much energy in the future rather than too little, with the environmental consequences remaining a subordinate concern.

A JOKE TOLD TOO MANY TIMES

CHAPTER 1

"LITTLE BITTY CARS"

The Department of Energy, Oil Decontrol, and the Anticonservation Backlash

The first public inklings of unease about America's energy economy appeared at the beginning of the 1970s. As American demand for oil had steadily increased through the 1960s, domestic production had concurrently been declining. This led to nascent fears in the 1960s about potential problems of coming resource scarcity. By 1970 the trends of increasing demand and decreasing supply meant that the nation could no longer produce enough domestic oil to sustain its current patterns of consumption. As oil prices slowly rose, national periodicals slowly began to examine the problem, but these gradual trends were virtually imperceptible to most American consumers. The few political leaders who engaged the issue disagreed both on its cause and on the best mix of solutions to address it, and without much concern among the public, politicians did nothing.[1]

Two years later, the problems on both the supply and the demand sides began to come into clearer focus. In 1972, resulting from shortages and price hikes engineered by foreign oil producers, crude oil prices in the United States began to increase much more noticeably. In June of that year, *Time* reported with alarm its discovery that the US demand for energy was doubling every fifteen years. The United States was consuming fifteen million barrels of oil per day, the magazine noted, but domestic production was currently only ten million barrels per day. Estimates showed that it would rise to only eleven million per day based on current reserves—not nearly enough to meet rising demand. The idea that the nation's energy security would only worsen over time led to concern among government officials. Interior Secretary Rogers C. B. Morton warned in 1972 that the nation could need to import half of its oil by 1985, and Undersecretary of State John Irwin II was even more pessimistic, claiming that the critical point would come as early as 1980.[2]

A severe energy shortage in the winter of 1973 brought the first major attention by the public. By January 1973, the prospective crisis that had seemed like a fantasy was becoming more real. According to *Time* magazine, "in scattered sections of the nation there were cold schools, unfilled jet-aircraft tanks, empty propane containers and a hasty scramble among high state officials to arrange emergency delivery of precious fuels." The periodical doubted that the nation's energy problems would somehow sort themselves out, arguing that the basic problem of soaring demand for oil "must somehow be slowed" in order to stabilize the American energy economy.[3]

On Yom Kippur in October 1973, during a disagreement over the fate of the Sinai Peninsula, Egypt struck Israel in a surprise attack. After a few days of fighting, a desperate Israel asked the United States for assistance. Secretary of State Henry Kissinger and Defense Secretary James Schlesinger agreed that the United States should supply aid but decided that any such support must be covert to avoid jeopardizing oil imports from Arab nations. US planes therefore would land at night, unload supplies for the Israeli military, and leave by daybreak. On 14 October, though, due to crosswinds at an airfield in the Azores, the transports delayed a half day and did not land until daytime. The immense white star on each transport signifying its US affiliation was visible to all observers, most importantly Egypt and its allies.[4]

The Arab nations decided to use energy supply as a tool of punishment, instructing their respective oil ministers to raise the price of oil by 70 percent, which they did on 16 October. The next day, the chief Iraqi delegate to the meeting proposed an even more radical idea: a total oil embargo against the United States and other nations friendly to Israel. Though the other ministers did not assent to such an extreme move, they did agree to cut production by 5 percent each month until Israel was contained within the borders agreed to in 1967 at the end of the Six-Day War. The United States received the "most severe" cuts of the graduated embargo. Panic quickly followed.[5]

Near the end of 1973, the Nixon administration—with a mandate from Congress—organized the Federal Energy Agency (FEA), which was authorized to determine allocations of petroleum products across the country.[6] The FEA's allocation plans, which included emergency rationing, hoped to balance the wide-ranging interests of small refiners, large refiners, distributors, and consumers. However, the managed shortage of oil alarmed American consumers who saw drastic disruptions to their regular habits. With the FEA's allocation plans in place, the most visible symbols of the embargo became the lines that appeared at gasoline pumps around the country. Not long after the embargo's onset, with oil rising steadily in price and the government rationing domestic oil, retail gasoline prices climbed by 40 percent, leading to shortages and lines of angry motorists waiting hours for the fuel needed to complete their daily routines.[7] Oil companies made huge profits during the crisis, which enraged suffering American consumers (although many of their profits were made in the Eastern Hemisphere, which was virtually unaffected by the embargo).[8]

The crisis in foreign affairs transformed the slow decline of energy reliability earlier in the decade into an outright disaster. As prominent energy analyst Daniel Yergin noted in retrospect, "the shortfall struck at fundamental beliefs in the endless abundance of resources" for postwar Americans. The embargo and the broader problems it caused "were an abrupt break with America's past, and the experience would severely undermine" public confidence in the future.[9]

To decrease US reliance on foreign oil, Nixon proposed Project Independence, a program to encourage conservation measures, increase reliance on nuclear energy, and encourage production of synthetic liquid fuels from coal and shale.[10] Also included was final approval of the Alaska oil pipeline, which had faced fierce environmentalist criticisms, and the president proposed that Congress exempt power plants from a number of environmental regulations. Nixon's clear ambivalence toward environmental regulation galvanized the coal industry to speak out against the Clean Air Act. Indeed, according to one historian of Nixon's environmental policies, the incentives for production in Project Independence dwarfed the encouragements for conservation, which were mainly limited to voluntary carpooling and thermostat lowering ideas.[11]

While Nixon was taking these steps, Egyptian and Israeli officials worked to resolve the conflict between their nations. As initial progress proceeded on the Arab-Israeli dispute and tensions began to dissipate, producers began to look to longer-term consequences of the embargo, and they did not like what they saw. President Anwar Sadat of Egypt urged an end to the embargo, arguing that the United States would assist only minimally in the cause of Middle East peace while under its penalties. He also believed that, if allowed to go on for too long, the embargo would eventually damage American relations with countries like Saudi Arabia and Kuwait, which would only hurt those nations in the long term. The Saudis in particular had never approved of the scale of the price increase, since it was not in their interest to perpetuate the cycles of recession and inflation that would be stimulated by further spikes in oil prices. Higher prices, they had concluded, would also spur conservation and the development of alternative energy sources, which would diminish the market for oil in the long term.[12] With the Saudis leading the way, the Arab nations relaxed the embargo in March 1974.

Some energy reformers took the embargo as an opportunity to stress the necessity of change. In May 1974, *Time* asked if the energy crisis could have been "a blessing in disguise" that could alert Americans to the current unsustainability of energy. It reported on a recent energy conference held in Williamsburg, Virginia, where prominent speakers argued that the embargo had "awakened Americans to long-festering energy troubles and started them thinking about solutions." Treasury Secretary William Simon told the conference that the United States had to increase domestic supplies of energy while curbing the growth in demand. The conference attendees clearly hoped that the panic at the pump of 1973 would compel Americans to recognize the structural problems inherent in the nation's production and consumption of energy.[13]

Yet for many Americans, as the foreign affairs crisis began to subside, so did the anxiety of high prices and the fear of shortages. Senator Jennings Randolph (D-WV), chairman of the Senate's Public Works Committee, "had his doubts" that the embargo would yield a lasting effect on the American psyche. On a recent road trip, the Senator said, he had conducted an experiment to determine the percentage of drivers who were exceeding the national 55 mile-per-hour speed limit, which was intended to reduce gasoline usage. He found that no fewer than 63 percent of all drivers were breaking the law. Americans' disregard for the speed limit was, for the senator, symptomatic of a more general disengagement from energy problems. Congress and the Nixon administration each remained "extremely reluctant" to impose mandatory conservation measures like gasoline rationing and taxes on energy-intensive machines, content instead to allow consumption patterns to return to pre-embargo levels.[14]

Ford tried to fold energy concerns into his broader economic strategy. His major domestic goal was to WIN, or Whip Inflation Now. With inflation running at about 12 percent annually and with unemployment at 5 percent, Ford made a pitch to Americans to stop wasting resources, fuel foremost among them. Given that oil was an essential input for both industrial production and transportation, Ford argued that more energy troubles would undoubtedly exacerbate inflation.[15] Ford attempted to persuade the country to voluntarily use less energy, imploring Americans to cut their driving to 5 percent fewer miles, which he claimed could save 250,000 barrels of foreign oil per day."[16]

Few Americans, though, heeded Ford's admonitions. They were busy enjoying the cheaper gasoline available after the embargo's end. Much of the public also became outraged a few months after the crisis when it learned that oil companies had profited enormously from it.[17] Because oil companies drilling in the Middle East split oil profits with their host governments, OAPEC's price increases brought higher profits to companies working in the region. These immense corporate profits reaped during the embargo allowed conservation-averse Americans to come up with an alternative narrative of the energy crisis, namely that oil companies had artificially created the problem in order to enrich themselves. In this version, corporate greed, not excessive consumption, was to blame, and thus changes in personal consumption habits were not necessary. Although Ford

"LITTLE BITTY CARS"

pursued several energy ideas, including a form of Nixon's Project Independence, few came to substantive fruition.[18]

Although Richard Nixon and Gerald Ford had proclaimed the necessity of energy conservation after the oil embargo, Jimmy Carter took the federal government's commitment to conservation initiatives to an entirely different level. He believed that the oil crisis was symptomatic of a much larger problem, namely that natural resources were running out, and that future energy shortages would be even worse than 1973. The cornerstone of Carter's energy policy was the establishment of a cabinet-level Energy Department to encourage Americans, through an extensive public campaign and a slew of new government programs, to use less energy in their daily lives. Carter coupled this formal policy initiative with regular rhetorical warnings that the sustainability of continued economic growth was in doubt. No longer could Americans use more and more energy every year, Carter argued; they would instead need to engage in acts of self-sacrifice and cut back on individual energy use in order to achieve collective energy sustainability. Altogether, the measures created a national energy policy more comprehensive than any that had come before.

Yet some Americans rejected Carter's admonitions. They denied that resources were running out and therefore rejected the idea that energy sustainability required drastic cutbacks in personal consumption. These Americans demanded that the federal government do more to secure energy supplies for the future, or that it get out of the way of private businesses. Other Americans were initially more receptive to Carter's warnings and accepted the idea that conservation might be necessary in order to achieve energy security. However, the Iranian hostage crisis of the late 1970s greatly damaged Carter's ability to convince the public of the necessity of his energy plans. Carter had promised that conservation and more responsible energy use would bring stability to energy markets, but by late 1979, Americans found themselves facing yet another horrendous national crisis.

As problems seemed to pile up with no solutions in sight, the Republican Party's conservative wing used the energy crisis to advance long-held ideas about the overriding importance of market solutions and the tragic inefficiencies of government planning programs. Denying the necessity of sacrifice and conservation, these market fundamentalists instead advocated for deregulating energy entirely, allowing the mechanisms of the free market and the creativity of the private sector to solve the nation's energy problems.

Market fundamentalists had to confront one major obstacle to exalting the righteousness of deregulatory politics. The 1960s had witnessed several landmark events, bookended by the 1962 publication of Rachel Carson's *Silent Spring* on one side and the Santa Barbara oil spill and the ignition of the oily Cuyahoga

River in Cleveland in 1969 on the other, that helped form a new environmental consciousness within the broader public.[19] Through the course of that decade, the human impact on ecosystems, including the effects of energy production and consumption, emerged as a major public concern. Always willing to exploit the prevailing political winds, Richard Nixon created the federal Environmental Protection Agency (EPA) in 1969. Environmental regulations, including the Clean Air Act, Clean Water Act, and Endangered Species Act passed in the early 1970s with broad bipartisan support, and 1970 was the inaugural year of the Earth Day celebration. Direct assault on environmentalism, especially in the early 1970s, was thus not a viable political option.

Republicans came up with a different strategy. While initially conceding to the potent political power of environmentalism, the GOP gradually turned against it as part of the embrace of energy deregulation. As Republicans increasingly criticized government regulation and cheered market-based solutions, they—especially those running the party's political apparatus—developed the strategy of using vague suggestions that energy development and environmental concerns could be "balanced" through careful mobilization of market processes. As Carter's conservationism increasingly appeared to have failed, Republicans spoke more forcefully about the power of market processes to keep the environment clean and guarantee abundant energy again. They began to cast the environmental movement, which had generally enjoyed wide respect since the early 1970s, as a radical force that was unwilling to make commonsense compromises that would get energy flowing to American consumers again. They also criticized federal laws protecting the environment as unreasonable constraints on business, and they argued that allowing the market to work would generally keep the environment clean, since the power of public opinion, not coercive federal laws, was the best way to regulate businesses' potentially damaging effects on the environment.

For Republicans, the rhetorical trope of "balance" was essential to their energy ideology. Businesses engaging in excessively dirty practices and unreasonable environmentalists each represented an equal threat to American life. Republicans generally offered few clues as to how this "balance" would function in practice, especially when energy production and environmental protection came into irreconcilable opposition. However, because most Americans did not understand the incredible complexity of America's energy economy and its relationship to environmental protection, the Republicans' strategy achieved wide political resonance despite its incoherence.

The GOP coupled its skepticism for environmental regulation with advocacy for decontrolling energy prices, especially the price controls placed on oil by Richard Nixon. Carter himself began his presidential term by proposing a quasi-deregulation of oil prices, but the initiative was defeated in Congress. During the Iranian Revolution, Carter redoubled his efforts to decontrol the price of oil in order to spur conservation, and he succeeded in instituting a schedule of gradual decontrol designed to ease companies and consumers into an unregulated marketplace without any major disruptions. Gradual decontrol was not acceptable to GOP presidential candidate Ronald Reagan, who advocated immediate decontrol of oil prices in order to create enhanced incentives for production. Taking advantage of the gradual and barely noticeable schedule of decontrol under Carter, Reagan downplayed Carter's deregulatory impulses in public statements and claimed that he, if elected, would come to the rescue of the private sector and release energy producers from the shackles of government regulation. American consumers responded and voted him decisively into office, though Carter's and Reagan's oil policies shared some overlap. Once in office, however, Reagan and the market fundamentalists transformed Carter's targeted deregulation into a more wide-ranging attack on government itself.

Environmental regulations and price controls are two very different types of government intervention into the marketplace. Yet both came under intense criticism and political attack in the late 1970s in the wake of multiple energy crises. Republicans and business interests argued that environmental protections were too broad and were harming the American standard of living. The discrediting of Carter's conservationist ethos, closely tied to respect for the environment and skepticism about the sustainability of perpetually increasing economic growth, helped allow the GOP's more antagonistic characterization of environmental regulation to gain traction in political conversation. Both Carter and Reagan agreed on the need to remove price controls on oil. The decline of environmentalism, coupled with the bipartisan acceptance of price deregulation, helped usher in an era of market-based thinking in American energy politics.

CREATING THE ENERGY DEPARTMENT

Though the 1976 campaign's major issues included cleaning up Washington after the Watergate scandal, fighting the Cold War, and especially addressing economic stagnation and inflation, Carter made energy a major priority upon taking office. Instead of thinking of energy as one public policy issue among many, Carter saw it as *the most* important facet of domestic policy, because energy functioned in every aspect of modern life ranging from homes and cars to factories and railroads. Carter especially thought that government had to step in to secure energy supplies, not only because of its connection to everyday economic and social life, but also because he believed that the world was running out of oil and gas. A comprehensive national policy, he insisted, was essential.[20] In addition to his emphasis on energy's economic centrality, there was also a moralistic dimension to Carter's energy focus. He thought that natural resources were a divine blessing and that humans had a responsibility to use them wisely. Americans, he believed, had been wasteful and profligate to the point of wickedness in their pursuit of individualized consumption. He was determined to alert Americans to their sins of excess and set the United States on a new course of righteousness.[21]

In fact, contrary to Carter's beliefs, resources—especially oil—were not in danger of imminent depletion.[22] Carter, along with much of the environmental movement, took the disaster of 1973 as proof that the world was running out of oil, thereby committing the logical flaw of casting a man-made event—a purposeful embargo—as evidence of natural limits. Nevertheless, the new president's focus on reforming energy remained paramount. He brought in James Schlesinger as an adviser in anticipation of the creation of a cabinet-level Department of Energy, which Schlesinger would head upon its establishment. Having served on the Atomic Energy Commission, and after subsequently skirmishing as secretary of defense with Henry Kissinger in the Ford administration, Schlesinger was one of the very few in Carter's team with substantial understanding of the realities of Washington politics. Most of Carter's other senior staff members had, like the new president, spent their careers in Georgia. They were inexperienced in the ways of national policy making.[23]

Carter's views on energy became apparent soon after his election, as he seemed to take every opportunity to articulate them publicly. A few days after taking office, at a briefing on natural gas legislation, for example, Carter spoke about his vision of the nation's energy future more broadly. He asked every American to lower the thermostat setting in his or her home, adding, "I must say to you quite frankly that this is not a temporary request for conservation." The nation's energy problems would not be resolved within a mere few years; "further sacrifices," the president said, "may be necessary." Carter exhorted all Americans "to cooperate in minimizing the adverse effect on the lives of our people." The next day, Carter informed a group of Pennsylvania students that Americans would have to learn to do without various things to which they had become accustomed, speaking of "small sacrifices" that all would have to share. Just before the two-week anniversary of his inauguration, Carter told the public, "I know that we can meet this energy challenge if the burden is borne fairly among all our people."[24] Practically all of Carter's early speeches on energy, which he famously dubbed the "moral equivalent of war" at the beginning of his term, echoed these austere themes.[25]

Schlesinger quickly developed skepticism for Carter's approach. As he later recounted, Carter, who had come to power promising to clean up government in the wake of Watergate, had a fresh attitude that was a double-edged sword, reflecting as it did a lack of experience in the rough-and-tumble of national pol-

"LITTLE BITTY CARS"

itics. Schlesinger noticed in Carter an immense intelligence and "a very quick mind" that, while allowing him to obtain a quick grasp on a wide variety of issues, also encouraged him to get involved in more activities than he should have. After determining that energy was the most important domestic policy priority, Carter attempted to tackle a number of other unrelated issues at the same time. He was unable to prioritize issues effectively and pursue them in a strategic manner, instead trying to solve a wide array of problems at once.[26] The White House's organizational structure, in which the lack of a chief of staff caused Carter to repeat the same conversations with a number of senior aides who drifted in and out of his office, also caused immense difficulties.[27]

In 1977, the first year of his presidency, Carter convinced the Congress, controlled by Democrats, to take up the task of creating a new federal Department of Energy with the main aim of encouraging conservationist goals. His strategies in constructing the department quickly drew criticism from members of his own administration. Before the department's formal establishment, for example, Schlesinger pulled select personnel out of the Federal Energy Administration (the re-named former Federal Energy Agency) and the Energy Research and Development Association (ERDA, established in 1975 to manage nondefense government nuclear programs) to form a proto-department and formulate a federal energy policy. Schlesinger, though, was outside the normal flow of the White House's domestic policy staff and thus had great trouble coordinating with other policy makers. Carter wanted Schlesinger's conclusions to remain secret until their rollout. At a practical level, though, entities like the Treasury Department, which would be affected by the establishment of new tax credits and other incentives, had no knowledge of or input into the plans. The ninety-day timeline to finish a proposal was, in domestic adviser Stuart Eizenstat's view, "inordinate."[28]

Perhaps of most importance, Eizenstat noted energy's minor role in the 1976 campaign: "And here we were putting together on a crash basis something that was going to become a centerpiece of Carter's domestic policy, and a centerpiece of his Presidency, when it had not reached the level of public attention as even being an issue."[29] Carter saw the president's proper role as that of a "public trustee," a chief executive who needed to avoid taking sides in disputes among special interests. Rather than act like the parochial members of Congress, who were concerned only about their groups of local constituencies, Carter believed he needed to make decisions with all of American society in mind. The by-product of this attitude, however, was that Carter did not see a need to persuade Americans and their elected representatives of the morality and virtue of his plans. He could simply act as he saw fit, he thought, ignoring the provincial desires and wishes of legislators. In a democratic society in which the public needs to be convinced of the necessity of major government action, however, this attitude slowed the movement of Carter's agenda through Congress and his ability to marshal public opinion.[30]

Once completed, Schlesinger's proposal called for a tax on all domestic oil production, a surcharge on automobiles that failed to meet federal minimum fuel efficiency standards, mandates for public utilities to switch to coal consumption from oil and gas, and tax incentives to encourage conservation. Carter declined to pursue oil company divestiture. Though he had supported divestiture during the 1976 campaign, once in office he generally accepted the argument that large, integrated companies were necessary to achieve optimal efficiency. Furthermore, he knew that passage of his energy bill would require marshalling the broadest possible support, including that of oil companies. The reorganization part of the plan proposed to consolidate the FEA, the ERDA, the Federal Power Commission (established in 1930 to handle licensing of hydroelectric projects), and several other smaller agencies under unified control. Carter presented the proposed bill to Congress and the public in mid-April.[31]

Public opinion on Carter's plan proved mixed. A Gallup poll in September found that 44 percent of the public approved of Carter's energy efforts, with 39 percent disapproving. A third claimed that the plan called for an "about right" amount of public sacrifice. Twenty-eight percent claimed that it called for too much, and another 28 percent claimed that it did not call for enough, nearly a three-way split. Though these numbers showed a sharp divergence in public opinion on Carter's specific plans, 38 percent of the public described the energy situation as very serious, and 43 percent described it as somewhat serious, indicating that Carter had at least some success in making energy a major public policy issue again. Only 15 percent of Americans claimed to be doing nothing to reduce their energy use, and another Gallup poll that same month found 66 percent approval for Carter's general performance thus far in office. After the national trials of Vietnam and Watergate, many seemed willing to give their new president some breathing room to implement his vision for the country's future, even given his moralizing exhortations for Americans to rethink their daily consumption. Four months after its initial unveiling, Carter's energy bill passed the House by a substantial margin.[32]

Yet the bill stalled in the Senate. One of the major points of contention was a mechanism designed to wean the nation from oil called the Crude Oil Equalization Tax (COET). The tax would have affected refiners, who presumably would have then eventually passed the cost down to consumers in the form of increased pump prices and home heating bills. With prices higher, Carter believed, consumers would use less energy. Though mimicking decontrol in many respects, this plan was not precisely the same thing. Carter held to his view that formal price controls should remain in effect so long as oil prices remained subject to

OPEC manipulation. The COET would still control the price of oil, allowed to rise no faster than the general rate of inflation. Sensitive to any increased taxation of the oil industry, southern Democrats from oil and gas producing states, especially the Senate Finance Committee's Russell Long of Louisiana, defeated the COET in Congress.[33]

In the time between House and Senate consideration of the bill, Congress also found that public support for the bill had declined significantly. Greg Schneiders, a member of the White House communications staff, thought he knew why. Having had more time to consider the proposal, the public would probably not be receptive to the idea that the nation was running out of fuel, he said. "There is significant disagreement among experts on this point," and furthermore, there were no longer any visible gas lines or rationing orders to compel alarm. "The public likes to think that technology will bail us out—and it might well." After the collapse of lengthy negotiations between the House and the Senate in May 1978, House Speaker Tip O'Neill threatened to divide the proposal into five separate bills. In October Congress finally sent Carter an energy bill, but one that emphasized tax credits instead of new taxes to provide incentives for conservation, and one without the COET. Carter somewhat reluctantly signed this National Energy Act into law, and he formally appointed James Schlesinger as the Energy Department's first head.[34]

REPUBLICAN RESPONSES

The Republican response to Carter's first plan was quite varied. Many Republicans conceded that energy consumption was too high but rejected the idea that government should lead the way in solving the problem. Other Republicans, especially those who believed in the importance of market solutions, presented forceful opposition to Carter's energy program. The rising prominence of the conservative wing in the party's public messaging campaign held significant implications for the party's self-identity.[35]

The GOP response to Carter's plan in the US Senate largely conceded to Carter's description of the energy problem. Calling the energy struggle "a fundamental crisis that threatens the American way of life," the Senate Republican Energy Initiative in 1977 generally agreed with Carter's characterization, foreseeing continued summer lines at gas stations, increased inflation, and shortages of food and agricultural problems. The plan included continued federal funding for solar research, demonstration, and commercialization as well as tax credits for the installation of solar heating, cooling, and hot water systems. It favored reducing the time to build and license nuclear power plants, along with an expedited program to develop uranium resources on public and private lands. Most significantly, the plan conceded that ending "unwise use and excessive consumption" of energy by Americans would be necessary.[36]

The approach was similar in the House of Representatives, with Republican members in the minority asking for deregulation of natural gas prices, provision of funds for mass transit, synthetic fuel development, and highway maintenance. House Republicans' main complaint related not to substance but to procedure. They angrily denounced the fact that the Democratic bill, running at around five hundred pages, emerged from the House Ad Hoc Energy Committee in less than three days, which to them meant that sufficient scrutiny was absent. The bill's content itself, though, received minimal objection. The House Republicans sought to position their proposal as moderate, claiming that both the Republican and Democratic plans agreed on the general goals of both reduced energy consumption and better use of natural resources.[37]

The tone of the Republican Party's statements targeted toward the public was markedly different. Anticipating the 1978 midterm elections, the party's electoral arm used the energy issue to draw a distinction with Carter. In June 1977, the GOP ran a "special broadcast" on the NBC television network, featuring some of its most promising rising stars, to criticize Carter's plans. The GOP's different factions united in the general belief that tax reduction could be the main catalyst of economic growth and opportunity, and that government regulation was almost invariably a stranglehold on business that caused more damage than it prevented. Unsurprisingly, much like most congressional Republicans, they castigated taxes meant to compel reduced consumption. However, they went even further in their criticism of Carter, denying the existence of excessive energy demand altogether. Representative Jack Kemp of New York, a former Buffalo Bills football player, claimed, "People in America work nearly five months of the year just to pay their taxes on the federal, state, and local level. It's obvious to me and quite obvious to the people I represent in western New York that we don't need higher taxes, we need lower taxes. . . . They also know that raising taxes on energy will not create one new barrel of oil."[38]

Governor Ronald Reagan of California, who had posed a stiff right-wing challenge to Gerald Ford in 1976 for the Republican presidential nomination, argued, "For the average family, the President's program could eventually cost over $1000 a year in new federal taxes. . . . Let's face it. This isn't an energy program. It is a tax program with the extra cost for gasoline and family-size cars amounting to the biggest tax increase in our history, over $70 billion a year."[39] The goal of Carter's tax policies was to disincentivize consumption, but Kemp and Reagan assumed that consumption would remain constant. They did not expect Americans to have to give up anything in their daily routines. Kemp and Reagan both disagreed with the idea that American energy demand was too high, and they characterized the tax increases as misguided government coercion against American families. Compelling consumers to decrease demand, whether voluntarily or through taxation, they argued, would do nothing but siphon capital out of the cycle of production and innovation, which could best solve energy problems.

Bill Brock, a former US Senator from Tennessee, appeared in the special too. After losing his seat in the 1976 election due to questions about his personal income taxes as well as a general post-Watergate backlash against Republicans in that cycle, Brock had assumed the post of Republican National Committee chairman.[40] He had marked himself as a strong partisan with an affinity for combative rhetoric throughout his Senate term. Equating the "erosion of our liberties" with "the growing power of federal regulatory agencies," Brock had once declared the federal government the main threat to freedom. In the energy special, although he spoke positively of the general idea of conservation, he concurred with Reagan and Kemp that it "should be achieved not through high taxes" to decrease consumption but instead through investment in mass transit, improvements in auto efficiency, and tax credits for home insulation. Brock did not address the difficulties of getting many Americans to accept mass transit without a tax on gasoline to raise the price of driving for consumers, and he ignored the fact that increased automobile efficiency usually came only through government mandate. Also like Reagan and Kemp, Brock extolled the possibilities for new fuel supplies, mainly fossil fuels. "Production of oil and gas, natural gas, coal, nuclear energy," Brock claimed, "all of them will be available to us in greater abundance if only the government will back off and allow producers greater opportunities to go after them."[41]

Notably absent from Brock's exhortations, as well as those of the other speakers, was a recognition that many of the regulations they deplored had only recently been put in place to protect the environment from the potentially harmful effects of energy production and consumption. Whether considering the impact of burning carbon-rich coal on the atmosphere, the potential for spilling oil into the ocean ecosystem, or the challenge of finding somewhere to store nuclear waste until it no longer posed a threat to human life, the extraction and use of energy sources was a very complex process. The simple demands to decrease regulation and increase supply did not adequately recognize this complexity. Carter's energy approach stood on the assumptions that both energy production and consumption, like all economic activities, involve trade-offs among competing values, and that environmental quality is one of them. The deregulatory ethos—and especially the later proliferation of the rhetoric of "balance"—obscured this fact.

In fact, to take Brock as an example, GOP views on the relationship among energy production, energy consumption, and the environment had often been difficult to discern. A 1974 press release from Brock, for instance, publicized an "unbelievable amount of duplication and overlap" in water pollution programs, claiming that water pollution research was being conducted and supported by at least twenty-five bureaus and offices in twelve government departments. Brock clearly saw such coverage as inefficient, and in 1975 on the Senate floor he deplored the fact that antipollution regulations would cost $60 billion per year by the 1980s.[42] For Brock, in the abstract, having multiple departments regulate pollution was a wasteful setup that impeded the efficiency of energy production and distribution.

In December 1974, though, Brock had called for the preparation of a comprehensive environmental impact statement concerning a proposed strip mining facility near Kentucky Lake in West Tennessee's Henry County. He expressed concern over the possible effects that strip mining might have on the lake especially, claiming that the lake was "critically important to Tennessee for its recreational facilities, and anything that might detract from its recreational value must be carefully examined." Brock asked that the Tennessee Valley Authority, the Bureau of Outdoor Recreation, and the Fish and Wildlife Service all participate in preparing the statement.[43] The slew of regulatory agencies that represented waste and inefficiency in theory became, in the case of Kentucky Lake, the guarantors of thorough analysis and action. Republicans were able to cast negative aspersions on the abstract idea of regulation while supporting it in specific, visible cases when it was politically prudent to do so. This obfuscation would allow the GOP to turn the energy issue into a powerful political weapon for use against Carter.

CITIZEN OPPOSITION

Carter enjoyed the usual post-election honeymoon during his first months in office, but it was not long before his approach alienated some Americans accustomed to cheap and abundant energy. Many made their views known to RNC Chairman Brock in letters that revealed voters' frustration with both Carter's policies and the Republican Party's emerging alternative vision regarding energy and the environment. Agnes Anderson, a member of the chamber of commerce in Burley, Idaho, wrote to Brock, for example, in reference to the construction of a coal-fired plant that had been halted because of "a few environmentalists." She castigated environmental regulation as the burden of a few forced upon the many, claiming, "The one thing that burned me up was the fact that a long-haired hippie type environmentalist can walk up and plunk down a $12 filing fee that will stop a multi-million dollar energy construction." She asked Brock what he could do "to get this show on the road, even if we have to breathe coal smoke for awhile, at least we won't be freezing."[44]

"LITTLE BITTY CARS"

Though most Americans did not share Ms. Anderson's cavalier attitude toward the environment, letters written to Brock indicated that the rhetorical strategy of glossing over environmental impact while discussing the virtue of increased energy production was achieving resonance. One Long Island woman wrote to ask Brock, "How, in Heaven's name, can [Carter] suggest that our citizens must sit still for higher taxes on gasoline and other forms of energy in an effort to 'FORCE' conservation and at the same time 'Force' producers and suppliers to forego enough profit so they can increase production which is so badly needed?" Taxes on oil ostensibly helped to account for its "full" cost, including not only the price of the direct environmental pollution created by its use but also the cost of defending foreign oil fields from security threats. This constituent's letter indicated that the image of regulation as a simple manifestation of governmental coercion was working as intended. Echoing GOP rhetoric back to Brock, she also commented, "It has been the all-out government intervention in every facet of our lives during the last 40 years that has caused the economic and social ills from which we are suffering!"[45]

Many constituents also saw Carter's program as a threat to the middle-class suburban ideal that had emerged in the postwar decades, a standard that included a spacious vehicle for personal use.[46] As a Pennsylvania man commented: "It is demagoguery to imply that a limited group of Americans are selfish, unpatriotic, wasteful citizens who are to be penalized for owning an automobile that can transport four to six people in reasonable comfort and safety." Similarly, a woman from Wisconsin asked, "If Mr. Carter is so much for 'women' and 'the family' I'd like him to explain to me why he's trying to get motor companies to make little bitty cars and do away with moderate/big cars." She wanted to know why Carter wanted to eliminate the freedom of choice to buy the size of car "I feel like buying in my future."[47]

Many Americans demanded that policymakers deal with the energy crisis in a way that did not impinge upon their existing standards of living, and Carter's calls to decrease consumption increasingly threatened this expectation. Carter's program was, for some, therefore not an economic agenda but an attack on the American way of life itself. Based on collective social responsibility, his energy philosophy came into conflict with the dominant post–New Deal liberal ethos that emphasized the primacy of citizens as individualized consumers. Although the New Deal had established a vibrant regulatory structure to control the excesses of capitalism, within this framework Americans were encouraged to consume freely in order to keep the economy growing.[48] Carter's calls for sacrifice and self-denial were at odds with the legacy of the New Deal. Recognizing this disjuncture, Brock proclaimed in reply to another correspondent that "the Republican Party has always taken the consumer and individual citizen into account first and for[e]most."⁴⁹ The market fundamentalists kept the New Deal's emphasis on consumption while discarding its regulatory impulses, creating a new vision of how society should function.

The letters that were more hostile to Brock's efforts, especially those coming from self-identified Republicans who distrusted the RNC's claims, demonstrate the complications inherent in the emerging strategy. A Pennsylvania man wrote Brock declaring that he, a registered Republican, was nonetheless convinced that the energy crisis was real and lasting. Further denial of this fact would simply increase the magnitude of the trauma in the future. Readily admitting that his vehicle, a Ford station wagon, was a "luxury" car in terms of gasoline consumption, he suggested that the GOP's rising stars were not acknowledging the new, harsh realities of energy consumption. He claimed not to understand the ideological consistency of the party in its current form, claiming that "a party that is concerned with conservation of our financial resources and preservation of our freedoms" would logically also be concerned with conservation of natural resources as well. Finally, he claimed to support Carter's plans and even argued that they did not go far enough. He ended his letter with a call for bipartisan efforts to ease readjustment to future realities. Brock's reply was a short, generic letter pointing to "differences in method" between Democrats and Republicans and criticizing regulation in general. It did not respond to the specific critiques of the letter.⁵⁰

A letter to Brock from a professor at the University of Massachusetts was even more scathing. He characterized as "cruel hoaxes" the rhetorical tropes of increased production and energy independence. He claimed that, while sounding pleasant in theory, they were unrealistic in light of the "waste and disregard" of American consumption habits. Brock's indignant reply to this missive claimed that conservation, while fine and necessary, was "naïve and sheer stalling" on its own. "What in the dickens are we going to conserve if the means to become independent of the oil cartel are ignored?" asked Brock. Curiously, while listing potential new sources of energy, alongside coal liquefaction and gasification, shale investment, and offshore oil and gas development, Brock mentioned "common sense approaches" to strip mining. Brock gave little indication of what these approaches might encompass, which is especially curious in light of his earlier concern with strip mining's environmental effects in his home state.⁵¹ Brock's responses to these correspondents showed that he and his political allies were largely avoiding the question of what trade-offs would be made in terms of production and environmental protection. They made a calculated gamble that this omission, given apparent consumer anger, would not matter.

Though not often considered a prominent member of the Reaganite political vanguard—likely because he never again held elective public office after losing his 1976 reelection bid—Brock had extolled supply-side economics and castigated Nixon's oil price controls quite early, long before most national Republicans. In June 1973, before the first oil crisis and while still a senator, Brock had asked listeners to "imagine, in a time of critical shortage and immense demand, it not being worth anyone's while to increase the supply. But that's what has happened. The Government has so over-regulated and stifled private initiative that what should be boom-time conditions look more like an era of oversupply."[52] Brock brought his skepticism of government to his new job of creating the party's public messaging.

More importantly, Brock's role as RNC chairman required him to act as conciliator among different factions within his party, and his rather striking adherence to and cheerleading for deregulatory ideas thus demonstrate how markedly that ideology was gaining favor within the Republican Party. It had only been a few years before that President Richard Nixon had established the Environmental Protection Agency and the Occupational Safety and Health Administration with the broad support of his own party. The rapidly rising influence of deregulatory economic ideas within the GOP's public messaging showed just how significantly market fundamentalists' views of the primacy of individual consumer decisions and the perniciousness of government regulation now pervaded the party's self-presentation.[53]

THE IRANIAN REVOLUTION

If Carter's initial focus on energy made slight ripples in public engagement with the issue, the geopolitical crisis that developed later in his administration generated a shockwave. Events through the course of late 1978 and early 1979 again brought energy back into focus as an important national policy issue just as viscerally as in 1973. In late 1970s Iran, rampant inflation squeezed the citizenry. The ruling shah's too-rapid and too-eager push for modernization led to Tehran streets perpetually jammed with traffic, a broken electric grid and blackouts, and an overwhelmed railway system. Although opposition to the shah ranged across the ideological spectrum within Iran, the Ayatollah Khomeini, a politically active fundamentalist who preached the idea of an Islamic Republic under the clergy's strict supervision, emerged as the chief opponent to the shah's programs. His hatred for the shah matched his rage at the United States, which he regarded as the entity responsible for propping up the shah's rule. During the first half of 1978, attacks on fundamentalist demonstrators protesting the shah only served to increase the ranks of those hostile to him. Early September protests in Tehran served as a key turning point, with the burgeoning unrest growing rapidly afterward. By October, strikes and demonstrations paralyzed the country.[54]

As the second-largest exporter of oil next to Saudi Arabia, with production of 4.5 million barrels for export per day, Iran's internal unrest dramatically affected the world's oil economy. Meanwhile, the Carter administration's Iran foreign policy was in disarray, having been preoccupied with the Camp David Accords, arms negotiations with the Soviets, and normalizing relations with China. As the scales of influence within Iran continued to tip in Khomeini's favor, a task force from the Oil Service Company began preparing an evacuation plan for expatriate oilmen and their families at the Fields, Iran's main oil production area. In the middle of December, evacuations began hastily, and petroleum exports from the country had stopped completely by Christmas Day. The revolution in Iran caused a second oil shock and worldwide panic as the uncertainty and instability spurred an upward price spiral. Gas station lines spread again across the United States. In the summer of 1979, they turned violent as consumers reached greater and greater levels of desperation. The nightmare of 1973 appeared to be repeating itself. Rising oil prices and the subsequent ballooning profits accrued by oil companies—from July to September, Exxon became the first corporation ever to earn a billion-dollar quarter profit—infuriated consumers just as badly as they had during the 1973 crisis.[55]

The crisis in Iran again raised the possibility of decontrol, with proponents arguing that this second oil shock demanded a drastic response. No longer could the United States, they said, afford to delay taking action. The OPEC nations would continue to dominate the American consumer indefinitely unless the United States could put itself on firmer energy footing. Recognizing the gravity of the situation, politicians opposed to decontrol reacted quickly to head off the burgeoning talk. In January 1979, potential primary challenger Senator Edward Kennedy (D-MA) gave a speech in New England condemning potential oil decontrol. The senator claimed to favor decontrol in a "free" market but argued that oil was presently sold in a market "controlled by OPEC," necessitating continued price regulation. Decontrol, he added, would mean a doubled average barrel price in the span of less than a year, which would be "nothing short of disastrous" for the New England states, which relied heavily on oil to heat homes and businesses during frigid winters.[56]

Kennedy then moved from regional concerns to a broader indictment of the current administration. Three successive presidencies, including Carter's, he said, had done "nothing" to challenge the hegemony of OPEC. Instead, US leaders had foolishly encouraged the popular belief that the world was running out of oil and thus justified higher prices, a misguided strategy that merely "play[ed] into OPEC's hand." Kennedy proposed the creation of a world oil exploration fund, which would cost the federal government about $33 million per year. The senator predicted that such a fund would add as many as four billion barrels of oil every year to the world oil supply.[57] The senator did little to explain how this fund would galvanize oil discoveries in a different or better way than the profit motive of private oil companies. Carter's aides were keeping files on the Massachusetts senator's public statements in anticipation of a primary challenge, and Kennedy's vague and easy promises of cheaper oil irked the president's staff.[58]

THE WINDFALL PROFITS TAX

Senator Kennedy's strong words notwithstanding, in April 1979 Carter delivered a major energy speech announcing his intention to initiate a gradual decontrol of oil prices beginning in June and ending in late 1981. Carter decided not to decontrol prices immediately, reasoning that during a time of double-digit inflation, such an abrupt change would further depress the struggling US economy. The administration also ruled out both gasoline rationing and mandated Sunday closings of service stations. The phased decontrol came with a "windfall profits" tax to keep oil company profits from ballooning simply because of a change in government policy. The windfall profits tax was in fact not a tax on profits themselves, but an excise tax on every barrel of oil pumped from the ground. Though Carter did not oppose oil companies acquiring other energy producers, he was worried that they would use their increased profits to acquire non-energy businesses like hotels and department stores. The president was determined to ensure that the money be used for reinvestment into further energy development, chiefly new alternative technologies and sources. The windfall profits tax would take a portion of the decontrolled revenues and put it toward federal investment in alternative programs.[59]

Interest groups lined up on various sides of the debate. Activist environmental groups, including the Sierra Club, supported decontrol, reasoning that the higher prices would force Americans to use oil more sparingly, ultimately improving the environment. They tended to favor a tax on oil company profits and urged that consumers, especially those with fixed or low incomes, receive a rebate from these funds. Although conservative Republicans as well as some Democrats from oil-producing states supported oil decontrol as a way to incentivize domestic oil production, they hated the tax, arguing that oil companies did not deserve blame for the consequences of overregulation. Lines at gasoline stations emerged because of government price controls, they said, and punishing oil companies for the government's broken policy was thus unfair. These conservative Republicans deemed the windfall tax excessive, claiming that the increased corporate income tax payments resulting from decontrol would be sufficient to pay for the proposed programs for alternative fuel research, low-income energy assistance, and mass transit.[60]

Consumer advocacy groups firmly opposed decontrol, pointing to the increased prices that would result. They especially castigated the effect decontrol would have on low-income consumers with little leeway for a higher cost of living, arguing that windfall profits rebates would be insufficient to offset the increased daily expenses. A Congressional Budget Office report supported this analysis, asserting that the president's plan would exacerbate both inflation and unemployment while failing to catalyze the amount of oil production that the administration predicted. A June meeting between the president and twenty-seven consumer advocates reportedly turned "argumentative," with former Johnson administration consumer affairs assistant Betty Furness commenting that she had "never heard anyone talk to [LBJ] the way they talked" to Carter.[61] Representative Edward Markey (D-MA) adopted consumer critiques, joining Senator Kennedy to criticize decontrol for its projected effects on New England.[62]

Consumer groups and New Englanders were not the only factions to oppose decontrol. Senator Henry Jackson (D-WA), chairman of the Energy Committee, also expressed his opposition, citing the "nearly out of control inflation" that decontrol would only exacerbate. He also acknowledged that he was in for an "uphill fight," since Carter possessed broad executive authority on the issue of prices.[63] The AFL-CIO, while supporting the "thrust" of Carter's energy security program, opposed decontrol for the effect that it would have on the purchasing power of the working class. Lane Kirkland, the organization's secretary-treasurer, warned that pursuing decontrol would be deleterious for the already strained relationship between the administration and organized labor.[64] The AFL-CIO called for nationalizing the oil companies, never a realistic solution. In what must have worried a Democratic president concerned about a primary challenge, the AFL-CIO coupled its opposition to decontrol with support for Kennedy's comprehensive national health care program.[65]

Carter had rarely been concerned about the public outcries of any particular moment and had pursued whatever policy he thought was in the long-term national interest. This situation was no exception. The multifaceted and myriad protestations of interest groups indeed did little to alter Carter's mind-set, and he pressed ahead with the gradual decontrol plan alongside the windfall profits tax. While consumer groups and New England politicians hammered Carter and strongly advocated keeping the controls in place, Carter faced criticism of an entirely different sort from his own energy secretary. Schlesinger favored immediate decontrol, which he said would allow the price mechanism to bring supply and demand into equilibrium immediately. Though this would generate higher electricity and gasoline bills for consumers in the immediate future, Schlesinger argued, it would be a wise move because of the high possibility of future energy shocks. Schlesinger pointed to the gasoline lines that cropped up around the country in summer 1979, arguing that phased decontrol was failing to prevent crisis. In August, he reiterated his position to Carter and urged decontrol immediately before "frustrating delays and political fall-out of likely gasoline shortages" the next summer. Carter rejected this advice, keeping the phased decontrol plan in place. Though Carter was able to institute the phased decontrol by executive order, it took until November to shepherd the windfall profits tax through Congress against the opposition of oil-state Democrats and conservative Republicans.[66]

Carter's 1979 and 1980 initiatives also contained a group of other ideas designed to increase energy supplies. To spur development, the federal Energy Security Corporation (later renamed the Synthetic Fuels Corporation) would make billions in investment incentives available to the private sector to produce liquids and gases from coal, biomass, peat, and oil shale. A tax credit would induce production of gas from basins in the Rocky Mountains, shale in the Appalachian Mountains, aquifers in the Gulf of Mexico, and coal seams across the country. The administration also established the Energy Mobilization Board, which could require quicker decisions on permit applications and ignore local environmental standards. This particular idea drew the ire not only of environmentalists, but also of state and municipal governments, which resented this encroachment on their own authority. It also antagonized some conservatives in Congress who saw it as a violation of the principle of states' rights. Members of Congress representing these diverse interests abolished the board in June 1980. Nonetheless, responding to consumer demands to remedy the dire energy situation, these initiatives were much more oriented toward production than had been the conservation-centric National Energy Plan in 1977.[67]

THE OIL INDUSTRY'S RESPONSE

Unsurprisingly, oil companies were the most vociferous opponents of the windfall tax. W. T. Slick Jr., the senior vice president of Exxon, testified before the Senate Finance Committee that it would hurt prospective energy development. The nation had exhausted all of its easily located oil assets, he said, and Congress needed to recognize that future energy projects would have to rely on "extraordinarily large investments, pioneer technology, long lead times, and high risk."[68] The windfall profits tax would drain needed capital from the oil industry, according to Slick, stymying energy development.[69]

Slick pointed to the Prudhoe Bay field on Alaska's North Slope, which was currently under development. The physical terrain there was frozen and hard only during the cold of winter. During the summer months, the ground became wet and unstable, and the cost of building reliable drilling and pipeline infrastructure there was complicated and expensive. Constructing each oil well there cost over $3 million, Slick said, more than *fifteen times* the cost of an average American well in the lower forty-eight states. Because the windfall profits tax was a flat tax on each barrel pumped out of the ground and did not take into account the wildly varying costs of drilling and exploration in diverse geographical areas, instituting it would be "extremely shortsighted." The oil industry would need larger amounts of capital to undertake riskier projects, Slick claimed, and the tax would hurt the industry's ability to reinvest in future production.[70] Carter discounted this criticism as well, insisting on the necessity of the tax. Because of the broad public disdain for oil companies resulting from their massive profits during this second oil crisis, the president worried little about the industry's hostile response.

Returning from a summer 1979 economic summit in Tokyo, Carter found his job performance and personal favorability ratings both miserable. He arranged with the networks to deliver a major address on the energy crisis on 5 July, but suddenly canceled just two days before the planned speech. At the urging of his personal pollster Pat Caddell, Carter decided to withdraw to Camp David and gathered a number of intellectuals and social commentators to reflect on the state of the nation. The new speech retreated to familiar tropes mobilized by Carter in the past. Delivered on 15 July, it addressed not just rampant energy use but broader moral and spiritual issues that the president deemed important. Carter decried what he saw as growing materialism, disrespect for government and authority, and the preference for self-interest over common values. Early reaction to the speech from both the press and the public was somewhat favorable.[71]

However, as its content began to sink in, Carter increasingly appeared as the sounding board for the "disorienting conditions" that had caused many Americans to seek new political leadership in the first place. Two days after the speech, Carter asked all of his cabinet secretaries for resignation letters. Although claiming to seek a "fresh start" and inspire renewed confidence in his administration, the move instead made Carter look panicked and desperate. Much of the public seemed to wonder whether he was competent enough to handle any problem at all. In September only 13 percent of Americans expressed significant confidence in Carter's ability to handle the energy problem, with only 10 percent feeling the same about his ability to handle the economy.[72] On 4 November, when revolutionaries at the US embassy in Tehran took sixty-three Americans hostage, things only got worse for the president.[73]

CARTER AND KENNEDY

Carter wanted to make it "very clear" that the issue of oil supplies would not weaken the US stand on freeing the Americans held hostage in Iran, and he drew a hard line. On 13 November, he banned the importation of any crude oil produced in the country.[74] Soon afterward, Senator Kennedy, who had announced his presidential candidacy on 7 November, again took the opportunity to castigate Carter on the decontrol policy.[75] Though "proclaiming his unity" with Carter on the Iran hostage issue, he deplored the "enormous giveaway over the coming decade, extracted from consumers" for the benefit of corporations. He attacked the administration for lifting controls before having the windfalls profits plan in place, implying that they should have come simultaneously. Kennedy then outlined his own plan, which included loans to businesses and consumers to install energy-saving equipment, increasing strategic petroleum reserves, and developing government plans to distribute oil during an emergency. Reaffirming his emphasis on Mexican fossil fuel supplies, he also proposed creating a "Northern Hemisphere energy alliance" to decrease dependence on foreign oil.[76] Carter and Jerry Brown expressed support for the same general idea.[77]

In the primary campaign of 1980, Carter and Kennedy skirmished throughout the spring. The president entered the Democratic National Convention with a solid majority (60 percent) of the delegates pledged to him, but Kennedy still refused to drop out, hoping that Carter's weakened public image might inspire some delegates to switch their allegiances on the convention floor. The incumbent had won several key primary contests in the early spring, but late April had brought disaster. On 24 April, Carter launched Operation Eagle Claw, a daring helicopter mission meant to rescue the hostages in Tehran. Several of the helicopters encountered mechanical problems while flying in the desert sand. As the aircraft were in the process of aborting the mission, one of the helicopters crashed into a transport vehicle, resulting in the deaths of eight American service members. The Iranians then scattered the hostages across Iran, making another such rescue attempt impossible. The resulting blow to Carter's perceived competence spelled grave consequences for the incumbent.[78]

Kennedy entered the convention believing that he had a strong chance of changing the minds of enough delegates to win the nomination. However, the senator underestimated the difficulty of ousting an incumbent president at a party's central gathering and was unable to mount a serious challenge to Carter's delegate lead. After a floor fight ended with the incumbent renominated, Kennedy delivered a speech that was passionate in support of liberal principles but halfhearted in support of Carter, leading to an awkward moment between the two at the end of Kennedy's address to the convention. The encounter between the two on stage after Carter's own nomination acceptance speech was even more uncomfortable.[79]

If Carter slipped by Kennedy's challenge, he ran into a brick wall against the Republican nominee, Ronald Reagan. Operation Eagle Claw and its aftermath may not have been enough to propel Kennedy over Carter for the Democratic Party's presidential nomination, but the ongoing sense of crisis was more than enough to tarnish the president in the eyes of the general electorate. Carter's inability to solve the Iran hostage crisis, the persistence of high energy prices, and a pervasive sense of general pessimism about the country's future combined to produce a landslide win for the former California governor, who received 489 electoral votes to the president's 49. John Anderson (I-IL), also on the ballot, earned zero electoral votes.

REAGAN AND ACCELERATED DECONTROL

Reagan's ascent to office changed the tone of decontrol opponents. Though Carter had advocated decontrol as a way to increase oil prices and wean the nation off of its use, Reagan's support for decontrol was a piece of his larger ideological opposition to government regulation. Instead of supporting decontrol to force consumers to use much less oil, he favored the policy—as did the congressional conservatives of Carter's time—to incentivize the private sector to produce much more of it. He had made his views very clear during the 1980 campaign, claiming that there had been no energy problem "from the days of the horseless carriage until" Nixon's imposition of price controls in 1971. With questionable logic and little supporting evidence, Reagan boldly asserted that decontrol would end the necessity of Middle Eastern oil imports entirely.[80]

While Carter had been somewhat willing to oppose members of his own party in Congress—and with the windfall profits tax moderating liberal Democratic criticisms—Reagan unsurprisingly cared almost nothing about congressional Democrats' viewpoint. Given the decisiveness of the election outcome and the surety with which Reagan believed in the power of private enterprise, the new president would pursue his own agenda regardless of how loudly Democrats in Congress protested. Recognizing the implications of the change in the Oval Office's occupant, Representative Markey now asked that decontrol merely slow. "The train for decontrol has long left the station," he conceded in an op-ed in the *New York Times*, and the argument now "is not whether we control the price of domestic oil, but how fast we accelerate the train." In a nation already "reeling from inflation and recession," the government should delay decontrol, Markey argued, until a more appropriate time. Failing to slow decontrol risked forcing companies to increase prices of consumer goods to make up for the increased cost of the oil input, thus "risking economic paralysis" in exchange for "dubious benefits" from decontrol.[81]

Reagan's administration paid little attention to Markey's requests. The new leaders in Washington turned out to be even more zealous than oil companies themselves in pushing for decontrol. Though James B. Edwards, the president-elect's designate for energy secretary, claimed that immediate decontrol of oil prices in January 1981 would mean "a lot more production," oil company executives disagreed. The price controls were already set to expire on 1 October, and one oil company chief financial officer noted that his company was already "drilling about as fast as we can" and would not be affected by immediate decontrol. Mesa Petroleum's chairman, T. Boone Pickens, added that his company already had all the drilling rigs working that were available. In fact, not only would immediate decontrol not significantly help oil companies, but the main beneficiary would be the federal government, which stood to collect an additional $9 billion under the windfall profits tax if decontrol was completed immediately. Executives speculated that part of the administration's impetus for immediate decontrol was that the extra revenue would assist Reagan in carrying out his promise of a 10 percent income tax cut. The oil industry asked that the new administration shift its priority from immediate decontrol to freeing more federal lands for oil exploration and simplifying drilling regulations. Reagan did this too.[82]

Surprisingly, joining the Reagan administration in highlighting the benefits of immediate decontrol were Robert Stobaugh and Daniel Yergin, faculty members at the Harvard Business School, who outlined their views in January contributions in the *New York Times* and the *Boston Globe.* Certainly not as dedicated to increased domestic oil production as Reagan's staff, their support for immediate decontrol lay instead with the effect it would have on dampening consumption. Under most assumptions, they reasoned, US petroleum prices would be the same, with or without immediate decontrol, after the 1 October deadline. However, they said, immediate decontrol would in fact likely help reduce US imports during the interim period, which would ease some of the inflationary pressures on the world oil market, which would in turn reduce the likelihood of a continued increase in world oil prices.[83]

In other words, they argued, "the US consumer would be facing the alternative of paying somewhat more now, or paying a good deal more later." While pointing to the long-term benefits of immediate decontrol, they warned that the Reagan administration would need to assist American consumers in making the transition, proposing expanded programs to make capital available for conservation investments. "Thus, even as prices go up," they said, "their effects can be offset through increased efficiency that results in less consumption."[84] However, Reagan's affinity for decontrol had nothing to do with conservation. It was a piece of his larger ideological commitment to freeing the private sector from government control. Stobaugh and Yergin later criticized Reagan for ignoring conservation and solar energy potential, though Reagan had never given any indication that he intended to pursue these routes.[85]

On 27 January, Reagan's director-designate of the Office of Management and Budget, David Stockman, indicated that a decision to lift the remaining controls immediately was "fairly imminent." Previous assumptions had turned on the possibility of an executive order to decontrol prices, but it was now likely that Reagan would also send a bill to Congress to address the "legally gray areas" of refiners' entitlements and the petroleum allocation system. The entitlement system subsidized small refiners by guaranteeing oil supplies to them at a price below market levels. Though the new anti-government administration had little sympathy for their federal subsidization, it also recognized that there would have to be some way to shield them from the effects of total decontrol, lest they disappear due to an inability to compete. The allocation system would share available supplies equitably nationwide; without some sort of transition, more remote areas of the country might find their energy supplies rapidly and drastically cut. With these stipulations in place, Reagan decontrolled oil price completely by executive order mere days after his inauguration, well ahead of Carter's schedule.[86]

THE END OF SACRIFICE

As the 1973 crisis faded from immediate memory and inexpensive energy returned, much of the American public seemed confused by Carter's rhetorical focus on conservation. Extravagant use of energy and reliance on unstable and hostile nations a world away remained unconnected in the minds of many, a disunity of perception that Carter was unable to reverse. Americans instead blamed oil company greed or government incompetence rather than their own consumption habits for any problems that appeared. After the second price spike in 1979, the nation seemed so disillusioned with Carter that many Americans stopped paying attention altogether. As *Time* reported in January 1980, despite a palpable "sense of urgency" in the nation in the wake of the hostage crisis–inspired energy spike, Carter administration officials began to argue that no new taxes or tariffs were needed to force a decrease in consumption, demonstrating how far the administration had conceded ideological and political ground. Eizenstat indicated that the White House feared that any "bold moves" would cost Carter votes in the upcoming primaries and general election. At every turn, Carter confronted voter demands that he solve the nation's problems without impinging upon established patterns of consumption and daily life. He seemed incapable of acting to address an obvious problem.[87]

Sensing an opportunity, the Republican Party sought to gain a political advantage from Carter's missteps. They charged that Carter's plan focused foolishly and needlessly on decreasing consumption. They instead emphasized increased energy production. Certainly, Carter's current plans included a healthy dose of production incentives, including tax credits for production and government support of synthetic fuels. Although Carter spoke hopefully in Seattle the day before the election about "new technology, new tools, new factories, [and] new industries that many of us have never even dreamed," it was far too late to overturn his image of unmitigated pessimism.[88] The GOP's image of Carter as an incompetent leader unfit for office had taken hold.

There is, of course, no way to know if the Iranian Revolution would have yielded such a devastating blow to Carter's presidency had he not so firmly insisted that conservation and sacrifice would make the United States more secure. However, the fact that Carter had made energy his foremost domestic priority, and that it had resulted in such disaster, was an impossible obstacle for the incumbent to overcome in the 1980 campaign. The Iranian Revolution and the second oil crisis seemed to prove Carter's wrongness. Though Carter worked to decontrol the price of oil, the process was too meager and too slow to counteract broad public distaste. A more general leveling of government regulation itself now seemed palatable in a way that it had not just a few years before.

Aware of many Americans' ostensible concern with environmental protection, many national Republicans spoke in vague language about "balancing" energy production with respect for the environment. The implication was that responsible market processes would naturally maintain environmental quality without the need for formal, overbearing public statutes. Some of the GOP's most prominent members went even further in downplaying the importance of environmental protection. In his speech accepting the Republican presidential nomination, Ronald Reagan touted domestic production of oil, natural gas, and coal. The nominee told prospective voters, "Make no mistake. We will not permit the safety of our people or our environmental heritage to be jeopardized." In a stunning redefinition of the term, however, he added, "We are going to reaffirm that the economic *prosperity* of our people is a fundamental part of our environment." The prominent journalist Elizabeth Drew remarked tersely of the Republican nominee, "There is no guide here to what choices he would make." It seemed not to matter. As historian Robert Collins has concluded with regard to debates about economic growth more generally in the stagnant 1970s, "balance was the key, but just what balance meant remained uncertain."[89] Because most Americans thought of themselves as inherently "environmentally friendly" but often saw the activist environmental movement as radical, the Republican strategy held wide appeal.[90]

Though Reagan had avoided appearing patently anti-environment during the 1980 campaign, his cabinet selections made his feelings more apparent once in office. Commerce Secretary Malcolm Baldrige, a former manufacturing CEO, released what one historian has called a "hit list" of basic environmental regulations he wanted to eliminate, including restrictions on hazardous waste, air pollution, and the distribution of potential carcinogens. Reagan's energy secretary concluded that the solution to ozone depletion was stronger suntan lotion. Interior Secretary James Watt spent the early 1980s rolling back protection of public lands in the West.[91] Though Reagan eventually fired Watt and disavowed some of his more extreme statements, it was clear that the virtually unconditional acceptance of environmentalism on the first Earth Day in 1970 had yielded to a more ambiguous view. Reagan could not have made such dismissive comments about environmentalism during the 1980 campaign had it been otherwise.[92]

At the 1980 Republican National Convention, candidate Reagan refused to acknowledge that energy shortages had ever existed, instead blaming the country's energy problems on what he deemed Carter's overzealous regulation. That it was Nixon who had instituted price controls on oil, and Carter who had worked to remove them, seemed irrelevant. The nation was so angry with Carter that it seemed willing to believe any antagonistic statement made about him. Carter's market initiatives paled in comparison to his pessimistic exhortations for sacrifice. The GOP depicted cheap and abundant energy as a fundamental component of citizenship in the postwar nation, and it characterized Carter as a hostile figure who threatened this basic right. Although American consumers in the Reagan years actually benefited from some of the conservation programs of the 1970s, like better insulation in their homes and improved gas mileage in their cars, the GOP's emphasis on "balanced growth" seemed to contrast favorably with Carter's conservationist ethos.[93]

As Meg Jacobs has argued of the slew of environmental regulations and price controls passed under Nixon, "it was precisely the persistence and, in many ways, the intensification of liberal reform in the 1970s that gave conservatives a ready target to attack." The conservative appeal to get "government off our backs," she claims, gained traction only in this world of growing regulation."[94] However, it was not just the expansion of regulation that helped turn American sentiment against government intervention in the economy. It was that both environmental regulations and oil price controls seemed to stand in the way of a more secure energy future. The ability of Reagan and the right wing of the GOP to capitalize on these changing sentiments helped bring them into power. The decline of environmentalism, along with bipartisan support for removing price controls, were integral components of the deregulatory, anti-government politics of the late 1970s and early 1980s.[95]

The oil politics of the 1970s were a key piece of environmentalism's diminished political power and the move toward deregulation in the American macroeconomy. At the same time, policy makers moved to enhance domestic production of other energy sources to reduce the nation's dependence on foreign oil. Attempts to reconfigure the American energy economy took place within an existing macroeconomy, and policy makers had difficulty aligning and satisfying the conflicting interests holding a stake in energy policy. Furthermore, the incredible complexities of energy infrastructures meant that policy changes had unexpected effects and consequences. The next chapter explores how these processes played out in the arena of coal policy.

CHAPTER 2

"RICH, BLACK VEINS OF THE FUTURE"

The United Mine Workers, Railroad Deregulation, and the Political Economy of Coal

Still pondering the shock of the 1973 oil crisis, Jimmy Carter sought to put the United States on firmer long-term energy footing by reducing its dependence on foreign oil. One initiative, the creation of the Department of Energy, would decrease consumer demand by incentivizing conservation. However, Carter realized that even given his best efforts, American consumption patterns were not going to change overnight and some transitional measures were necessary. Reflecting this reality, another of the main components of Carter's energy security plan was to encourage American utility companies to convert their equipment to burn coal, which the US could produce in abundance, instead of oil. Though the images of consumers in long lines at gas stations had highlighted the nation's oil problems, in the 1960s low oil prices had catalyzed utilities to burn huge quantities of it.[1] The replacement plan seemed on its face to be a perfectly rational and reasonable strategy, but for a variety of reasons, it proved much more difficult to execute successfully. Environmental regulations passed only a few years before impeded the transition, as did the coal industry's volatile workforce and the nation's crumbling railroads. This chapter examines the political economy of coal in the late 1970s and argues that some of the problems Carter encountered in implementing his energy policy related to the internal tensions within the nation's systems of energy supply. By focusing on Carter's attempts to replace imported oil with domestic coal, this chapter mobilizes political and labor history to examine the Carter administration's energy policy problems.

Encouraging utilities to substitute abundant domestic coal supplies in place of imported oil seemed to be a straightforward and reasonable idea to many contemporary analysts, especially the president. However, coal, which is much more carbon dense than oil, generates significantly more atmospheric pollution, and there was no cost-effective way to allow utilities to convert to coal and simultaneously comply with contemporary clean-air regulations. Coal mining companies also found their costs increased by the expenses associated with black lung disease, the debilitating and deadly malady caused by years of breathing in coal dust. The administration was rather unwilling to compromise on protections for vulnerable miners—in fact, Carter supported even stronger black lung measures in 1978—but never came to a firm conclusion on how to balance increased coal use with existing environmental and labor regulations, leaving utility and mining companies greatly confused. The administration attempted to increase domestic coal production while maintaining strict environmental protection standards, a virtually impossible task.

The United Mine Workers of America (UMWA) strike of 1977–1978 further complicated the Carter administration's plans to achieve energy security. A new labor contract proposed by coal employers would have slowed the growth of workers' wages over the coming years and, more importantly, would have curbed the union's right to strike in the future. Over a hundred thousand miners walked off the job to protest the contract's objectionable provisions. Though initially reluctant to intervene and poison relations with organized labor, Carter eventually invoked the Taft-Hartley Act to try to force the miners back to work, an action that no US president had taken against the UMWA in nearly thirty years. Most miners responded by simply ignoring the order, and an association of coal mining companies launched a blistering public relations campaign against the union. The unstable and contentious atmosphere generated by the longest coal strike in US history cast the administration's oil replacement plans into serious doubt. Even when the lengthy and often violent strike was resolved in the spring of 1978, national periodicals pointed to the heightened antipathy between union miners and coal companies as a potential problem going forward.

Coal politics also intertwined with the economic debates about deregulation in the late 1970s, specifically with regard to railroads. With rampant inflation in the 1970s wreaking havoc throughout American industry, businesses pushed for loosened government control over their daily operations. Railroad owners saw deregulation of their industry as a necessary step that would keep the nation's rail infrastructure from falling deeper into dilapidation. They could no longer afford to break even or even lose money operating unprofitable routes, and they sought greater leeway to operate the routes of their choice and to charge competitive prices. However, electrical utility companies opposed deregulation of railroads. They saw deregulation as a giveaway to the rail companies, since deregulation would force utilities to pay more for coal and subsequently pass on the cost to irate consumers. There was fierce competition to gain the upper hand in reconciling these two viewpoints into a coherent deregulatory policy. The outcome, which largely deregulated the railroad industry, nonetheless kept coal prices in particular under the control of the Interstate Commerce Commission. This outcome meant that coal prices would remain artificially higher than the prices that would have prevailed in an unregulated market, again impeding the immediate shift from oil to coal in the short term.

These factors all complicated the Carter administration's ability to deal with the energy issue effectively by obstructing a main thread of the president's energy security plan. Caught between competing interest groups in the private sector, Carter's staff struggled to come up with solutions amenable to all involved, and it often settled on resolutions that pleased no one. Focused on the international implications of oil, the administration was ill equipped to address the domestic facets of coal and oil production and consumption. Understandably worried about what was happening in Iran, Iraq, and Saudi Arabia, the administration paid too little attention to—or was simply unable to handle—the political issues simultaneously playing out in West Virginia, Pennsylvania, and Ohio. Thus, many of the Carter administration's political problems came not simply from problems with Congress, but also from an inability to align the conflicting interests embedded within significant policy changes.

The UMWA strike and the railroad deregulation debate were linked in another profound way. One of the effects of the broad 1980 railroad deregulation law was to catalyze a new wave of railroad mergers, which generated greater coordination and efficiency in the rail industry. Non-union coal from the West, a region that had never unionized to the same extent as West Virginia and Pennsylvania, had not theretofore been cost effective to ship in large quantities to the eastern United States. However, this new railroad integration made it much easier to transport coal inexpensively. The rising availability of non-union coal seriously weakened the UMWA, much more than Carter's invocation of the Taft-Hartley Act had done. Although Ronald Reagan often receives credit for implementing deregulatory economic policies and crushing the political strength of organized labor, actions taken during the Carter administration helped make these outcomes possible.

THE CONFUSION OVER ENVIRONMENTAL REGULATION

One of Carter's first ideas to achieve energy security was simply to use existing industrial facilities to generate more electricity than was being produced under the status quo. Soon after his inauguration in 1977, Carter launched a plan to introduce financial and other incentives to encourage large industries, such as the chemical and steel sectors, to generate their own electricity. The targets of the plan were large factories already equipped with steam boilers, which are often essential for providing power to factories from within. Carter called for legislation that would give these industries tax credits to install equipment to harness the excess energy not needed for industrial production, and that would also require utilities to buy the surplus power. Administration energy officials estimated that within ten years this industrial cogeneration could reduce US imports by 500,000 to a million barrels of oil per day.[2] With minimal reconversion, large industries could earn additional income by generating needed electricity, creating a win-win situation for all involved. However, utility companies were generally skeptical about this plan. They routinely went through periods in which they generated surpluses of power not needed by the public, and they worried about the prospect of having to buy industry surpluses in times when they could not sell even their own power.

The larger problem with encouraging increased use of coal, though, was the cost of cooperating with the environmental and safety regulations that had recently passed Congress and been signed into law. Some legislation dealt with protections for coal miners. The Federal Coal Mine Health and Safety Act of 1969—passed in the same surge of safety legislation that established the Occupational Safety and Health Administration—targeted black lung disease, the crippling condition caused by years of breathing coal dust. The act required stringent federal inspections of mines several times per year and provided compensation to miners disabled by the disease. The 1972 Black Lung Benefits Act strengthened compensation for black lung victims. In 1978 Carter signed a new Black Lung Benefits Reform Act that allowed more liberal medical eligibility criteria and eased the claims process for working miners and miners' widows.[3]

Other legislation targeted the effects of coal mining on the nation's physical landscape. Responding to eye-opening press accounts of the destructive effects of strip mining, Carter signed the Surface Mining Control and Reclamation Act in 1977, which strengthened the permitting process and required coal companies to post a bond equivalent to the cost of cleaning up a site before mining could begin.[4] Strip-mining, a process by which mountaintops are removed for easy access to coal deposits inside, was widely criticized not only for its effect on the aesthetic quality of mountains, but also for its deleterious effect on water quality when debris trickled down mountainsides into waterways below.[5]

The cumulative effect of black lung and strip-mining laws on the price of coal was not negligible. The Tennessee Valley Authority (TVA), the quasi-public regional utility based in the Southeast, estimated in 1977 that these laws together had increased its cost of purchasing coal by around $7.50 per ton, a significant amount given that the spot price of coal in 1969 had been about $100 per ton. Clean air regulations threatened to increase costs further, and utility executives warned that converting boilers and power plants to use coal instead of oil without relaxing clean air requirements would be impossible.[6] For utility companies, the possible benefits of coal conversion paled in comparison to the headaches caused by the cost of cooperating with environmental regulations. Coal industry spokesperson Carl Bagge warned in 1977, for example, of a coming "collision" between Carter's optimistic coal projections and the demands of environmental protection.[7]

Carter did not budge in the face of the utilities' ire and prodded Congress to proceed with the oil replacement plan. His solution to the regulatory problem was to propose—within the mammoth 1977 National Energy Plan bill—taxes on oil and natural gas that would raise their prices to equal that of the more environmentally expensive coal, which would remove the financial obstacle to power plant conversion. To prevent the costs that would flow to consumers from becoming a burden, the administration wanted the revenues from the tax rebated directly to the public. However, the Finance Committee chairman, Senator Russell Long (D-LA)—a stalwart defender of his state's oil and gas industries—suggested using the money to promote alternative energy resources, including extracting gas and oil from coal, extracting oil from shale deposits, and investing in solar energy. Since Louisiana was a major oil and gas producer, Long preferred an option that would subsidize research and development for these businesses instead of having the revenues confiscated and distributed to consumers. The committee split on the question, some siding with the administration and others agreeing with Long, who in turn decided to leave the issue to the Senate-House conference committee that would eventually reconcile the two versions of the entire energy package.[8]

This conference committee, which consisted of more conservative members than the Finance Committee, in turn voted for neither idea, instead deciding overwhelmingly to provide tax credits and tax cuts to utilities instead of new taxes to induce conversion. The technical costs of converting utility equipment from oil to coal use would pass to rate-paying customers, and giving utilities cuts and credits rather than taxing them directly would not generate revenue for rebates to consumers to ease the transition. Carter was thus disappointed in this vote. Later in the month, though, the full Senate gave Carter a "surprise" victory when it voted in favor of a modified, more limited version of the originally proposed tax. There was more support for the Carter energy program in the full Senate than in the Finance Committee, and the public perception that the Senate had been lagging in adopting an energy program spurred the Senate to resolve the tax issue quickly.[9] Carter was in this case successful in pushing for specific taxes on utility oil use, although to a more limited degree than he had initially hoped, as the full 1977 energy bill emphasized tax credits instead of new taxes. However, burning coal first required obtaining it from underground, no easy feat in itself. Indeed, coal miners would soon attain a central position among the Carter administration's main political worries.

THE UNITED MINE WORKERS ON STRIKE

While environmental regulations posed challenges to the coal conversion idea, another political development would prove much more momentous. In the spring of 1977, Carter's energy advisers were looking optimistically at the possibility of doubling yearly domestic coal production within ten years. The "major pitfall" threatening this forecast was the UMWA, a unionized force organized in 1890 that was currently mining about 54 percent of the nation's coal supply. The UMWA comprised, according to one contemporary journalistic assessment, the most militant workers in all of American organized labor, and their contract was due for renegotiation.[10] The UMWA indeed had a long tradition of combining militant strikes and sabotage with coordinated national bargaining every three years to pressure the coal industry during contract negotiations. A likely strike during this round of negotiations would interrupt Carter's plans to convert American utilities to burn coal instead of oil.

There is a distinction between industrial militancy and political radicalism. Through most of its history, the UMWA pursued the former as an organizing strategy and eschewed the latter. While using strikes and violence during contract disputes, it has largely avoided a radical politics of economic redistribution, instead focusing on reliable wage increases and retirement protections for workers. The UMWA in the 1970s was different in one particular way from previous eras, namely the effectiveness of the UMWA head to channel militant impulses into a productive negotiating position. Longtime UMWA boss John L. Lewis had well understood his workers' confrontational tendencies, harnessing his workers' militancy to keep pressure on the government and the Bituminous Coal Operators Association (BCOA), an alliance of several powerful mine operators who had organized themselves in 1945 to coordinate bargaining with the UMWA.[11]

However, current UMWA chief Arnold Miller was not nearly as effective at mobilizing his workers' militant tendencies, bringing a new complication to government and business efforts to negotiate the UMWA's labor contract. First elected as UMWA chief in 1972, Miller's troubles had begun as early as 1974 amid accusations of financial mismanagement of the union's assets, which continued to dog him into 1977. Much of his administrative difficulties owed to his meteoric rise—his only other executive position had been running a local chapter with numbers in the dozens—which, while impressive, had also left him unprepared to lead a feisty union with tens of thousands of members scattered across the eastern half of the country. A former miner suffering from black lung disease himself, Miller's sympathies certainly lay with rank-and-file workers, but his inexperience left him unready to combat the union's enemies head-on and predisposed him to seek compromise instead of conflict. Local union leaders came to see the UMWA boss as too conservative and willing to give in to corporate and government demands at the expense of miners' rights and financial security.[12]

There was indeed good reason for Carter's policy makers to worry as 1977 contract negotiations approached. The resolution to the 1974 negotiation served as a grim harbinger for his domestic policy staff. It had failed to bring lasting peace to miner-employer relations, with wildcat strikes (strikes originated by the regular members and not sanctioned by union leaders) continuing afterward. Strikes during negotiations were routine for the UMWA. Strikes after a contract's ratification were not, and they indicated the UMWA's dissatisfaction with its central leadership. Wildcat strikes in anticipation of the contract renegotiation three years later exploded in late April and early May 1977, shutting down a number of mines in West Virginia and Ohio. Roving pickets soon extended the shutdown to some fifty mines employing fifteen thousand workers. National UMWA officers tried to get strikers back to work but met resistance in the coalfields. At the same time, a tight three-way struggle for control of the UMWA was in progress with an election set for June. The internal fight meant that a stable UMWA seemed doubtful. The election result, which saw Arnold Miller earn a second term, would have stark implications for the union's internal coherence in the very near future. Miller won the three-way race with only 40 percent of the vote, hardly a ringing ratification of his first five years in office.[13] In the fall, wildcat strikes continued across West Virginia, with Miller ordering miners back to work and miners largely ignoring his protestations.[14]

As expected, the following winter the UMWA as an organization went on strike during the negotiation of a new labor contract. On 7 December 1977, 160,000 UMWA members walked off the job in protest. The BCOA had offered the union wage increases of about 27 percent over the span of a proposed three-year contract. Carter had recently called on the nation's industries to keep wage and price increases to a minimum in order to combat inflationary spirals, and BCOA's offer followed in this spirit. Yet macroeconomic worries mattered little to UMWA miners. The union demanded a 44 percent increase. Wayne Horvitz of the Federal Mediation and Conciliation Service, which was helping to facilitate negotiations, pointed skeptically to this "very wide gap" between the UMWA and the BCOA. For the miners, however, financial concerns were secondary to the right to strike itself. The contract three years earlier had curbed the possibility of illegal walkouts, but the new proposed agreement went much further. This new contract would have given the coal operators wide latitude to fire wildcat strikers, a provision the miners refused to accept.[15] As miners came to distrust their leaders' motivations and general competence, wildcat strikes stood as a last resort of guaranteed effectiveness in labor negotiations, and they refused to assent to this provision. There is little evidence that the UMWA specifically exploited Carter's calls to increase domestic coal production as a bargaining chip to extract higher wage gains. The issue of wildcat strikes stood at the center of the UMWA's objections.

The first strong pressure for government intervention appeared at the end of January, about seven weeks into the strike. Midwestern and Appalachian states suffered the brunt of a particularly cold winter, and residents feared the impact a coal shortage would have on their ability to stay warm. In early February, recognizing that no quick settlement was in sight, Carter instructed his administration to plan for cutbacks in electric power and coal supplies. He did not plan, at this point, to invoke portions of the 1947 Taft-Hartley Act, which gives the president power to intervene in strikes that constitute a "national emergency." UMWA strikes every three years to increase its bargaining advantage during contract negotiations were routine, and Carter hoped this walkout might likewise end in the near future. The president's orders for the moment included suspending some air quality regulations in Ohio for thirty days, asking all federal facilities in the area to reduce power consumption to a minimum, and directing the EPA to "speedily review" any requests for temporary relaxation of Clean Air Act regulations.[16] In West Virginia, the epicenter of the strike, miners mainly produced "soft," or bituminous, coal. Relaxing environmental regulations intended to speed the burning of non-union "hard," or anthracite, coal from northeast Pennsylvania. Anthracite coal burns cleaner and produces less soot than does bituminous, but it also tends to have a higher content of poisonous sulfur. By this point Carter considered longer-term problems of air quality less important than the immediate emergency.

Reports began to emerge that the strike was exacting a broader toll on the nation's economic health, especially in the Midwest. The nation's automakers predicted production cuts and some resultant plant closings by the end of February if the strike did not end soon, due to expected power shortages in Ohio and Indiana. General Motors (GM), for example, expected a mandatory 50 percent reduction in the electric power supplied by Ohio Edison Company, which would reduce production or force closures entirely at seven GM plants employing 27,000 hourly workers. To make matters worse, GM said that some of the plants in question were the only source of specific parts, meaning that the closings of only a few scattered plants could halt the production of entire cars if a key piece or two went unmade. It also warned that a "serious interruption" of supply could close GM's operations completely, which would generate layoffs of more than 300,000 employees. Chrysler predicted a closedown of all of its US and Canadian auto and truck assembly facilities by early March, which would idle about 150,000 employees.[17] While its impact was at first confined to the energy industry, the UMWA's strike threatened to generate broader ripples across the US economy.[18] Despite the negative impact the UMWA strike was having on the auto industry, the United Auto Workers did not blame the coal miners for hurting their trade. In fact, in an act of labor solidarity, the organization pledged $2 million to a relief fund for the families of UMWA workers.[19]

The auto industry news changed Carter's tone dramatically. On 14 February, he demanded that the UMWA and BCOA convene at the White House immediately to resume "serious negotiations." In a statement at the White House, the president began by speaking of the "increasing hardships" that the strike was causing, declaring emphatically that "it cannot be allowed to continue." Asked if he was ready to invoke Taft-Hartley, he replied tersely, "That's one of the options available to me, yes." Attorney General Griffin Bell, no particular friend to organized labor, did not rule out the use of federal troops in ending the strike, which had traditionally only been done during a wartime emergency. "I will have no choice but to resort to stronger measures" if the strike did not end, threatened Carter, and he instructed Labor Secretary Ray Marshall, a pro-labor union sympathizer, to participate more directly in the negotiations.[20]

There were several options available to Carter, and none of them seemed good. He could invoke Taft-Hartley, but the consequences of doing so were impossible to predict. The law had been used against the UMWA only three times before and not since 1950. Two of the three invocations resulted in miner defiance and eventual federalization of the mines. Harry Truman broke the last Taft-Hartley impasse in 1950 by threatening to seize the mines again. Invoking the law would have certainly damaged Carter's already tense relationship with organized labor and was not guaranteed to yield any practical result.[21] The disastrous status quo was no better choice. Carter looked weaker every day that he could not resolve the conflict. It was no small wonder, then, that he continued to urge the UMWA to reach agreement on the labor contract as soon as possible. Unfortunately for Carter, his aides had failed to reach management bargainers before Carter's 14 February announcement, and the first the bargainers heard of the demand to resume negotiations was therefore over national television, along with the rest of the country. Embarrassed by the unexpected demands, the operators' association rejected the proposed meeting but, realizing the public relations disaster that would ensue from appearing intransigent, quickly relented.[22]

THE STRIKE TURNS VIOLENT

Carter soon had even more to worry about. Drawing on a long tradition of sabotage and violence to strengthen its negotiating position, some members of the UMWA engaged in aggressive acts against non-union coal producers on a daily basis. Meant to impede coal from being mined or moved anywhere until the strike was resolved, which would preserve the UMWA's bargaining leverage and ramp up pressure on the BCOA, violence spread across the Southeast and Midwest. Some of the violence directly targeted non-union producers themselves. A few days after the strike began in December, for example, UMWA strikers formed a caravan of more than one hundred vehicles and drove from Kittanning, Pennsylvania, northward through western Pennsylvania toward Clarion. On the way, they stopped at several mining operations and ordered each to close down until the strike had been resolved. Unsurprisingly, each site complied with the armed miners and their demands. At some sites, the roving miners inflicted damage to equipment or buildings. A firebomb was believed responsible for a 6 January blaze at Boonville, Indiana, that destroyed two independent coal-hauling companies, with total damage estimated at $500,000.[23]

UMWA members also targeted railroads to stop mined coal from getting to its intended destination. On 3 January, a bomb destroyed a section of the Norfolk and Western Railroad tracks at Ada, West Virginia. On 16 January, an L&N train traveling from Loyall to Corbin received gunfire while traveling over the Emerling Bridge. On 23 January, reports indicated that a bridge carrying a section of track leading to the Tennessee Valley Authority plant at Paradise, Kentucky, was on fire, and about two weeks later, this bridge was set ablaze again. On 8 February in Pikesville, Kentucky, someone threw a basketball containing fifteen pounds of dynamite at a loading dock of the Elkhorn Fuel Company, but the fuses burned out and the bomb did not explode. These examples represent only a small portion of the union violence. FBI reports documenting incidents from 8 December to 5 March record four incidents of bodily assault, thirty-four bombings, and seventy-two incidents of "disruption," which were mainly forced closings of mining operations.[24]

The night after Carter's tense speech, on 15 February, the two sides did indeed convene at the White House to continue talks. The coal operators—in the White House's view, the most vehement holdouts—returned at the behest of what White House press secretary Jody Powell graciously called a "concern for the general welfare." Another senior White House aide, however, noted that Carter might issue a public denunciation of the coal operators if they spurned his request to return to the bargaining table. Five days later, the talks fell apart again. This set of talks hinged on three-way negotiations among the UMWA, the government, and the Pittsburg & Midway Oil Company (P&M), a subsidiary of the Gulf Oil Corporation. Although the P&M was not part of the Bituminous Coal Operators Association, the government hoped that if the P&M and the UMWA could come to an agreement, one or more other independent operators would support it. The government believed that subsequent combined public and corporate pressure would force the BCOA to retreat from its perceived hardline position. However, the talks came apart when the P&M itself worried that it was being used for "pattern-setting" by the government and that the BCOA members might end up with a more favorable deal. Also not helpful to a resolution were the whispers of secret caucuses among UMWA officials opposed to UMWA's president, Arnold Miller, as well as rumors of a "conscious effort" among federal mediators to bypass him. With the coal operators unlikely to budge and the UMWA fractured and disorganized, hopes for a resolution remained dim as ever.[25] Miller's shaky control of his organization and seemingly endless conflicts with his top lieutenants did little to alleviate an already tense situation.

Two days after the talks resumed, 17 February, Labor Secretary Ray Marshall received a confidential memorandum from Mary Lawton, a high-ranking official in the Justice Department's Office of Legal Counsel (OLC). The memo responded to preliminary inquiries into the possibility for federal seizure of the mines if the issues could not be resolved. Marshall's general sympathies lay with unions, and there was a strong chance that threatening to seize the mines would compel the BCOA to compromise and offer the miners a more favorable settlement. Lawton was skeptical about the idea, noting that previous presidents had only seized industrial facilities in times of war. The president had no authority to seize an industry in a strike situation, Lawton noted, if Congress had provided alternative means of settling the strike, which the Taft-Hartley Act and other legislation obviously provided. On 24 February, Assistant Attorney General John Harmon, also from the OLC, wrote members of Carter's domestic policy staff to warn against seizure. The government had to decide at the outset just how far it was willing to go if it encountered resistance to seizure, Harmon said. "Would the government be willing to nationalize the mines on a permanent basis if either the operators or the mine workers refuse to comply with a seizure law?" he asked. Was it prepared to dismiss miners who refuse to work, and to staff the mines with government personnel? Could it use the army as miners until a settlement was reached? "Is the President prepared to call out troops to protect the mines" against militant workers? Harmon hoped that the administration would not need to consider these questions, but time to resolve the crisis was running out.[26]

On the night of 24 February, Carter scheduled a 9:00 p.m. television appearance to announce "drastic and unsatisfactory legal action" to end the strike, presumably meaning Taft-Hartley. At 7:00 p.m., though, the president made an unannounced appearance in the White House press room to discuss a last-minute proposed settlement and warned that he would follow through with the promised "drastic steps" if it fell through. Carter's about-face was due to his confidence in his own intense two-day effort to push the settlement through, which included getting the governors of Ohio, Pennsylvania, and Kentucky to phone company executives and urge them to accept an agreement.[27] Carter's maneuvering gave him cautious optimism that a breakthrough was imminent, but the margin for error was slim.

Most commercial customers had possessed three-month stockpiles of coal when the strike started, which they had believed would be ample. Having been accustomed to regular work stoppages of varying length every three years as the UMWA renegotiated its labor contract, commercial customers had learned to keep excess coal on hand. The 1974 strike had lasted a mere twenty-eight days, but this particular walkout was approaching its three-month anniversary. Because of the strike's unexpected duration, electrical utilities and other industries dependent on coal were running dangerously low in Ohio, Indiana, Tennessee, and Pennsylvania. Utilities and industries in Virginia, West Virginia, Kentucky, and Michigan were not far from the point of panic either. In the meantime, P&M had also relented in its opposition and had finalized a separate agreement with the UMWA after the company dropped controversial provisions giving management the power to punish all workers in a mine if they participated in a wildcat strike. The *New York Times* seemed cautiously optimistic about the settlement, but also was sure to note that the divisive Arnold Miller, a man with increasingly less influence within the union, had negotiated it. Even more damagingly, the union's thirty-nine-member bargaining council was not consulted, and it apparently learned of the "break-through" by watching television, a major insult to the regular members. Nevertheless, Carter urged the union members to ratify the agreement immediately.[28]

Even as it appeared that the strike might be ending, national media took a decidedly pessimistic tone about the broader prospects for the coal industry moving forward. As the *New York Times* reported, ending the strike in this way would do nothing to effect wider reform of the coal industry's "volatile" labor relations. The idea that labor tensions could erupt again seemingly at any time would be a major impediment to Carter's continued efforts to convince the nation's industries to switch from oil to coal. Administration economists also worried that the strike would set a pattern and that the Teamsters, for example, might see the coal strike as a sign that they could get a more generous contract simply by waiting until a trucking shutdown created a national crisis as well.[29]

Carter's economic advisers—namely Council of Economic Advisers (CEA) Chairman Charles Schultze and special inflation adviser Alfred Kahn—were also concerned that sizable wage increases in the industry of such an essential economic input as energy would generate broader inflation. These costs, they argued, would eventually "work their way" through to higher prices for a "broad spectrum" of goods and services.[30] Schultze made a similar argument about a 1978 labor law reform bill that would weaken the power of Taft-Hartley and make it harder for employers to fire striking workers, claiming that an increased number of strikes leading to higher wage settlements would yield deleterious macroeconomic consequences.[31] The UMWA's actions, in the eyes of these government officials, therefore threatened nothing less than the lasting destabilization of the US economy. It was of the utmost importance that the situation come under control as soon as possible before further damage occurred. Just what "control" would mean, though, still seemed elusive. Both the BCOA and the UMWA seemed unlikely to budge from their respective positions in the near future.

SPORADIC PROGRESS

Administration officials began making contingency plans in case the miners rejected the deal. Wayne Horvitz, the federal official leading the negotiations, wrote to Secretary Marshall on 1 March to warn against the possibility of seizure legislation. The miners would not return to work under a Taft-Hartley injunction if they knew that seizure legislation was in the works, he argued, since the federal government would negotiate a settlement under seizure and would not be concerned about maximizing profits. If Marshall decided that seizure was necessary, Horvitz said, the legislation should not spell out the specific conditions of employment that federal control would mean for the UMWA. Rather, UMWA members should hear as little as possible about how their working conditions might compare between seizure and the proposed contract, as the uncertainty of the former might lead to resigned acceptance of the latter. Marshall agreed with this analysis, and Stuart Eizenstat, a senior domestic adviser to the president, wrote to Carter two days later to outline the consensus view. A simple Taft-Hartley injunction was the "step most likely to get coal moving immediately," Eizenstat said, and legislation was premature since Taft-Hartley alone might end the strike. "Taft-Hartley satisfies the need for action without involving us in a legislative imbroglio and the unknown but certainly unpleasant consequences of owning the mines."[32]

Furthermore, any legislation seemingly too generous to the miners, Eizenstat said, would likely generate opposition from pro-business members of Congress. Eizenstat feared that alienating pro-business conservatives would jeopardize unrelated pieces of legislation under consideration on Capitol Hill. The administration, he said, had already exerted "great pressure" on the industry to accept a contract that it already considered a sellout. "We cannot credibly turn around and force them to back off even further under threat of seizure." Eizenstat also believed that the miners could not hold out much longer, predicting that the strikers "will surely seize upon the government order as an excuse to return to the work they so desperately need."[33]

Eizenstat was immediately proved wrong. The miners voted overwhelmingly against the settlement. On 5 March, a Sunday, Press Secretary Jody Powell appeared in the White House pressroom to proclaim that Carter had called both a cabinet meeting and a bipartisan meeting with congressional leadership. In the words of the *Los Angeles Times*, the "restrained euphoria" of the tentative settlement had transformed into a "mood of grimness" pervading the White House. Miners seemed to be generally satisfied with the wage provisions of the contract. However, many objected to dropping free medical care in favor of a deductible on all medical costs, provisions implementing the operators' demands to punish leaders of wildcat strikes, and the "strike-baby clause," which deprived miners' families of maternity benefits for children conceived while the strike was going on.[34] To the miners, preserving broad latitude to strike in the future was still much more important than an immediate resolution that would put them back to work. They refused to take the promise of imminent relief, to the detriment of their long-term bargaining position.

Relying on welfare payments and food stamps, as well as loans from relatives, many miners had apparently decided to hold out longer to get a contract they liked better, one that preserved their right to mobilize wildcat strikes when deemed necessary. Union leaders predicted "chaos and bloodshed" in the coalfields if Carter tried to invoke Taft-Hartley. One West Virginia miner said of the prospects of forcing miners back to work, "No doubt in my mind, it's going to cause violence." David Forms, the former head of a UMWA local in West Virginia, told *Time* magazine, "You've got $250,000 pieces of equipment in each of these mines, and it wouldn't take much to tear them up. I'm not making any threat. That's just the way it is."[35] The UMWA would go back to work only on its own terms. Given the level of UMWA violence and sabotage that had already occurred, the accompanying threats were credible.

The next day, Carter formally invoked the law, which obligated the president to name a fact-finding panel to report on the impact of the strike before taking action. From that report, he could ask a federal court ordering the strikers back to work for an eighty-day "cooling-off period." Taft-Hartley also required the resumption of collective bargaining. Three days later, on 9 March, Carter received the panel's written report, which predictably indicated the prospect of "little chance" for prompt settlement. Carter directed Attorney General Griffin

Bell to enjoin the strike immediately. The US District Court for the District of Columbia directed the UMWA to halt the strike and commanded the UMWA's officers to instruct all members to "resume normal employment." It also ordered the UMWA to return to the collective bargaining table "in all good faith."[36]

The threatened violence in response to this order largely failed to materialize, yet miners found other ways to resist the order. They simply ignored it. Although miners and union officials who sought to incite support for continuing the strike might receive fines and jail time, the government could do nothing to punish those who simply stayed home. On 8 March, Doug Huron, senior associate counsel in the White House Counsel's office, again broached the possibility of seizure legislation. "We had earlier decided to defer seizure until we had firm evidence whether the miners were returning to work under Taft-Hartley," he noted, and "it seems relatively certain that only a small percentage will go back."[37]

On the surface, the UMWA treated the order to return to work disdainfully and took steps to preserve absolute resistance to the injunction. The *Christian Science Monitor* told the story of Robert White, a miner from Ohley, West Virginia, who, although his wife supported their family sufficiently during the strike by working at an insurance company, simply wanted to go back to work. White invoked the memory of his father and grandfather in proclaiming that "I'm fighting for their beliefs and my beliefs in getting a decent contract," but he also had a more practical reason for resisting the urge to return to the mines: "I got a call saying if I went back to work, my home would be blown up and everything in it." At a rank-and-file meeting of UMWA Local 9111 in Sesser, Illinois, Barney Beard sarcastically proclaimed, "As local president I have to ask you to go back to work." Amid laughter at Beard's sardonic command, one member shouted, "And we can tell you to go to hell." On 13 March, the first Monday after the injunction, fewer than one hundred striking miners returned to the mines.[38]

However, there were other things happening behind the UMWA's fierce façade. That same Monday, both the coal operators and UMWA senior officials had reported "some progress" in talks. The shift likely had to do with the fact that the Carter administration planned to cut off food stamps for strikers, which drew the threat of a court action from AFL-CIO President George Meany. Many of the UMWA strikers' savings and family support were by this point also running low, and they could hold out for only so long. Furthermore, non-union mines, especially in the West, had been steadily increasing production to take advantage of the shortages of union coal coming out of the Southeast and the Midwest. The longer the strike went on, the UMWA was beginning to realize, the less important Eastern coal would become in the end, and thus the more the UMWA was putting its own future livelihood in danger.[39]

The next day, negotiators for both the UMWA and the BCOA announced that they had reached agreement on a new contract proposal, one that would likely win rank-and-file approval. The new three-year agreement would boost miners' wages and fringe benefits by about 39 percent, significantly more than the 27 percent increase under the rejected contract and only slightly less than the 44 percent the miners had originally demanded. The new settlement also scaled back changes to health and pension benefits. Most importantly for the miners, the new contract virtually eliminated the crackdowns on wildcat strikes. UMWA members still did not let up with their campaign to impede coal production until they had their say in the rank-and-file vote. In Somerset County, Pennsylvania, a caravan of about 150 vehicles traveled from mine to mine to make sure they stayed closed. On 17 March, the Justice Department, anticipating the ratification of this new contract, asked Judge Robinson to extend the temporary restraining order for another two weeks rather than issue a final Taft-Hartley injunction, which would have cut off food stamps to strikers. This extension would allow the status quo to prevail until the scheduled 24 March ratification vote.[40]

On the day of the vote, the UMWA's regular members voted 57 percent in favor of the agreement, effectively ending the strike. By 28 March, the *Los Angeles Times* reported that miners were returning to work and operations "were beginning to return to normal." A *Washington Post* headline spoke of Carter's relief at the strike's end, but the paper also noted that the final agreement did not contain earlier industry demands for curbs on wildcat strikes and other "labor-stabilizing" measures. The possibility for future upheavals was still very much present. "Restlessness" within the UMWA, the *Christian Science Monitor* opined, "could continue to block operations in the hills and tunnels where coal is dug" and "where the nation's energy future lies in rich, black veins."[41]

LABOR'S POLITICAL POWER IN THE 1970S

Carter and his staff seem to deserve some of the blame for the duration and severity of the strike. As John Dumbrell and Carter's own staff have noted, Carter was a "populist" in one sense of the term. As "tribune of the people," he saw himself as a champion against "special interests" and "inside deals."[42] Wary of concentrated power in any form, he considered the BCOA, an alliance of private businesses, and the UMWA, an organized group of well over a hundred thousand miners, to each be a "special interest" in its own right.[43] He was reluctant to intervene on behalf of one or the other in their disagreements, instead preferring to urge both to return to the bargaining table after every breakoff in negotiations. Shortly before taking office, President-elect Carter and Ray Marshall had decided that, in the event of a coal strike, collective bargaining should run its course. Coercive government intervention would be only a last resort. This was an approach also recommended by CEA chair Charles Schultze, as government intervention would encourage miners to increase their demands. However, there was an obvious downside to this strategy. By the time Carter threatened to invoke Taft-Hartley, the miners had already prepared themselves for an extended struggle.

Historian Burton Kaufman describes the strike as an event "over which [Carter] had little or no control."[44] To be fair, the government had played a minimal role in coal bargaining ever since Truman's last invocation of Taft-Hartley in 1950. Yet Carter had failed to anticipate that the intractable disagreement between the BCOA and the UMWA over wildcat strikes, combined with the precarious position of embattled UMWA chief Miller, might lead to a prolonged and protracted battle. It did. The coal replacement idea was such an integral part of his energy security plan that Carter's seeming cluelessness about the UMWA's internal strife brings his political acumen into question, especially when his administration had specifically warned him about the possibility that the UMWA might impede his coal conversion plans. The failure of his administration to coordinate labor and energy politics was also clear. By contrast, in 1974 the Ford administration had diligently monitored the changing internal politics of the UMWA, then used intermediaries, most notably the high-ranking United Steelworkers of America official Meyer Bernstein, to gain information about Miller and to formulate strategies for resolving the expected strike. Though Ford administration officials had discussed invoking Taft-Hartley if deemed necessary, the 1974 strike ended before such an action. In the case of handling coal labor policy, the president from Georgia was far less effective. However, to be fair to Carter, the provisions against wildcat strikes negotiated in 1974 made resolving the 1977 strike much more difficult than it otherwise would have been.[45]

Existing scholarship on the 1977–1978 strike casts it as another episode in the UMWA militancy that began in the early years of the twentieth century, a discrete but familiar point in a decades-long stream of coal miner violence and defiance.[46] While such a broad chronological approach has its benefits in placing the strike in wider historical context, it also ignores the way in which the 1973 oil crisis affected the way Carter approached the strike. Carter's troubles in getting the miners back to work made him appear politically weak and contributed to his declining public image of competence, as analysts of the strike have already argued.[47] However, Carter's desire to improve his standing in the electorate's eye was not the only reason for his frantic approach to the strike's resolution. The union's propensity for walking off the job and its deteriorating relationship with the BCOA also served, according to the administration, as significant roadblocks in the way of securing the nation's long-term energy future.[48]

The strike revises our understanding of labor history in the late 1970s. A sizable body of historiography has cast the 1970s as a period in which the political power of organized labor fell off precipitously, owing largely to the United States' decreasing dependence on its manufacturing base, as well as to corruption and malfeasance by union leadership. Judith Stein, for example, has recently argued that national Democrats in the late 1970s abandoned their direct support of organized labor, "replac[ing] the assumptions that capital and labor should prosper together with an ethic claiming that the promotion of capital will eventually benefit labor."[49] At the same time, public opinion turned against the perceived greed and corruption of union members, symbolized most viscerally by the shocking murder by UMWA boss Tony Boyle of his rival Jock Yablonski, and his wife and daughter, in 1969.[50]

This narrative is accurate to some extent. Political leaders, including the historically labor-friendly Democrats, paid less attention to the demands of labor's highest-ranking officials in the 1970s than they had in the decades before. Much scholarship on Carter's labor policy focuses on his deteriorating relationships with AFL-CIO head George Meany and United Auto Workers chief Leonard Woodcock due to his perceived anemic labor initiatives.[51] However, turning attention to how Carter's labor policies intersected with his signature domestic priority of energy security yields a different view of labor's agency in the Carter years. As the UMWA strike shows, the fact that labor leaders wielded less influence in Washington did not mean that the regular members did not hold alternative ways of making their dissatisfactions known. The United Mine Workers in this era paid little attention to the wishes of its ostensible spokesperson, Arnold Miller, anyway. Its acute ability to disrupt a major domestic priority of the incumbent administration must give pause to analyses that cast the early 1970s as the effective terminus of organized labor's power in American politics. While UMWA leader Miller found himself marginalized within his own organization and ignored by high-ranking federal officials, the regular members proved feisty and combative opponents for both the coal mining companies and the Carter administration alike.[52]

The consequences for both Carter's energy policy and the UMWA's future were significant indeed. In the strike's aftermath, industrial and utility coal customers worried about the favorability of the settlement for the UMWA, predicting that their victories would encourage and embolden future militancy. Another three years would bring another contract renegotiation, so it would not be long until the viability of labor-management peace was again tested. Moreover, given its rippling effects in slowing down the auto industry and other manufacturers, the strike itself had hamstrung broader economic activity, and recovery would be slow.[53]

RAILROADS AND DEREGULATION

Though the labor issue was resolved, the regulatory-economic structure of the coal industry itself presented another layer of difficulty for Carter's coal conversion plans. This specific structural problem had deep historical roots. In the face of the astronomical profits reaped by railroad operators like Cornelius Vanderbilt and Leland Stanford, in 1887 Congress passed the Act to Regulate Commerce to set rates at a "just and reasonable" level. It created a new regulatory body, the Interstate Commerce Commission (ICC), and charged it with upholding this standard, allowing wide latitude to determine just what was reasonable and what was not. Nearly a century later, in the second half of the 1970s, the federal government began to retreat from its role in overseeing transportation, along with communications, banking, and energy. Crushing inflation made competitive pricing seem much more attractive and necessary than it had during the ample prosperity of the immediate postwar years.[54]

In February 1976, President Ford signed the Railroad Revitalization and Regulatory Reform Act (4R Act), designed to bolster the nation's "ailing" railway industry, which, partially because of the rise of airlines, had sunk into disrepair. Airlines could ship many consumer goods more quickly and provided a faster transport method for passengers, too, which cut heavily into railroad traffic. However, many larger items—including shipments of coal—were immovable by air, and saving the railroads was necessary. The law committed $6.4 billion for the purposes of rehabilitation and modernization, including $1.6 billion in grants to finance improvements to the Northeast Corridor line running between Boston and Washington, $1 billion in loan guarantees to finance facility improvements across the nation, and $200 million to electrify routes between Pittsburgh and Harrisburg in Pennsylvania. The law also included provisions for deregulation of rail routes, allowing railroads substantial latitude to explore rate increases of up to 7 percent annually without substantive ICC supervision. This figure helped railroads gain more revenue from coal to compensate for slim profits, or even losses, in carrying other items for which there was more competition.[55]

As Carter encouraged the switch to coal, he met obstacles with the railroad industry as well. Over the previous few years, the desire for increasing production of domestic sources of energy had generated several proposals to build slurry pipelines from the West. Coal slurry is a thick, black liquid that looks like crude oil, created by grinding coal to the consistency of sugar and adding water. Among the proposals was a thirty-eight-inch pipeline stretching over a thousand miles from Wyoming to Arkansas, which would prospectively carry twenty-five million tons of coal per year. In 1978 the nation's rail infrastructure was largely in disrepair, but railroads were loath to give up "their private domain" of transporting Western coal. They uniformly refused to allow slurry pipelines to tunnel beneath their tracks, and the pipeline advocates resorted to looking for "windows" (stretches of track where the railroads did not hold title), purchasing rights from the owners, and taking the issue to court. Although the pipelines were victors in a majority of the cases they filed, it was a long and slow process.[56] Dealing with the ailing railroads themselves seemed the only viable option.

In June 1978, the ICC rejected an industry request for a 7 percent increase on coal shipments to electric companies. Instead, the commission allowed a 4 percent increase, citing coal's status as a "basic energy source" and the inflationary impact of an increase it deemed "not fully justified." In August the ICC fined the Louisville & Nashville Railroad Company $1 million for violating requirements to move freight cars into coal mining regions. Members of Kentucky's congressional delegation had been in to speak with ICC officials the previous month to relay the complaints of coal mining companies, which had claimed that the L&N was using cars for more profitable endeavors. The mining owners alleged that this caused them major financial difficulties, as they could not ship the coal they had mined. The ICC agreed with them, claiming that repeated efforts to get L&N to move cars faster went ignored.[57]

L&N responded in October, claiming that it lacked the equipment to move coal sufficiently, therefore requesting a 22 percent hike in coal freight rates to pay for it. L&N's chairman cited the large discrepancy between his company's average charge for moving a ton of coal ($3.57) and the national average ($6.49), and he claimed that the increase would provide $425 million over the next five years to pay for locomotives, freight cars, and facilities. Utilities vehemently resisted L&N's claims, as any increase in freight rates would lead to a rise in the price of coal, which would cut into utility profits. The senior vice president of finance for Georgia Power, for example, announced his opposition to the proposal, claiming that the boost would reduce his company's profit by $7 million over the next year alone. Despite the opposition, though, the ICC approved the increase within a matter of weeks.[58]

In the midst of the oil crisis resulting from the Iranian Revolution of late 1978, the ICC allowed railroads to give priority to hauling food and fuel supplies at the expense of manufactured products, and allowed railroads more leeway in coming up with rates to achieve this end. To utilities, it seemed as if railroads' power was out of control. As the Tennessee Valley Authority noted, for example, the average transportation cost of a ton of coal rose over 60 percent from fiscal year 1977 to fiscal year 1979, from $2.60 to $4.22. Though TVA claimed to be trying to control rail-rate increases through negotiation of long-term rate agreements, such goals were difficult to achieve in the sour and unstable economic climate of the late 1970s. Taking a frustrated tone, TVA noted that it had become increasingly difficult to work with the railroads, particularly the L&N Railroad, TVA's major rail carrier. "TVA is currently in the process of negotiating new long-term agreements with the L&N," it claimed in a summary of its coal procurement program, and it reported with exasperation that "there has been no response to [our] last proposal." While the railroads contended that the costs were justified, TVA's own studies on the matter concluded skeptically that the increases were "excessive."[59] Utilities had little power to resist the railroads' rate increases, and in their view, the railroads were exploiting economic uncertainty.

In November 1979, Representative Bob Eckhardt (D-TX) launched a direct attack on the railroads. He asked the Supreme Court to overturn some of the recent ICC decisions affecting rail rates, which he claimed had artificially increased coal prices and utility bills. In doing so, he joined in a case brought by Houston Lighting and Power and Arizona Electric Power Cooperative assaulting a 1978 ICC decision. This decision had approved a rate increase request by Burlington Northern Incorporated, which Eckhardt claimed had then catalyzed further increases by other railroads. He deemed these recent price hikes unwarranted and harmful. Eckhardt's argument revolved around his interpretation of the 4R Act's requirements that the ICC consider both a railroad's profitability and the "general public need," and he claimed that the ICC had ignored the latter in coming up with their decisions.[60]

He seemed to have a point. Because of the decisions, coal-hauling rates in the Southwest in 1978 had more than doubled over what 1974 projections had predicted. According to Eckhardt, his constituents subsequently paid $40 million a year in higher utility bills than they should have. Eckhardt's accusations quickly gained traction. The same month, the Department of Justice asked a federal appeals court to overturn the decision, along with several related ones. Its antitrust division joined the City of San Antonio in accusing the ICC of ignoring the needs of consumers. The appeals court agreed with the ICC's critics, deeming the 7 percent figure of latitude in exploring costs arbitrary, and ordered the ICC to come up with an approach that it could more solidly justify.[61]

The ICC thus found itself under assault and quickly acted to make amends. In May 1980, for example, it ordered two rail companies, Burlington Northern Incorporated and the Chicago & North Western Transportation Company, to repay nearly $3 million in overcharges on coal shipments to an Iowa utility. The two railroads had proposed a rate of $10.69 a ton for coal shipped from Wyoming to Iowa, effective in September 1978. When the utility protested, the ICC investigated and found that the rate was illegally high, and it required that the rate decrease to $8.23 a ton. The railroads pleaded with the ICC to reconsider the decision, arguing that Congress wanted the financial stability of the railroads restored, but the commission demurred, arguing that the policy of restoring the railroads' solvency only went to certain limits before increases became unacceptable.[62] Railroads' financial health, while a major concern, could not impinge too directly on consumer energy costs. Though the railroads had achieved some measure of victory in the deregulation debate, it was partial at best. The necessity of maintaining affordable energy meant that railroads would not have total freedom to set their own rates at will.

Congress, prodded by the Carter administration, in mid-1980 proceeded with rail deregulation that went even further than the 4R Act. Though Carter knew that enacting such measures could increase the cost of coal to utilities and thus to consumers, he was also interested in doing more to fix the nation's ailing railroads. His domestic policy staff recognized that they were taking a gamble, balancing fears of consumer anger in the short term against the hopes of achieving economic health for the railroad industry in the long term. In their analysis, in the long term the choice would not be between expensive rail service and cheap rail service, but instead between expensive rail service and no service at all.[63]

In early July, the House debated an administration-backed bill that would give railroads freedom to set rates without ICC review, except on specific rail routes where no competition existed. Importantly, the definition of "competition" at stake was rather wide. As written, it would mean not just that competing rail lines would be present in an area, but that railroads could simply show that the shipper could obtain goods from another source at a price near the cost of transporting the goods by rail. Eckhardt and his coal industry allies challenged this definition. They argued that it overestimated the feasibility of water movement, which was only useful near navigable waterways, as well as truck transport, which, due to size and weight limitations, was only useful at distances of less than a hundred miles. Eckhardt introduced an amendment in the House to strike this wording, seeking to perpetuate the ICC's strong jurisdiction over coal shipping, but it was easily defeated. At the end of July, he succeeded in passing a different amendment that hinged upon the issue of "trigger prices," the ceilings above which shippers could appeal rate increases to the ICC. The administration-backed bill would have set the ceiling far above current levels with the intention of helping to revitalize the rail industry.[64]

Eckhardt's amendment, whose victory came as a surprise to administration officials, reduced the trigger prices to levels that approximated the average freight rates in the country, which were significantly below the administration's proposed rates. In September, Eckhardt and his opponents reached a compromise on the bill as a whole. While largely deregulating the railroad industry, the compromise (known as the Staggers Act of 1980) gave the ICC stronger powers in dealing with shippers served by a single railroad, which included many coalmines in the East. The administration was disappointed with this compromise, believing that it was not in the railroads' long-term interest to remain subject to partial regulation in general and fearing the effect of continued regulation for the coal conversion plans in particular.[65] Though the administration achieved the goal of boosting the railroad industry as a whole through deregulation, this compromise did little in the short term to help the specific goal of coal conversion. The administration found its plans stymied by the complex interplay of the divergent interests at stake, which it had again failed to consider adequately at the outset of debate.

THE UMWA'S FUTURE

The confusion of Carter's staff in the railroad deregulation debate, and its sluggishness in understanding the concerns of the various interest groups involved, were symptomatic of the administration's general orientation toward energy. The policy makers in the Carter administration conceived of coal as a commodity whose domestic abundance could help wean the nation off imported oil. The administration's plans reflected a simplistic approach to the fuel that sought increases in coal production and distribution in order to replace oil as an input in the process of electricity production. As a symbol, coal represented a more secure position in the international arena, as it would cleave the United States from dependence on oil from an increasingly unstable region of the world. Carter administration policy makers' first and most glaring error was in not considering how increasing coal use would be constrained by existing environmental regulations. There were many other problems as well. Later conflicts over coal reflected deeper differences over conceptions of its essential nature and demonstrated how control of the fossilized material represented underlying power relations.

UMWA miners saw coal in terms of the sweat and toil they had expended while mining it from the ground, a brutal and backbreaking job further exacerbated by the constant lurking threats of explosion and gaseous poisoning.[66] For miners, the dangers involved in providing the material to heat homes and businesses and allow Americans to live in comfort entitled them to reasonable compensation in return. What they lacked in everyday job safety, they believed, they were entitled to in economic security. Increasingly unfavorable contracts in the tightened macroeconomic environment of the 1970s threatened this long-standing expectation. Unionized miners thus sought to exert control over the fruits of their labor, interdicting shipments of non-union coal in order to obtain concessions in contract negotiations. They sought to use the black rock as a tool of preserving their economic standing in an era of increasing inflation and decreased consumer purchasing power.

Their corporate foes, by contrast, saw coal in terms of the capital investment they had made to obtain it, and they resisted the miners' demands in order to secure what they saw as their legitimate return. The inflation of the 1970s brought smaller and smaller profits for corporations across the economic spectrum, and coal companies resisted miners' demands to maintain what the coal companies saw as overly lucrative labor contracts while company profits shrank.[67] Miners' and coal mining companies' fundamental disagreements over the allocation of coal mining profits had a stark effect on Carter's energy plans and generated problems that continually frustrated Carter's domestic policy staff as well as his legal advisers.

There was still another group involved in the economic debates, one whose interests lined up with neither the miners nor the coal mining companies. Railroad interests saw coal as a potentially useful profit maker, but only if they were allowed significant leeway to set the rates for what traveled along their tracks. This desire brought the railroads into nearly irreconcilable opposition with coal companies, for each extra dollar charged by the railroads to haul coal was a dollar out of the coal companies' pockets. Because coal companies paid the miners, each extra dollar charged by the railroads to ship coal also represented money out of coal miners' wallets down the line.[68] Coal miners, mining companies, and railroads all battled for economic hegemony, with the Carter administration caught in between all of them. For all these private-sector constituencies, the conflicting understandings of coal relied on divergent ideas about its control. UMWA miners sought to control the commodity their dangerous labor had yielded, coal-mining companies sought to control the returns on their industrial investment, and ailing railroads sought to control their rails and what rode upon them.

Conflicts over the meaning of coal thus reflected disagreements over ownership of the natural world and especially the physical landscape. Coal was a commodity whose extraction, transportation, and burning all had intensely localized effects, and major controversies in the late 1970s turned on how profits generated by this natural resource would be distributed. The administration's emphasis on coal's increased importance, and its calls to expand production and distribution, only exacerbated these underlying tensions. The lacuna in the administration's thinking meant that it could not appreciate the clashes that would result when its energy agenda reconfigured the power relations embedded within the political economy of coal.

The UMWA strike and the debate over railroad deregulation were linked in an unexpected and profound way, one that became apparent after Carter's reelection defeat and the inauguration of his successor, Ronald Reagan. It was during the Reagan administration that the UMWA's power fell off precipitously, much more than in the Carter years, but it was not Reagan himself who crushed the union. Indeed, the Reagan years began as a time of optimism for the UMWA. In response to its 110-day strike in 1977–1978, the union had received a quite favorable contract that both guaranteed significant wage increases and preserved protections for wildcat strikers. The UMWA was therefore emboldened when Reagan announced huge federal cuts to black lung benefits shortly after his inauguration in 1981. New UMWA chief Samuel Church, a man much more respected within the union than his predecessor Arnold Miller, invoked the specter of the April–May 1977 strikes to warn that the union would not have victories "taken from us by an administration that apparently has no concept of coal mining and what it does to the people who are simply trying to make an honest living."[69]

As the 26 March deadline to negotiate a new contract approached, a broader set of concerns emerged. The BCOA had agreed to a contract giving a 36 percent raise over the next three years, along with a new dental plan and increased pensions. The BCOA had been generous with financial benefits in the new contract for a very particular reason, one that infuriated the miners. The new contract would allow BCOA members to process non-union coal at preparation plants located at union mines. Miners balked at the idea of having non-union coal in unionized workspaces. Even worse in the eyes of the miners, though, the coal companies were at present required to pay a royalty of $1.90 into a pension fund for retired miners for each ton of union-mined coal that was processed, and the new contract exempted non-union coal from this royalty. Though non-union workers would mine the coal in question, UMWA members were the ones doing the processing, and the proposed exemption thus represented to the miners both an underhanded jab at their financial security and an insult. The union went on strike to prevent this provision from going into effect.[70]

The 1981 strike lasted seventy-two days, which, while shorter than the 1977–1978 walkout, still made it the second-longest coal strike in US history. The final settlement restored union rules governing the processing of non-union coal, although it also for the first time allowed coal companies to farm out some work to non-union contractors. The aftermath of the strike also revealed a larger story about the UMWA's diminished power, one rooted in Carter's deregulatory actions. The Staggers Act of 1980, which had crippled the ICC, had also catalyzed railroads across the country to pursue mergers, which brought various routes under tighter control and better management, and made them more efficient. Though the Staggers Act had kept regulation in place in cases where there was no effective competition for rail service, the improved coordination of railroads crisscrossing the country resulting from mergers brought down costs gradually but significantly. Mergers rendered railroads more profitable and made it easier to speed non-union coal from the West around the country, even with formal ICC regulation of some route prices still in effect. Furthermore, the Staggers Act freed railroads to enter into long-term contracts not subject to constant ICC oversight, which made prospective future revenues much more reliable and predictable. The West had long been a major center of coal reserves, but the high cost of transporting it back east had limited its contribution to the national coal economy. The Staggers Act largely removed that obstacle.[71]

This development brought the UMWA's fears about the growing influence and power of non-union coal to fruition. In 1970 the share of total US coal covered by the union's contract had been 70 percent, but by March 1981 it was a mere 44 percent and falling. Coal executives and government officials alike predicted that the UMWA's propensity for striking would continue to drive demand for non-union coal, especially with improved rail service taking it easily eastward for wide distribution.[72] Oil companies, noticing decreased petroleum reserves and more difficult oil field exploration, had begun to enter the coal market. They owned many non-union Western coalmines. Due to these oil companies' diverse revenue streams, they were much better equipped to resist Western miner defiance than eastern coal companies, which relied totally on revenue from coal. Western coal, like that of Appalachia and the Midwest, is generally bituminous, making it an easy substitute for that of the East. National periodicals that had expressed fear and awe of the UMWA's power at the end of the 1977–1978 strike now described the 1981 strike as a pained gasp of a suffering and weakened entity.[73]

The mergers spurred by the 1980 Staggers Act thus represented a grave threat to the UMWA's bargaining power in the future. In contemporary media coverage, the UMWA seemed increasingly to be a relic of the past, and perhaps it was. The UMWA's initial organization efforts in the 1890s had occurred with the blessings of the myriad small mine operators extracting coal in Appalachia and the Midwest, who saw a unionized workforce as a way to stabilize their intensely competitive industry. Overproduction and seasonal variations in demand made operating coalmines a risky entrepreneurial choice, and unionization of disparate miners was the best hope to steady the political economy of the industry. The 1920s and 1930s witnessed a consolidation of eastern coal producers that eliminated these structural problems, but by then the UMWA was firmly entrenched in the region. By contrast, the West's remoteness spared it from this battle of small operators ever occurring. Instead, a handful of large companies developed the Western coal industry. Far from encouraging unionization, these companies suppressed it.[74] Nearly a century later, newspapers predicted that this non-union coal would power the country's future. Striking during contract negotiations had once appeared to be a powerful bargaining tool for unionized miners. Now, at the beginning of the 1980s, the UMWA, by insisting on striking during every contract negotiation, seemed to be speeding its own demise.[75] The feasibility of using western coal as a replacement for that mined by the UMWA brought a new paradigm to the domestic coal industry.[76]

These consequences, and the tone of the national press after the strike's settlement, cast Jimmy Carter's relationship with the UMWA a few years before in an entirely different light. In February 1978, with the 1977–1978 strike ending, the *Chicago Tribune* had indignantly accused President Carter of unfairly applying pressure "principally to one side, the mine operators" and of "help[ing] the UMWA get its way."[77] In the *Tribune*'s opinion, Carter had gone much too far and had flirted with extortion of the coal companies to help the miners achieve their demands. Although the *Tribune*'s accusations were overblown in light of Carter's invocation of the anti-union Taft-Hartley Act, at several moments during the strike Carter indeed lashed out at the BCOA, demanding that they do more to accommodate the UMWA's wishes. The Carter-supported settlement saw the BCOA giving the miners almost every substantial provision that they had gone on strike to achieve. Ironically, though, the Carter-supported Staggers Act did more to weaken the power of the UMWA than anything the BCOA did during the tense and violent 1977–1978 walkout, and even more than Carter's use of Taft-Hartley.

These developments remind us of the deregulatory continuities between the Carter and Reagan administrations. In popular perception, Ronald Reagan transformed the political landscape of the United States, ushering in an era of deregulation and undercutting the economic and political power of organized labor. However, the intertwined history of the UMWA and rail deregulation reveals that Carter contributed significantly to both of these developments, even if his actions in this particular case brought about decreased UMWA influence quite by accident. For all his other anti-union measures elsewhere, Reagan himself barely had to do anything at all to weaken the public image of the UMWA, and he was not nearly as involved in settling the 1981 strike as Carter had been in ending the one of winter 1977–1978. The Staggers Act passed under Carter practically took care of the task of undercutting the UMWA's political and economic standing for him. That Carter pursued the Staggers Act to help the railroads does not make its indirect effect on the UMWA's lasting viability any less noteworthy. The deregulation of railroads, not the shocking image of Jock Yablonski's murder, Carter's ambiguous relationship to unions in general, nor Ronald Reagan's anti-union exhortations, is what helped truly weaken the UMWA.

This chapter demonstrated how attempts to achieve energy security intersected with existing political and economic arrangements, and how such attempts had unexpected consequences. It also showed how the Carter administration's political missteps impeded the execution of energy policy and how perceived

"RICH, BLACK VEINS OF THE FUTURE"

incompetence led to the president's declining public reputation. However, another factor intruded into debates about energy policy, namely predictions of future energy use. Since future energy use relies on a number of dynamic factors—population growth, economic growth, and rates of technological progress, among others—wildly divergent predictions of future energy needs could all seem reasonable. Even if some analysts determined that a certain technology was not needed decades in the future, stakeholders who had an interest in that technology could present competing analyses to suggest that it would be needed after all. The next chapter explores how disagreements about future energy needs intersected with the Carter administration's energy policy, using the case of plutonium-based nuclear reactors. It also examines the limits of environmentalism's political power in the midst of energy crisis. Though environmentalists strongly opposed plutonium reactors, they were powerless to halt funding for them as long as there were reasonable concerns about future energy needs. After the oil embargo, nebulous American support for environmental values did not necessarily translate into policy successes.

CHAPTER 3

"THE MODEL-T OF REACTORS"

The Clinch River Breeder Reactor Debate in Congress

The United States Congress approved plans in 1970 for an experimental plutonium reactor on the Clinch River in East Tennessee. It then appropriated initial funds in 1972. Tennessee's representatives in Congress, especially the powerful Republican senator Howard H. Baker Jr., ensured that money kept flowing reliably for years afterward, much of which supported local engineering and design jobs. More than ten years after the initial appropriation, and after continual infusions of cash for the reactor, Congress voted to discontinue further money, effectively ending the project. After more than a decade, although an Indiana manufacturer had produced some of the necessary components and a portion of land along the Clinch was cleared, no structures were ever installed. Congress spent hundreds of millions of dollars developing the project, with nothing to show for the money save for some assorted reactor parts sitting in a Midwestern warehouse, along with a bare spot of land in East Tennessee. This chapter examines the political debate surrounding the Clinch River breeder from the Nixon administration's attempted cancellation in 1973 to the project's ultimate demise in late 1983.[1] It argues that the local concerns of securing federal money and jobs transcended the competing ideologies at the heart of energy policy in the late 1970s, and that these local concerns helped derail the Carter administration's attempts to influence US energy policy in the late 1970s. It also shows that, in the same period, environmentalism's political power declined in the face of energy concerns.

The breeder debate created strange coalitions among political interest groups. The standard intellectual history of environmental debates in the late 1970s nearly always pits environmentalists on one side against conservative thinkers on the other. Environmentalists concerned with endangered species and the fate of pristine wilderness advocated for strong federal intervention to protect the interests of the natural world, even at the expense of local property owners. They generally believed that the federal government was the appropriate body to assume control and protection of environmental quality, arguing that a strong and centralized effort was necessary to counteract the rampant destruction of the natural world. Conservative intellectuals and think tanks countered that this environmental approach was wrong, for two reasons. First, it was legally wrong, since federal regulations enabling environmental protective actions without compensation unduly deprived landowners from using their own private property as they desired, a violation of constitutional rights.[2] Second, it was misguided and ineffective, since localities and landowners could be wiser and more efficient stewards of their own surroundings than some distant federal regulator ever could.[3]

The breeder controversy made political allies out of these two seemingly antagonistic groups. Environmentalists argued that plutonium was much more dangerous than uranium and that even a tiny amount of plutonium waste released into the environment could yield catastrophic consequences. As the estimates of the project's final cost ballooned in the early 1980s, conservative think tanks and political organizations broke with Reagan and spoke out against the project. The alliance of environmentalists with anti-tax conservative groups against the technology in the early 1980s spurred a shift in congressional sentiment that finally led to the breeder's demise. Competing ideologies took a back seat to the vagaries of practical politics in the breeder debate. More importantly, the breeder battle exposed the limits of environmentalism's political power in the 1970s. Though Americans broadly claimed to support environmental principles, environmentalist groups were unable to halt or even cut back funding for the breeder until fiscal conservatives in Congress turned against the project. The history of the breeder suggests again that public support for environmental values did not necessarily translate into policy successes after the oil embargo made energy a more pressing priority.

Examining the breeder debate also advances our understanding of nuclear politics and the role of expertise in making public policy in the postwar United States. In one of the seminal analyses of nuclear power in the United States, historian Brian Balogh focuses on the period from 1945 to 1975 as a time when "professionals and administrators" guided the course of nuclear development and "staked proprietary claims to this new federal policy." An "unprecedented reliance on expert guidance" directed the course of nuclear politics, with focused and insulated congressional committees providing close support to nuclear development. The decline of nuclear power, Balogh argues, came when the vast proliferation of experts reached its logical conclusion and generated a critical overload of information going out to the public. With so many scientific and social-scientific fields of possible expertise, each with its own assumptions and epistemologies, it was inevitable that the opinions of experts from different specializations would come into conflict with one another. Regular citizens were understandably ill equipped to evaluate competing experts' claims, and thus expertise itself lost its influence in the eyes of the public. If trained experts could not agree on virtually any complicated issue, in other words, then expertise itself had little practical value.[4]

Balogh ends his analysis in 1975, with "policymakers . . . deadlocked" and "experts seemingly on all sides of every issue."[5] Using the example of the breeder reactor to extend Balogh's chronology helps reveal what happened next. Pork-barrel politics in Congress took over with legislators standing to benefit from nuclear dollars, wresting the debate out of the hands of experts and pushing to construct projects that economic analysis often deemed unnecessary. Congressional breeder proponents' power to guide the US nuclear program as they saw fit was vast. Balogh focuses on insulated science and technology subcommittees to explain nuclear power's rise, but after his period of interest, the contentious floors of the House and Senate held the fate of nuclear politics. Tennessee politicians, to whom the breeder meant economic opportunity for their constituents, guided the debate at all times.[6]

The breeder debate is also a reminder of the continuing importance of local politics in the postwar United States. Even with the federal government's massive growth and bureaucratization through the course of the New Deal and World War II, representatives in Congress still had an overriding need to deliver services to local constituents in order to secure their own chances for reelection. The efforts of Tennessee's congressional delegation kept the breeder going long after most rational economic analysis had recommended that it end. The effort created some very odd sights indeed. For example, Al Gore, who would later become one of the most prominent anti-nuclear voices in the world, strongly supported the Clinch River project alongside his Tennessee colleagues. Congressional desires to preserve federal jobs near Oak Ridge, Tennessee, drove a sizable component of US nuclear policy in the late 1970s and early 1980s. To be sure, the Clinch River debate intersected with other aspects of nuclear power in the late 1970s, including safety concerns, declining energy demand, and plummeting uranium price. The Clinch River case also shows that, when it came to the international dynamics of energy policy, local concerns still mattered too. Carter's multiple failed attempts to kill the breeder caused his public image to suffer accordingly and represented another blow to his attempts to convince Americans to trust his energy plans. With Americans generally unable to evaluate and adjudicate competing scientific claims, Carter became merely one voice among many. Carter, the General Accounting Office, pro-breeder members of Congress, anti-breeder members of Congress, pro-breeder scientists, and anti-breeder scientists all received roughly equal weight in media narratives, with media outlets unable to adjudicate disagreements over very complicated scientific and technical questions. The breeder debate thereby further impeded the president's ability to implement and execute his energy agenda.

THE PROMISE OF BREEDER TECHNOLOGY

Following the end of World War II, Oak Ridge National Laboratory, the site of the Manhattan Project's uranium enrichment, served as a major federal center of scientific and technological research under the supervision of the Atomic Energy Commission. In the midst of the 1973 energy crisis, the Nixon administration took steps to eliminate experimental energy programs that it concluded were not sufficiently promising, a decision that affected the research center. Nixon's assessment, and the implications it would hold for the high-paying jobs at Oak Ridge, drew the attention of Tennessee politicians, most notably Howard Baker. Baker and other Tennessee legislators protested general cuts in technological funding but reserved special disdain for the administration's decision to terminate a Molten Salt Breeder Reactor (MSBR) on the Clinch River. The MSBR was one of two backup efforts to another major experimental nuclear project on the Clinch, the Liquid Metal Fast Breeder Reactor (LMFBR). The MSBR, the less promising of the two reserve efforts, found itself under the budgetary axe.[7]

Proponents of breeder technology had claimed that the concept posed an ideal solution for future energy needs because of its ability to extend dwindling supplies of fissionable uranium nearly indefinitely. They argued that breeder technology possessed the capacity to extract *sixty times* as much energy from uranium ore than could conventional reactors and thus, even without any further mining, could supply the United States with electricity for two hundred years just from uranium "tailings" already stored as waste. This striking efficiency derived from the breeder's use of plutonium to regenerate fuel continually. Conventional reactors, breeder boosters noted, subjected to the fission process uranium-235, an isotope that splits when struck by a neutron at low speed, giving off heat. Water under high pressure slowed down the neutrons and then carried off the heat to a steam turbine in order to generate electricity. Such reactors depended on the scarce U-235, which made up only 0.7 percent of uranium ore. The rest existed as a heavier isotope, U-238, which does not fission.[8]

By contrast, the breeder design made productive use of this plentiful U-238. The core of a breeder reactor consisted of plutonium fuel rods surrounded by a "blanket" of U-238 atoms waiting to be "impregnated" by neutrons shot off from the plutonium. Each time an atom of plutonium-239 fissioned, in theory, it would give off heat to turn water into steam for electricity production, but the Pu-239 atom would also emit two or three neutrons. One of these neutrons would hit another Pu-239 atom in the core, sustaining the reaction, but the remaining one or two neutrons would be captured by the "blanket" of U-238 atoms, each of which would then be transmuted into Pu-239, the very fuel the reactor had started with. The breeder process thus generated both energy and still more Pu-239, more indeed than when the reaction had begun. The plutonium in the core would be "spent" at the end of the reaction and would have to be disposed of, but the new Pu-239 was usable in future reactions; all that was required was fresh U-238, of which there was no shortage. The breeding ratio at Clinch River was expected to be 1.24, meaning that the reactor would produce 1.24 atoms of Pu-239 for every one that it consumed.[9]

In theory, then, by producing more Pu-239 than it had started with and by making use of the abundant U-238, the breeder could serve as a self-sustaining source of energy and fuel the creation of electric power for years and decades into the future, decreasing US dependence on foreign oil. However, the outcome was necessarily uncertain. New scientific technologies often see their costs fluctuate rapidly throughout the development process as unexpected roadblocks arise, and it is nearly impossible to know if a technology that seems to work in theory will actually function properly in physical form. The breeder idea was a gamble from the start. The Nixon administration, determining that the technology would be neither ready nor necessary until many years later, took the steep immediate cost as a signal to abandon the less-promising MSBR and simply write off the money already spent. Baker and Tennessee's other senator, Bill Brock, subsequently pledged in tandem to "rededicate" their efforts to obtain funding for the MSBR, as well as a radio-isotopes program that also faced elimination. They made the primary reason for their efforts abundantly clear, citing the termination of the approximately seven hundred employees that would occur should the cuts go through. Nixon's staff in the Office of Management and Budget replied tersely that they were "not unaware" of the "difficulties imposed on the affected personnel" by the MSBR's termination and reiterated the fiscal logic of shutting it down.[10]

Advocates claimed that the breeder's recycling of plutonium waste made it more environmentally friendly than traditional reactors. The breeder's use of plutonium in place of the uranium used by traditional reactors, however, drew prominent environmentalist critics, since in small amounts plutonium is much deadlier than uranium. The consumer advocate and anti-nuclear spokesman Ralph Nader penned a scathing June 1975 piece in the *Chicago Tribune* warning against the use of the "fiendishly toxic" element of plutonium in the breeder design. Though Nader opposed nuclear power broadly, he singled out breeder technology for special criticism. "A millionth of a gram [of plutonium] has caused cancer in laboratory animals; police state measures will be necessary" to control the dangerous substance, he predicted.[11] Famed biologist Barry Commoner estimated in his 1976 book *The Poverty of Power* that if the US nuclear power program adopted the breeder design as its base in the future, nationwide nuclear power generation would involve about 130 million pounds of plutonium. If only one one-millionth of this material were to be released into the environment in the course of normal operations, Commoner said, it would generate 1,600 new cases of cancer per year. The release of four parts in ten thousand, according to Commoner, would generate *600,000* new cases of cancer per year.[12]

Nader's and Commoner's exhortations seemed to gain little traction initially. Despite plutonium's dangers, the environmental journalist and lawyer Sheldon Novick declared in a 1976 analysis of the nuclear industry that the experimental LMFBR likely represented "the next stage in nuclear development" in the United States, given its bright promise for recycling fuel.[13] The breeder appeared to be an integral component of US energy policy moving forward. However, the presidential election of 1976 changed the situation quickly and dramatically. After the short Gerald Ford presidency came to end at the hands of Jimmy Carter, the newly elected Georgian moved even more forcefully than Nixon had to shut down not only the backups to the LMFBR, but the LMFBR itself. The significant amount of raw plutonium involved in the breeder's operation unnerved politicians worried about nuclear proliferation, especially the new president. For the same reason, Carter also opposed the development of technologies to reprocess spent nuclear fuel for reuse.[14] The federal Energy Research and Development Administration (ERDA), the Tennessee Valley Authority (TVA), and a group of private utilities were jointly financing the project and would lose their investments if the Clinch River project ended. They were all dismayed by the decision and mobilized to stop it.[15]

CARTER PULLS HIS SUPPORT

In April 1977, soon after taking office, Carter declared that the United States would halt construction of the reactor as part of an appeal to other countries to renounce plutonium themselves.[16] Carter was a Democrat, a party that included many anti-nuclear politicians, most notably Earth Day co-founder Gaylord Nelson of Wisconsin. The new president himself was not quite so predisposed against nuclear power, claiming in 1977 that he considered nuclear power a major frontline energy source rather than a last resort. Nonetheless, he felt strongly that this specific project was not worth funding and could in fact be quite dangerous to long-term national security. According to Carter and other commentators, the spent plutonium from the breeder design was much easier to convert into weaponized form than spent uranium from more traditional reactors, and the breeder would prove much more dangerous to international stability than reactors that created uranium waste.[17]

Other criticisms of the breeder centered on the fact that West Germany, Britain, and especially France were further along in developing the breeder technology and would likely be able to license it to the United States at a lower cost than that of developing the technology in the US. Furthermore, by the time the complicated technology was completed, it might not even be needed, since some better alternative would likely be available.[18] Carter continually invoked these two critiques, the proliferation threat and murky cost-effectiveness, in his anti-breeder push. Though Carter especially emphasized the nonproliferation argument early in his term and shifted to an emphasis on cost inefficiency later in his presidency, he consistently cited both throughout his years in office.

Carter's passion for ending the project is unquestionable. However, from the beginning of its involvement in the breeder debate, his administration seemed to struggle to understand basic facts about the reactor. The administration subsequently gave off mixed signals about the project in the media, weakening its negotiating position vis-à-vis breeder proponents. For example, on 7 April, Carter released a statement declaring that the reactor would revert to an "experimental basis," which conflicted with other declarations in which he had said that the project would be ended completely. In the question-and-answer session that followed this particular pronouncement, Carter suggested that he was open to an option that did not involve complete termination of the Clinch River plan, suggesting that a uranium enrichment facility intended for addition to a gaseous diffusion plant in Portsmouth, Ohio, might be constructed at the Clinch River site instead. Jessica Tuchman, director of the National Security Council's Office of Global Issues, later informed the president that such a plan was "technically impossible," as the proposed enrichment facility was not freestanding.[19]

Likewise, on 8 February a group of Princeton scientists had written the newly inaugurated Carter to suggest that he consider adapting Clinch River to experiment with thorium cycling instead, which would keep the facility operating but minimize the proliferation problems presented by plutonium cycling. However, in a 16 April cabinet room general meeting to resolve issues in the energy program, when Science Adviser Frank Press recommended to Carter that he consider adapting Clinch River to experiment with thorium instead of plutonium, Carter seemed confused and responded merely by indicating "that this option had not been presented to him before." According to Carter's staff secretary's records, there was no evidence that the president had ever received the Princeton letter, read it, or referred it to his staff.[20] With the relevant information so badly delayed by administrative disorganization, this idea seems to have never received any serious consideration. By the time it came to the attention of pertinent staff, the dynamics of the debate had progressed in other directions.

The administration's troubles in managing the flow of information notwithstanding, the project drew intense skepticism from a number of national periodicals, many of which adopted President Carter's criticisms. A June 1977 *Washington Post* editorial, for example, castigated the breeder, calling it a "peculiarly ominous symbol." The editorial argued that if the project was built, the "main damage" inflicted upon the United States would be not the plutonium waste itself but "the signal that it sends to the rest of the world." No scientific knowledge would be lost should the breeder be cancelled, the *Post* opined. The only purpose of the project was to demonstrate on a commercial scale the breeder process already in operation at a smaller test facility in Hanford, Washington; but there were other, safer options for future commercial use. If the project continued, it would mean that Congress was undercutting President Carter's wishes, which would "knock the bottom out of the President's attempts to restrain the proliferation of plutonium"—and the weapons made out of it—"throughout the world." If Congress authorized funds for the reactor, the *Post* darkly predicted, European nations might see Carter's position on nonproliferation as nothing more than a ploy to delay European nuclear development in order to allow the United States to pull into the technological lead.[21]

As might be expected, Tennessee's congressional delegation was loath to let a multibillion-dollar project sponsoring scores of local jobs die so quickly. In June, in the Senate's Subcommittee on Public Works, Senator Jim Sasser proposed a $150 million appropriation, a compromise between the $237 million that President Ford had requested to continue the project and the $33 million that Carter wanted appropriated in order to wind it down. Although a number of senators indicated their support for the compromise, Chairman John Stennis (D-MS) decided to wait another week to put it to a vote.[22] Stennis's delay gave the breeder's boosters time to plan their counteroffensive, and they mobilized to scuttle the compromise and ensure the full original amount of funding allocated for the breeder.

One of the most vocal senators in favor of the project was Frank Church (D-ID), dubbed "Capitol Hill's star player" in the Clinch River saga by the *Washington Post*. Church, for his part, argued that two experimental breeders—EBR-1 and EBR-2—had already been making plutonium and power quite safely for twenty years in Idaho. The viability of breeder technology was proven in 1953, when it was discovered that EBR-1 was producing additional fuel during the fission process, a result that had not been anticipated. Church supported the construction of the Clinch River facility as a larger and more advanced manifestation of this proven underlying idea. Church's liberal environmentalist past as the floor sponsor of the 1964 Wilderness Act had caused White House aides to believe that he would be against the project. They attributed Church's support for the plutonium breeder to the $500 million in research grants that Idaho would receive for ongoing research on the EBR reactors should the Clinch River reactor stay on the books. His vehement support for the breeder project stood in stark contrast to his extant legislative career, to that point filled with sharp accusations of corruption aimed at entities ranging from the Pentagon and the US intelligence apparatus to private corporations.[23]

In July, Congress set the project aside to consider Carter's critiques, and the *Washington Post* took the opportunity to argue against continued funding, once more on national security grounds. It asked the Congress to take the opportunity to undo the mistakes of the past. "For years, mindlessly, we promoted abroad the very technology [plutonium] we have now recognized as dangerous. . . . We oversold it." Now, part of America's obligation, the *Post* proclaimed, was to undo "some of the distortions of that oversell." The United States, it said, could hardly hope to convince the Europeans and Japanese to turn away from a plutonium-cycle future if it was unwilling to abandon such a path.[24] The *Post* saw the domestic debate over the breeder reactor as a turning point, arguing that continued funding would unleash grave danger in the international arena. No longer able to trust the United States, the newspaper darkly predicted, America's allies would develop unstable and perilous technologies, exhortations to do otherwise falling on unhearing ears.

The middle of 1977 also saw the public release of a report authored by Burns and Roe, the architectural-engineering firm running the project. The forty-two-page report was written in 1973 but kept confidential for several years, and it was very critical of the project's management and execution. The proposed site at Clinch River was, in the words of the report, "one of the worst ever selected" for a nuclear plant. Varying rock conditions, voids and cavities pockmarking the landscape, and slope stability were all concerns, any one of which could render the site unacceptable. Finally, the document predicted safety problems for the reactor due to infighting between regulatory and research staffs within the AEC that could not agree on safety standards.[25] In a terse statement before a Senate subcommittee on nuclear regulation, Burns and Roe's vice president declared that, "contrary to misleading impressions left by the media," the issues highlighted in the 1973 report were fixed in the intervening four years. Given later problems with the site's physical condition, though, there was reason to doubt the honesty of the vice president's comforting reassurances.[26]

Though the public release of the report was intensely embarrassing, it was also surprisingly inconsequential. The July delay proved short lived, even in spite of the multilayered criticism. On 20 September, the House of Representatives voted down an administration proposal to defund the reactor entirely and proceeded to allocate $80 million to continue the project. House Speaker Tip O'Neill claimed disappointment with the vote. It is impossible to know why each member of the House voted the way he or she did, but what seems clear is that post-1973 fears of energy crisis, along with the longstanding practice of legislators to support one another's local projects, combined to produce a congressional majority in favor of the project. The debate had taken a notably bizarre turn when Thomas Downey (D-NY) held up "what appeared to be a soccer ball with holes into which plutonium could be placed," menacingly demonstrating to his colleagues "how simple it is to make a nuclear weapon." Mike McCormick (D-WA) seemed to speak for the majority view, however, in downplaying the risk of nuclear proliferation. "The fact is that there are three dozen nations today that could make nuclear weapons for $50 million, 5 percent of the cost" of the cheapest possible breeder reactor, he claimed, and ending the breeder would not make a difference in Carter's efforts toward plutonium nonproliferation.[27]

The *Los Angeles Times* disagreed with McCormick's analysis, calling the vote "shockingly irresponsible" and claiming that Carter's campaign to prevent the spread of nuclear weapons would be "hopelessly undermined." It emphasized the risk of plutonium waste falling into the clutches of malevolent non-state actors, a risk that McCormick had not addressed. The *New York Times* struck a similar tone, calling the vote "an excellent target for Mr. Carter's first veto." Leading scientists also joined the debate. Edward Teller, one of the world's foremost nuclear power advocates, was less concerned about proliferation but more worried about the technology's future effectiveness. A significant voice due to his longstanding support for nuclear power even in the face of intense opposition, Teller joined in the tide of criticism and dubbed the Clinch River project obsolete before it had even been started, arguing that more promising alternatives were readily apparent. Though breeders promised to produce fuel indefinitely, developing the technology was, as rising cost estimates indicated, incredibly expensive. By the time the technology was necessary decades in the future, Teller claimed, a better and safer alternative would almost certainly be available.[28]

CONGRESS ADAPTS

At the end of October, following the House's vote, the Senate's Appropriations Committee voted to require Carter to spend $80 million to keep the breeder project alive for at least another year. Although Carter vetoed this bill, both chambers later added the funds to a larger $6.8 billion appropriations bill, meaning that dozens of other federal programs would die alongside the breeder should Carter again exercise his veto power.[29] After this vote, the *New York Times* disappointedly dubbed the breeder "the reactor that would not die." Carter was in a bind. The *Washington Post*'s early prophecy looked likely to come to fruition. Europeans received with cynicism the president's initial promise not to build the reactor. The perception across the Atlantic was that Washington was trying to get other industrial powers to renounce a technology in which they led and the United States lagged behind, giving the US time to catch up.[30] Were Carter to backtrack now, he would have granted great credence to these theories about the ominous nature of US intentions.

Carter's only options besides simply signing or vetoing the bill were to ask Congress to defer the use of the money or to propose that Congress rescind the appropriation for the breeder only. Given the breeder's popularity in Congress, both options seemed incredibly unlikely. The *New York Times* declared that Carter must either "deliver an early finishing blow" to the breeder or "find a graceful way to yield" to the demands of Congress. Continuing the constant demands to defund the project only to receive a public rebuff, though, would certainly harm the president's domestic political standing.[31]

The president felt compelled to sign this bill for the sake of the other appropriations and did so. After negotiating with key House members, the administration came up with a new compromise that it hoped would end the impasse. The funds allocated for the plutonium breeder in the coming fiscal year would go toward building a smaller, demonstration breeder reactor powered by uranium instead of plutonium. In addition, Congress would allocate an additional $160 million to a two-year design study for a larger, different breeder based on some other fuel than weapons-grade plutonium. To alleviate fears of local job losses in East Tennessee, Energy Secretary James Schlesinger promised that this proposed study plan would employ 90 percent of the professionals currently on the Clinch River design team.[32]

The *Los Angeles Times* voiced support for the compromise, claiming that, should the design study prove successful, "the technology could be made available to other countries that are genuinely convinced that breeder reactors are essential to meeting their future energy needs" without increasing the risk of plutonium dangers. It advised Carter to use an upcoming scheduled trip to Oak Ridge to argue that "if a breeder reactor is to be built in Tennessee, surely it's better that it be one that will contribute to a safer rather than a more dangerous world." Likewise, Walter Flowers (D-AL) "hailed" the compromise as an opportunity to break the impasse. However, Marilyn Lloyd (D-TN), in whose district the Clinch River site lay, was skeptical. She deeply distrusted the administration's motives. Redirecting the funds toward a study, she feared, might simply be a stalling tactic, and an actual facility might never come to fruition. The bill also split anti-nuclear advocates in the House, with some opposing funding for *any* breeder plant and others seeing the compromise as a way to end the controversy and move on to other energy issues marginalized by the breeder battle.[33]

Less than a month later, Representative Lloyd offered an amendment to the 1979 fiscal year authorization for the Department of Energy to reject the administration's compromise and authorize $172.5 million to fund the breeder for another year.[34] With anti-nuclear forces divided and pro-breeder advocates united, the amendment passed. Mike McCormick claimed boldly that the vote indicated that "it's time now for the administration to recognize the Congress is not going to roll over and play dead on the breeder." Expressing his own support for the project, Representative Barry M. Goldwater Jr. (R-CA), son of the former Republican presidential candidate, pointed to the widespread United Mine Workers' strike interrupting coal shipments as evidence that nuclear power had to receive even greater emphasis in US energy strategy going forward. In Goldwater's eyes, the unreliability of militant coal miners made developing the more dependable nuclear power option necessary, even given the increased risks of disastrous public health hazards.[35]

John Wydler (R-NY), the ranking minority member on the House's Committee on Science and Technology, wrote Carter that same April to warn about the nuclear progress that America's Cold War adversary was achieving. Wydler had conversed with high-ranking Soviet officials in Moscow during the last week of March. The information conveyed was alarming. During the visit, the Soviets had victoriously touted the 350-megawatt breeder plant that had been operating on the Caspian Sea for three years, as well as their plans to complete and begin operation of a massive 600-megawatt plant in 1980. Wydler warned President Carter that the United States' own program paled in comparison to the aggressive approach pursued by the Soviets. He felt it was "frightening to speculate on the degree of control of the world market" for distribution of breeder technology that the United States' Cold War adversaries might achieve by successfully implementing their program.[36]

By contrast, Representative Wydler warned, the United States was foolishly "limping indecisively" on the nuclear option. Imperative action was necessary to counter this ominous trajectory. He advised the president to "commit strongly" to breeder technology to head off Soviet hegemony in the nuclear sphere.[37] That Wydler may have been subject to a carefully choreographed and possibly exaggerated presentation to exaggerate the Soviet nuclear program and intimidate the Soviets' Cold War enemy seemed not to have occurred to the representative. In fact, a long 1983 exposé in the *Atlantic Monthly* on the problems within the US breeder program also revealed that the Soviets had experienced "greater than expected" problems with their own efforts and had scaled back their previously bold plans.[38]

Wydler's demands for the breeder's continuation rested on an ideological belief that the United States must not fall behind the Soviet Union in the development of any nuclear-related technology. It may be surprising that weapons concerns did not initially figure more prominently in US fears, given the decades-long nuclear standoff between the two nations. Yet by the late 1970s, the United States and the Soviet Union each possessed a stockpile of weapons that could virtually wipe the other off the face of the planet. In this context, the main concern for each nation was that the other could launch a rapid and comprehensive attack to wipe out main cities and missile storage areas before there was even a chance to react or respond. The nuclear arms race between the two nations in the 1980s therefore centered on building sleeker, faster, and more accurate missiles with a bigger payload in the warhead, along with developing reliable missile defense systems.[39] Since the Soviet Union already had thousands of nuclear weapons, any fear that it might use the breeder to create more nuclear material for military use would be redundant. For Carter and other critics of the breeder, the technology's primary danger was always the potential compromise of plutonium shipments on the way to or from a power plant, followed by their handoff to nonnuclear states or non-state actors.

Almost as passionate about the project as Representative Marilyn Lloyd was John Duncan, the representative for Tennessee's second congressional district. Having served as mayor of Knoxville in the early 1960s, Duncan assumed a seat in the US House of Representatives in early 1965 after the death of Howard Baker Sr., who had represented the district since 1951. Duncan's district included Knox and Loudon counties, among others, which were adjacent to the counties (Anderson and Roane) containing Oak Ridge represented by Marilyn Lloyd. Many of Duncan's constituents commuted into Oak Ridge for work or otherwise benefited from the economic activity that the site generated for the region, and his office received a number of letters asking him to advocate for the Clinch River reactor's completion. In October 1977, for example, one of Congressman Duncan's newest constituents wrote him in support of the project. David Norcutt informed the representative that he was a "newcomer" to the Lenoir City area of Loudon County and was already concerned about the potential curtailment of the Clinch River project, which would be "very det[rime]ntal" to the area's economy. "I would appreciate anything you could do," wrote Norcutt to Duncan, to assure the project's continuation.[40] Norcutt had little to worry about, as Duncan was among the project's most ardent boosters and continued to be so.

In late May 1978, Carter visited Oak Ridge for the very first time, as president or otherwise. Prior to his arrival, the dean of research at the nearby University of Tennessee, along with the head of the Department of Nuclear Engineering at the institution, sternly argued that the "opportunity for senior scientists" at Oak

Ridge to speak with the president was "long overdue." The University of Tennessee's engineering school had a close relationship with the Oak Ridge installation, and the two university officials took an intense interest in research projects there. They hoped that Carter's presence at the site in East Tennessee would lead him to recognize the necessity of the breeder and its important role in the future of US energy policy, and they cautiously anticipated that the visit would be illuminating for the chief executive.[41]

Carter used the visit to speak about the importance of a wise nuclear policy for US national interest. However, on balance, the university officials must have been disappointed, along with many other East Tennessee residents who supported the project and its economic benefits. Carter said virtually nothing about the controversial Clinch River project in particular during his visit. Knoxville resident Dianne Turner wrote to the local newspaper, the *Knoxville News-Sentinel,* to register this complaint. She noted that the president did not bother to mention the Clinch River reactor by name in his visit to the area and, even worse, "did not even allow scientists and engineers the courtesy of mentioning, let alone expressing their opinion on" the project. He had merely spoken *at* them, not *with* them, not taking time to hear their perspectives and opinions about the important work completed there. This alleged muzzling of the Oak Ridge employees outraged Turner. "How our Senators and Representatives could stand for this is a mystery to me," she fumed. In addition to sending this letter to the newspaper editor, she sent a copy to Congressman Duncan.[42]

Duncan's reply made it clear that he did not stand for it. He called Turner's letter "one of the best" he had received on the Clinch River project. Carter's refusal to discuss the project with the scientists and engineers at Oak Ridge was, in the representative's estimation, an "act of stubbornness," since they had important perspectives to provide. He told Turner that she could "be assured" of his continuing support for the Clinch River reactor, regardless of the president's position on the issue.[43]

NEXT STEPS

In early June 1978, the Senate Energy Committee resurrected the compromise plan rejected in the House, voting to allow Carter to scrap the breeder if he planned for an alternative. Administration officials, exasperated with the ongoing controversy, frustrated with the House's perceived intransigence, and continuing to demand the project's unconditional cancellation, indicated that the proposal did not go far enough and could invite another presidential veto. However, Carter himself indicated his approval for the compromise the next month. To assuage congressional fears that the administration would stall the design study of the alternative demonstration breeder reactor until it simply died, the vote required that the study be completed by 31 March 1981. Opponents of the breeder seemed hopeful that this would *finally* conclude the controversy. A few days later, though, during consideration of a $4.3 billion fiscal authorization for the Department of Energy, the House rejected the compromise, again reiterating its inflexible demand for full funding of the original project. The president was unsurprisingly shocked and disappointed, the political controversy seemingly no closer to resolution now than months or years before.[44]

Newspapers continued their assault on the reactor after the failed compromise, pointing to the lack of material results even after so much funding from Congress. A December 1978 story in the *Washington Post* reported critically that the site chosen for the breeder reactor along the river had yet even to be cleared of trees; "meanwhile," though, "fabrication of the huge pieces of machinery that were designed and ordered for Clinch River chugs along." At an Indiana plant that was manufacturing the reactor's components, construction of the 470-ton reactor vessel was reportedly 90 percent complete, which put it ahead of schedule. The stainless steel vessel designed to house the plutonium fuel bundle had already reached its full girth of twenty feet and its full height of fifty-four feet. "But when it is finished, in a few months," opined the *Washington Post*, "it will be placed in storage like an antique vessel that nobody wants."[45]

Most of the holdup in preparing the site traced back to the Nuclear Regulatory Commission (NRC), which required the breeder to meet strict safety licensing standards before construction could start. One of the side goals of the project had been to procure an NRC license to prove that breeders could meet federal health and safety standards, which would remove one of the key arguments against future breeder projects. However, the contractors building the breeder had neglected this licensing goal. Breeder proponents seemed to have few answers to the disjuncture between the rapid manufacturing of the reactor itself and the lethargic preparation of its home on the Clinch River, lending growing credence to the complaints of critics who dubbed the project both a mismanaged mess and a waste of money.

The following spring brought a renewed push against the breeder by the administration. In the face of the compromise plan's failure, Carter and his staff returned to a hard-nosed approach favoring total cancellation. In April, Carter reiterated to his vice president, Walter Mondale—also, of course, the president of the Senate—that the $15 million per month spent on the breeder needed to end, and asked him for help in achieving this outcome. The same day, Secretary Schlesinger sent legislative language to Senator Henry Jackson (D-WA) that would remove basic authorization for the Clinch River breeder reactor project and provide for "intelligent use" of those components that could be put to use in other nuclear designs. Attempts to combat the breeder in the Senate had little effect on continued support for the breeder in the more rambunctious House. Despite the administration's push, two days after these actions, the House's Science and Technology Committee voted to proceed with initial construction on the Clinch.[46]

Carter's public statement the next day overflowed with irritation. Returning to his nonproliferation critiques, he called the vote a "significant setback to a rational and responsible nuclear energy policy" because the vote would antagonize European nations that had trusted Carter's calls to abandon breeder technology. Carter publicly urged Congress to press ahead with uranium-fueled light water technology, an alternative to plutonium, and to ignore the "special interests"—namely, Tennessee politicians and utility companies—driving continued funding.[47] Carter's words must have come merely from frustration, as there was little reason to think that Congress would deviate from its support. The "special interests" were firmly in control.

It might be surprising that the nuclear meltdown at Pennsylvania's Three Mile Island (TMI) plant in March 1979 had little direct effect on the breeder debate through the rest of 1979. The accident caused many American citizens who had been ambivalent about nuclear power to turn against it, and it galvanized the national anti-nuclear movement to new levels of protest. Defenders of nuclear power raced to defend the industry. Yet there is evidence that the impact of TMI has been exaggerated in retrospect. It is true that no new nuclear plants were approved for decades following the accident, but declining energy demand in the late 1970s and early 1980s did more to contribute to this outcome. Indeed, the meltdown did not catalyze the shutdown of any other existing plants in the United States, and in 1985 Consolidated Edison succeeded in obtaining NRC authority to restart the TMI-1 reactor despite public protest. (The meltdown had occurred in the TMI-2 reactor; both reactors had suspended operations after the accident.)[48] Though some communities took the TMI accident as a signal to resist future nuclear construction projects, Oak Ridge had long embraced its identity as an integral component of the Manhattan Project, with the massive Y-12 plant lying just outside the town.[49] Residents embraced the idea of being at the forefront of a new nuclear technology. The prospect of the breeder being constructed near their community seems to have caused residents little worry, and Tennessee representatives pressed ahead wholeheartedly with their support.[50]

Indeed, the Carter administration's position took another major blow in May 1979, when a report from the General Accounting Office (GAO), Congress's investigative arm, urged legislators to press ahead. The project appeared to be operating on sheer inertia at this point. Citing the $674 million already spent on the project, the GAO concluded that terminating the project would represent an enormous waste of resources. The United States should simply finish the project, it said, and reap whatever salvageable benefits remained at the end rather than simply lose what had been expended. To support its pro-construction analysis, the report also addressed the risk of nuclear proliferation and asked the Carter administration to recognize practicalities. Other countries were proceeding with their own plans to build such reactors and would continue to do so whether or not the United States developed its own technology, the GAO said. The United States should not find itself stymying its own energy future, since breeder technology was going to be a reality whether or not the US participated. Though plutonium proliferation might be a legitimate concern, the GAO argued, the idea that US refusal to support breeder research would make the world safer was simply wishful and foolish thinking. The GAO report also disputed administration contentions that the reactor was not large enough to be practical, since part of the point of the Clinch River project was to prove the feasibility of the underlying design before larger, more expansive reactors received funding allocations from the government.[51]

Two months later, in July, the *Washington Post* again criticized the Clinch River breeder and disputed the GAO's conclusions about the need to continue funding the project. The newspaper estimated that the break-even point (the point at which the revenue generated by the breeder would match the funds invested) would not come until 2020, when the design would be fifty years old. Channeling nuclear scientist Edward Teller's earlier critiques, the *Post* claimed that the breeder would end up as the "Model-T of reactors," more suitable for museum display than for practical use. "This year," the *Post* opined, "Clinch River should be sent once and for all to its grave." Later that month, though, the House voted down Carter's latest compromise plan. By a voice vote, it also rejected a proposal offered by Morris Udall (D-AZ)—a major congressional critic of nuclear energy in general—to kill the Clinch River complex without launching the new breeder project, which never had a chance.[52]

Another GAO report in May seemed to bear out at least some of Ralph Nader's ominous "police state" warnings from four years earlier. Although the Energy Department and NRC required special security measures for shipments of weapons-grade plutonium that reached a specified quantity known as the "strategic level," the GAO warned that the theft of multiple shipments below that level could provide enough material to construct a bomb. The safeguards, the GAO said, also did not distinguish among enrichment levels of assorted plutonium quantities. Because the more highly enriched plutonium is, the less of it is necessary to build a bomb, shipments less useful for making a bomb might be protected while more useful shipments would not.[53] With hundreds of millions of dollars already spent on the project, this warning seemed to have little impact on the political debate.

The GAO's conflicting, divergent analyses of the complicated project seemed now to reflect the mindset of the president himself. In the middle of 1979, Carter gave off new, mixed signals about his ideas for the breeder's future, making all concerned interest groups suspicious. After years of losing battles with Congress, Carter proposed using the breeder's current funding to develop a more "modernized" version of the reactor instead of the current design, giving little indication of what exactly this meant. Part of Carter's new proposal was to delay construction to allow time to complete this redesign. He argued that declining energy demand meant that the breeder would be necessary later than originally envisioned, and that this delay would thus not negatively affect the project. The delay would instead lay the foundation for an increased chance of lasting success. However, the president wrongly anticipated the reception of this idea. The reaction to the new plan was not favorable at all. The nuclear industry, rather than welcoming the president's change of mind, instead saw Carter's move as simply another delay tactic. Environmentalist groups unanimously abhorred this new position, saying that Carter's abandonment of opposition to breeders was a dangerous and unprincipled sell-out to his political opponents.[54] Carter had maintained the support of environmentalist groups throughout the breeder debate; with this new compromise proposal, he lost their backing.

Through the rest of 1979 and the first few months of 1980, the politics surrounding the breeder proceeded according to this general pattern. Carter would try to forge some sort of compromise option to delay or kill the construction of the plutonium breeder, and the House would insist on reliable continued funding by including money for it within larger appropriations that Carter could not veto. For example, Carter recommended no money for the project in the Energy Department's budget for fiscal year 1981, but the House Committee on Science and Technology voted to include $155 million in the department's budget instead. A veto would obviously have meant cutting off all funding to the entire Energy Department.[55] It would clearly take some kind of structural change to the situation to alter the underlying dynamics that had guided events on a steady path of conflict between the anti-breeder executive and the pro-breeder legislature for the past several years.

REAGAN'S SUPPORT AND CHANGING SENTIMENTS IN CONGRESS

The election of 1980 was just such a change, but not in the way expected given the new president's campaign rhetoric. The newly elected Ronald Reagan had come into office promising a rollback of government spending, and a long-delayed, over-budget, and ostensibly outmoded federal project appeared to be a prime target for cost-cutting measures. However, in February 1981 Reagan instead decided to put his backing behind the initiative and to propose completing the reactor. The new chief executive appeared to support the project as a favor to Senator Baker, who had become senate majority leader with the Republican takeover of that body after the 1980 election. Reagan, of course, required Baker's help in moving his anti-tax and anti-regulatory agenda through the legislative process, and support for the reactor was a necessary price to pay to ensure Senate attention to his larger priorities.[56] In July, Reagan also announced that the United States would stop trying to impede breeder development in Europe.[57]

Reagan's support for the project was an embarrassment to his powerful budget director, David Stockman, who as a congressman three years earlier had denounced the project both as "totally incompatible" with a free-market approach to energy and as a "large economic subsidy" to the power industry. Stockman's previous opposition notwithstanding, the project's future stood in "an entirely different light." The administration even promised to try to obtain an exemption from the National Environmental Policy Act, which would have required updating the analysis of the project's environmental impact with every major change in plans. The numerous utility companies that held financial interests in the project, and that had long dreaded its cancellation under Carter, welcomed the pro-breeder statements coming from the new administration.[58]

As the executive branch finally gave its blessing to the project, the tide of opinion in Congress slowly began to turn against the breeder. The shift traced to larger trends in energy consumption that had resulted from the Carter agenda. Over the course of the previous administration, Carter's conservationist policies—tax incentives for insulation and various home improvements in energy efficiency, better standards for energy use by home appliances, and other initiatives—had taken effect, with the nation's aggregate energy use declining markedly. Utility companies found themselves unable to fund planned ongoing construction, as declining energy usage meant less money paid to utilities by consumers. Utilities also scaled back projections for future growth in energy demand, meaning that fewer new plants would be necessary. With utilities both scrambling to deal with demand that had failed to materialize in the present and reducing expectations for future demand, an experimental technology that would likely not be ready for decades seemed much less necessary than it had just a few years earlier. Members of Congress who had hailed nuclear power as a source of energy that would be "too cheap to meter" now found their enthusiasm for the breeder dissipating. Furthermore, the French, who had previously stood boldly at the forefront of breeder development, were experiencing economic problems with

"THE MODEL-T OF REACTORS"

their own program, causing US proponents to rethink the practical usefulness of the technology.[59]

The *New York Times* continued its assault on the program with renewed vigor, warning the Reagan administration not to "plunge ahead" with the project before settling on its overall plan for nuclear nonproliferation. The *Times* spoke apprehensively of a coming vote in the House Science and Technology Committee for $254 million to start construction. "A favorable vote will probably assure that the Tennessee demonstration plant progresses to completion," the periodical predicted, but a contrary vote "may finally turn Congress against this costly, ill-conceived technological turkey." Opponents of the breeder also faced two stark consequences of the 1980 election: first, Baker's ascension as the Senate's powerful majority leader, and second, Tennessean Marilyn Lloyd's assumption of the chairmanship of the House's Subcommittee on Energy Research and Production, which had significant sway in allocating federal dollars to energy projects.[60]

The fears of anti-breeder activists notwithstanding, there were signs that some members of Congress were beginning to turn against the project. On 7 May, the House's Science and Technology Committee narrowly voted to de-authorize the reactor and spend a mere $20 million to terminate the program. The significance of this vote is difficult to pinpoint. Although the *New York Times* characterized the vote as a "major blow" against the project—and some opponents overreached by calling the result "a major shift of sentiment away from nuclear power" altogether—in July the full Congress voted to spend $250 million to fund continued development for another year. Though one important committee had clearly turned against the breeder, the full Congress had not yet done the same. In the meantime, the projected cost of the reactor had ballooned to $3.2 billion, from an initial estimate of $669 million in 1973.[61]

With congressional sentiment now in flux, media reports on cost estimate increases and logistical roadblocks provided more fodder for breeder opponents. In an article entitled "The Staying Power of the Clinch River Breeder," the *Wall Street Journal* noted that one of the ancillary goals for the reactor, procuring a license from the Nuclear Regulatory Commission in order to prove that breeders could meet federal health and safety requirements, could add *another* $1.6 billion to the project and delay it by another forty-three months. Obtaining an NRC license had been a goal of breeder proponents since the Carter years, but this also proved an elusive goal.[62] To the breeder's opponents, the project had always been a waste of money, and mounting evidence seemed to validate their predictions. Every time the breeder project seemed primed to make a productive contribution to US energy policy, some new complication would push the day of ultimate benefit just a bit further into the future. The difference in this new era was that opposition statements casting continued funding as simply throwing good money after bad were beginning to find a foothold in Congress.

The Washington Post joined the journalistic assault on the project, dubbing it a project that "deserve[d] to lose." The rationale for the plutonium breeder, if there had even been a solid one to begin with, according to the *Post,* was now gone. In the past few years, projected electricity demand had fallen sharply and new discoveries of natural uranium reserves had raised estimates of future uranium availability. The two factors combined to make the price of uranium plummet. While a potent argument in the mid-1970s, casting the breeder as a solution to the problem of scarce uranium supplies now made little sense. Furthermore, private utilities' share of the expenses of the reactor had dropped to 9 percent, sticking taxpayers even more unforgivingly with the cost of a project that was becoming more outdated. The initial funding plan for the breeder had capped private utility contributions at a flat $250 million, and as the project's costs continued to balloon, the proportion of the total cost billed to taxpayers climbed higher.[63]

However, in a 24 July vote the full House again voted to fund the project, approving a $13 billion appropriations bill for energy and natural resources that included money for the reactor. Representative Al Gore (D-TN), who had won a seat in the House in the election of 1976 and whose district housed many of the Clinch River project workers, helped ensure the outcome. Citing "massive uncertainty with respect to energy supply and demand in the future," Representative Gore led the charge against Lawrence Coughlin's (R-PA) amendment, which would have killed the project. With a somewhat overblown rhetorical flourish, House Majority Leader Jim Wright (D-TX) attempted to warn his colleagues of the dangers of ending the breeder project by raising the specter of the ancient Hebrews: "They wearied of the costs of wandering in the desert. Some wanted to turn back," but they pressed on, Wright said, "and now some want to turn back" on the reactor.[64] The implication of this comparison—that finishing the breeder would lead the United States to some glorious "promised land"—must have been particularly galling to environmentalist critics who emphasized plutonium's potential for dystopian terror.

More succinct was the Nader-affiliated group Congresswatch, which dubbed as "hypocrites" the 129 members of Congress who had voted in favor of the breeder "boondoggle" while simultaneously cutting programs for the poor and elderly. In November, over the objections of vocal breeder opponents Daniel Patrick Moynihan (D-NY) and Charles Percy (R-IL), the Senate approved the same $13 billion appropriation passed by the House. The Senate simultaneously voted to shelve an amendment offered by Paul Tsongas (D-MA) that would require private industry to pay half of the $180 million tab for the coming fiscal year.[65] Since the breeder was becoming more uneconomical by the day, its supporters almost certainly knew that additional private sector contributions would be scarce. The costs would continue to be borne almost completely by taxpayers, who had yet to see any benefit.

On the eve of the vote, the *Wall Street Journal* reported the abrupt resignation of the Clinch River's project director, along with the reassignment of the assistant director for engineering to a job with fewer responsibilities. These developments were not surprising in light of the level of mismanagement already demonstrated. An executive director in the Energy Department's nuclear energy office refused to say whether the Clinch River's director had resigned willingly or was fired, which tends to imply the latter. The mysterious announcement seemed to have little impact on the Senate's vote. Commenting on the outcome, the *Washington Post* noted the extent to and rapidity with which the Senate's newfound "budget-cutting zeal" was tempered by "old-fashioned pork-barrel politics and senatorial courtesies." The *Journal* attributed the result to the persistent work of Howard Baker Jr. Lobbyist Jill Greenbaum for the anti-breeder National Taxpayers Union concurred, claiming, "We would win easily if it weren't for Senator Baker."[66]

CONGRESSIONAL OPPOSITION COALESCES

However, by the next spring, with still no work done to prepare the reactor's intended site, a more concentrated opposition emerged in Congress. Anti-breeder voices attempted to cancel the contract among the Energy Department, TVA, and private utilities to build the reactor on grounds that the cost had doubled over the previous years, only for the GAO to tell them that the contract did not specify cost overruns as a legitimate reason for abrogation. In what must have been a frustrating piece of information for anti-breeder advocates to hear, the *New York Times* reported that the Energy Department had not provided several critical documents needed by the GAO in its review of the contract.[67]

In June the *Times* reported that an "unusual coalition" of thirty-six Republican and fifty-five Democratic representatives had mounted a campaign to kill the breeder, sending a letter to Reagan asking his administration to withdraw a $252 million request for fiscal year 1983, part of which was intended to fund groundbreaking on the Clinch River site. There was much urgency, since one of the major roadblocks facing the project's construction had fallen. The NRC had twice rejected administration requests to expedite groundbreaking, but in August, on the third try, the NRC voted to allow construction to begin. The deciding vote in this shift was Reagan appointee James Asselstine, a longtime staff attorney for the NRC. At the May vote, Asselstine, who had just been appointed to the review panel, had voted no on the administration's request. He claimed that the speed of his appointment and confirmation by the Senate might raise ethical questions if he voted in favor before having sufficient time to study the project. In August Asselstine shifted his position, tipping the balance of the five-member commission in favor of the administration. According to an assistant secretary in the Energy Department, site clearing, grading, and excavation would start as soon as possible. Obtaining a permit and a license from the NRC to operate the plant would still take several more years, ensuring continued uncertainty about the project's timeline.[68]

On 22 September, bulldozers finally began clearing the reactor's intended site. An outside environmental group had obtained an order halting construction to that point, but after an Atlanta appeals court judge overruled the order, the bulldozers went to work immediately. Percy Brewington Jr., the acting director of the project, divided a red oak—the first tree to fall at the construction site—into segments and distributed them to longtime proponents of the reactor. The same *New York Times* article that reported this news also noted that a sports shop in town was selling T-shirts that read, "I've been to Oak Ridge; I glow in the dark," demonstrating the pride that Oak Ridgers had for their place in atomic history.[69] In response to the beginning of construction, an "odd coalition" of the Heritage Foundation, the National Taxpayers Union, and environmental groups joined forces to cut off funding in the Senate. Conservatives were reportedly looking for a way to punish Senator Baker, who had pushed a 1982 tax increase through the Senate. The 1982 midterm congressional election, which saw twenty-seven incumbent Republicans lose their seats to Democrats, seemed to present another opportunity to anti-breeder advocates. Many incumbent Republicans had depended on Reagan's support in their reelection battles. Now freed from the requirement of maintaining favor with their party's leader, lame duck Republicans ideologically inclined toward budget cutting found their hands untied. According to one House staffer, "the leadership can put us off once, but on something this controversial, they have to allow a vote eventually."[70] With significant coalitions in both houses opposed to the project, the breeder's future looked more uncertain than in many years.

The *Chicago Tribune* took the initiative to recap the costs of the project so far: though the cost of the project was $2 billion in 1977—and $2.6 billion as recently as mid-1979—the current figure used in congressional debates now stood at $3.6 billion. Much more alarmingly, a new GAO estimate put the total cost of completion, which included expenses for NRC licensing, at up to $9 billion. The *Tribune* warned Senator Baker, known to harbor presidential ambitions for 1988, claiming that "he'd do well to kill this thing and show that he's responsible enough to put the nation's interests ahead of his state's." With more than a hint of sarcasm, the paper predicted, "He won't get far running

"THE MODEL-T OF REACTORS"

for president of Tennessee." Indeed, the lame-duck session of Congress saw the House finally vote down the reactor, and the Senate decide to continue funding by a single vote. The *New York Times* happily described the project as "dangling by a thread" and advised that "the next Congress will do well to sever it without regret," which would only require one changed vote in the Senate.[71] While these periodicals had long assailed the breeder, their criticisms were now gaining traction in Congress.

With momentum on their side, congressional critics redoubled their efforts to kill the project, knowing that "once concrete is poured and more than 4,000 workers are hired for construction," the project might be impossible to stop. Senator Baker's announcement in 1983 that he planned to retire from the Senate was just the catalyst that critics needed. In a major turnaround the following June, the Senate for the first time in a decade approved annual appropriations for the Energy Department that included no money for Clinch River. In an even more telling sign of how congressional opinion had shifted, Senator Baker did not attempt to restore any part of the $270 million cut from the appropriation by the administration. The *Boston Globe* reported that the reactor's future was "in serious doubt" unless the electricity industry agreed to share a major portion of the cost. Given that the plutonium breeder required uranium prices of $200 per pound to remain economical and that uranium prices currently stood at only $20 per pound, an infusion of private-sector cash seemed extremely unlikely. Alvin Weinberg, a former member of the Manhattan Project and the former administrator of the Oak Ridge National Laboratory, claimed that the nation needed breeder technology. He insisted that the technology was not "that far from being economic" if one considered the timeframe not in the short term but in terms of decades into the future. This protestation rang hollow with those who had long felt that the technology was already largely outdated.[72]

Weinberg's insistence on continuing to fund the breeder had more to do with flailing attempts to bolster the nuclear industry after Three Mile Island heightened safety concerns and declining energy demand lessened the need for future nuclear capacity, not with any specific economic analysis. Weinberg, among others, argued that the TMI disaster need not be taken as the end of nuclear power in the United States, but instead as an opportunity to inaugurate a "second nuclear era" characterized by more stringent safety regulations, an era that would presumably include the breeder.[73] Despite Weinberg's status as a major figure in the history of American nuclear administration, his exhortations had little effect on the new wave of sentiment within the House and Senate, one based on economic concerns.

Representative Marilyn Lloyd posed in September for a bizarre media opportunity that was very much out of step with the new realities of the breeder's status. A cheery Oak Ridge news release reported on the wondrous scale of work recently completed to prepare the reactor's site on the Clinch. More than 350,000 pounds of explosives blasted 675,000 cubic yards of limestone and siltstone from the area to create space for the reactor, the news release proudly proclaimed. More than 2,400 steel rock bolts and bearing plates were installed to prevent rock from newly formed vertical rock walls in the area from moving. Representative Lloyd was given the honor of tightening the last rock bolt and completing the preparations necessary for construction to begin.[74] Since the breeder's future now appeared quite bleak, the jovial tone characterizing news releases about the completion of the reactor's intended site seemed like willful ignorance of the situation. Another news release announcing that a scale model of the breeder would be on display at the Oak Ridge Public Library, while also highlighting Oak Ridge's deeply rooted nuclear identity, seemed even stranger, given that it was doubtful that the structure would ever exist in full-scale form.[75]

SCIENCE AND SOCIETY

With the turn of congressional opinion against the project, Clinch River's advocates turned to increasingly desperate measures. The project's managers were reportedly planning to attach further funding for the reactor to urgent legislation, perhaps the continuing resolution to keep the government funded after the fiscal year concluded at the end of September. This plan failed in the face of general congressional opposition. To assuage concerns about federal spending, reactor backers had also supposedly come up with a new financial plan that included greater contributions from industry. This latest plan would supposedly raise $1 billion, or 40 percent of the now $2.5 billion total cost, from private industry, with the money being repaid to industry with revenues from the project's eventual electric output. Closer inspection, though, revealed that the "support" consisted mainly of loans covered by broad federal guarantees, meaning that the government, not private investors, would be responsible for losses if the plant failed to reap projected revenues. The director of the Congressional Budget Office testified to Congress that this private support program would indeed cost the government *more* than conventional appropriations, and the plan thus unsurprisingly gained little support.[76]

The last lifeline to the project had failed. At the end of October, the Senate definitively voted by a tally of fifty-six to forty to cut off funding to the project. Breeder backers reluctantly recognized the finality of the vote. "The Senate has spoken," Senator Baker conceded tersely; "I will not prolong it at this point." With both houses of Congress on record against the project and refusing to give it any more money, Clinch River's future came to a quiet end.[77]

The only remaining question had to do with the costs of shutting down the project. After the Department of Energy put out the word that the project would end "in an orderly manner," just how much more money would be required was uncertain. The director of the DOE's nuclear planning division said that the department had once figured shutdown costs at between $200 and $500 million. After the Atlanta appeals court's decision had allowed construction to begin, the local site manager had rushed outside around midnight and knocked down trees with a bulldozer. Subsequently, a large cavity had been blasted out of rock, as Representative Lloyd's symbolic tightening of the last rock bolt had highlighted, and a foundation had been laid. Now that the breeder was dead, the site required some environmental repair and stabilization before abandonment was possible. The DOE director predicted that Congress would have to vote another small supplemental appropriation for 1984, since Clinch River's current budget would expire in a few weeks.[78] This shutdown cost was a small inconvenience in light of the hundreds of millions already spent.

With the saga of the Clinch River project finally finished, critics of congressional waste turned their attention to a $10 billion uranium enrichment plant that the Department of Energy was building in Portsmouth, Ohio. Carter had discussed this same plant at the outset of his involvement in the Clinch River debate. Like the breeder, the plant's capacity would not be needed for decades, and prospective development of new technologies in the future threatened to make the plant obsolete long before it would be necessary. The Natural Resources Defense Council, a longtime opponent of Clinch River, argued at a House hearing that spending so much money on the Portsmouth plant would siphon money away from more promising experimental projects.[79] Though Clinch River was dead, environmentalist battles against suspected pork-barrel nuclear projects in Congress continued.

The Clinch River breeder was, of course, only one component of the nuclear debate in the United States in the 1970s and 1980s. Reagan and his successor, George Bush, were both strong supporters of commercial nuclear power. Each used a combination of executive orders and bureaucratic appointments to assist the nuclear industry, even with the 1979 Three Mile Island disaster and the 1986 Chernobyl incident in the Ukraine turning public opinion against nuclear power.[80] The Clinch River breeder was only one federally subsidized exception in a field that Presidents Reagan and Bush wished dominated by private enterprise. However, as this chapter has shown, despite its uniqueness, the Clinch River project stood as one of the cornerstones of US nuclear policy in the late 1970s. Its story reveals much about the intricacies of the history of energy in the United States.

The Clinch River reactor was a multibillion-dollar public initiative. More importantly, it was also a test case for future endeavors. If the Clinch River reactor had been constructed and deemed a success, it would have served as the model for future similar reactors, each also receiving some measure of government support. The story of the Clinch River reactor thus serves as a window into politics and policy making in the late-twentieth-century United States. The era encompassing the New Deal and World War II witnessed an explosion in the federal bureaucracy, with experts of every profession populating a seemingly endless array of new agencies. Yet the Clinch River saga demonstrates the limits of the influence of this new rationalized and insulated expertise in the federal government. Even as expert consensus within the government, bolstered by the admonitions of critical periodicals, turned against the project, money still flowed freely from the coffers of Congress. Hundreds of millions of dollars spent over years yielded little more than a hole in the ground in East Tennessee, a wasteful outcome that the Carter administration was powerless to halt.

One obvious question begged by the Clinch River saga is how congressional supporters were able to maintain ongoing funding even as many economic analysts cast the project as more and more transparently a waste of resources. The answer has to do with the nature of science, and more specifically the challenge of predicting the future. Many analysts predicted that patterns in the rate of technological change meant that, by the time the output of the breeder technology was needed, there would likely be some more efficient, cleaner, and safer alternative available. Congressional supporters of the project, assisted by conflicting GAO analyses, successfully claimed in response that no such assumption was reliable. They noted that uncertainties in future population growth and future electricity demand, along with the growing unreliability of Middle Eastern oil, meant that the breeder could not be so easily abandoned. No analyst can say for sure what the political-economic situation of a given area will be decades into the future. There are simply too many interconnected variables to consider.

Congressional proponents were thus able to maintain an argument for continuing to pour resources into the breeder, even against vehement political and bureaucratic opposition and amid the unrelenting criticism of newspaper commentators.[81] The fact that most breeder supporters in Congress had little or no scientific training mattered little, confirming historian Brian Balogh's observations about the diminished influence of trained expertise in this new era. As the Italian-born microbiologist Salvador Luria wrote in a May 1977 analysis of science's public standing, the thousands of scientists laboring in their individual laboratories had become like "the uncountable numbers of coral polyps that are continuously working under the waves," operating out of view and cloistered from scrutiny, which made competing assertions hard to evaluate.[82] Because of this inscrutable facade, in the breeder debate it seemed as if all claims were created equal. Jimmy Carter's energy policy and public image suffered accordingly.

"THE MODEL-T OF REACTORS"

The combination of Carter's vehement opposition to the breeder and his inability to cut off funding for it made him appear weak and ineffective in the pages of national newspapers, and they represented another blow to his ability to formulate and execute a coherent energy policy.

The Clinch River story demonstrated that environmentalists could not be sure of policy successes in the post-embargo era, especially in light of uncertainties about future energy needs. When it came to decisions about funding new energy technologies, it seemed that many Americans believed that erring on the side of caution was the wisest course of action, especially if a repeat of 1973 was avoidable. Environmentalists found that even with fervent appeals to health and safety, funding for the plutonium breeder flowed freely from Congress for years. However, it was not just general political support for environmentalism that declined after the oil embargo. Specific laws found themselves affected too. When the new regulations of the environmental era seemed to impede energy security, many Americans came to believe that they were too broad and generated outcomes that seemed to defy common sense. They demanded that the scope and power of the laws be rolled back to a more reasonable level. The next chapter explores the politics of hydroelectricity to examine how concerns about energy security reined in the Endangered Species Act.

CHAPTER 4

"DELIBERATELY INFLEXIBLE"

The Tellico Dam and Endangered Species Law

As it was for all domestic energy sources, the mid-1970s was a moment that held potential for dynamic change in the hydroelectric economy of the United States. Keynoting the 1976 annual convention of the Colorado River Water Users Association (a group of representatives and officials from western states and Native American tribes), US Bureau of Reclamation Commissioner Gilbert Stamm declared emphatically that hydropower was significantly underdeveloped in the United States, with untold numbers of rivers primed and ready for useful hydroelectric construction. He optimistically predicted that remedying this problem of underuse could play a large role in solving the nation's energy woes, dependence on foreign oil foremost among them. Citing the key role of hydropower in the historical development of the American West, Stamm warned that "we would be grossly irresponsible if we ignored its undeveloped potential in planning for future generations." Noting that only a third of the nation's identified hydroelectric capacity had been exploited, Stamm extolled the potential for water to make an "important and unique" contribution to energy security.[1] Though Commissioner Stamm specifically touted the untapped hydro capacity of the Colorado River Basin in the West, he also expressed broader optimism about the potential of flowing water to help solve the nation's energy problems. If the numberless rivers crisscrossing the country could have their waters harnessed for human use, the nation's dependence on oil from across the world could quickly dissipate.

Not all observers shared Stamm's zeal for hydroelectric power. The mid-1970s also witnessed tense debates surrounding several large hydroelectric projects, whose potential effects on the landscape and wildlife in their proposed construction areas generated controversy. Environmentalists often mobilized to block the construction of these huge structures, which brought them into conflict with public agencies funding and supporting the projects. Environmentalist opponents of the dams were often unable to prevent the construction of hydroelectric projects by appealing to general environmental sensibilities. They resorted to using a relatively new piece of regulatory legislation, the Endangered Species Act (ESA), to preserve undeveloped wilderness areas.

Passed in 1973 as a key piece of the broader wave of environmental legislation in the United States, the ESA was meant to protect imperiled animal and plant species. Supporters of the law argued that allowing species to go extinct was shortsighted. One pragmatic reason given was that they might provide some yet-unknown benefit to humans at some future date; another was that species had an inherent right to exist, and humans did not hold the moral authority to wipe them out.[2] Once passed, the ESA prevented federal agencies from taking any action that would kill endangered animal or plant species or destroy their habitats. Though the law passed with virtually universal acclaim from the public, several facets quickly became controversial as the legislation was put into practice. Chief among the contentious aspects was that the law protected endangered species indiscriminately with no regard for their relative usefulness to humans. This provision at first seemed noncontroversial. How can one compare the relative inherent monetary value of one endangered species to another? Yet its enforcement soon irritated many Americans who came to believe that it was too broad. Not long after the law's passage, endangered species—which often had negligible differences from similar species whose populations were abundant— delayed or halted massive, multimillion-dollar economic projects.

Endangered species' ability to dominate and marginalize all the other facets and issues embedded within a complex debate soon made many observers question the scope and power of the law. Even publications that may have had mixed feelings about a given economic project came to opine that such debates should pivot around weightier concerns than one seemingly insignificant species. This chapter examines the case of the Tellico Dam, which revolved around the power of the Endangered Species Act. A small fish called the snail darter delayed the Tellico project and put its eventual completion, for a time, at risk. The dispute over the dam made its way to the US Supreme Court, which ruled in favor of the tiny fish. The snail darter's ability to dominate public debate and supersede all other concerns about the future of the two projects made many observers, including individual citizens and national periodicals, come to believe that the act protecting them was too powerful. These cases turned many Americans' opinion against the idea of environmental regulation, as many observers came to believe that regulations, while admirable in the abstract, did not, in practice, consider the imperatives of human economic need.

As the endnotes for this chapter indicate, the Tellico story has already received significant attention from historians and political scientists. Such analysis generally focuses on narrow aspects of the story, such as the history of legal litigation on the dam or the internal discussions among Tennessee Valley Authority officials as the story played out. This chapter instead places Tellico into the larger unfolding story about the declining political power of environmentalism after the oil embargo. When environmental guidelines did not seriously endanger Americans' standard of living, they were relatively uncontroversial. However, when environmental values and economic comfort came into conflict, some Americans came to believe that recent regulations were unfairly predisposed, against the dictates of common sense, to favor the former at the expense of the latter. The Tellico controversy led to the deterioration of the Endangered Species Act's reputation and legal power. With it, the reputation of environmentalism suffered a serious blow.

THE TENNESSEE VALLEY AND RIVERFRONT DEVELOPMENT

The Tellico Dam project, as an initiative of the quasi-public TVA, had deep historical roots. By the mid-1960s, the time of the project's inception, the agency had developed a central and nearly mythical position in the history of the US Southeast. During the economic disaster of the New Deal years, many of President Franklin Roosevelt's top advisers had developed a theory to explain the seemingly insurmountable poverty of the American South, the wealth of which persistently lagged behind the industrial centers of the Northeast and Midwest. They concluded that urban industrial centers in other parts of the nation had kept the "resource-rich hinterlands" of the South in a perpetual state of underdevelopment by appropriating its raw resources with little concern for the residents of the region. The Southern states had exhausted their soils and forest resources to produce material—mainly cotton—for refining and processing in urban industrial centers. To equalize incomes between farm and factory, therefore, meant that agricultural regions must "retain the right to their own resources" and use them effectively. New Dealers also decided that the federal government would have to be the agent of change, as the South, focused intently on preserving strict nineteenth-century racial hierarchies through maintenance of a farm-based economy, lacked the political will to achieve its own forward-thinking economic uplift.[3]

As historian Sarah T. Phillips has argued, no single New Deal initiative better embodied this thinking than TVA, a government corporation created during FDR's first hundred days. Created to "restore and develop the resources of an entire watershed area," according to Phillips, TVA built multipurpose dams, supplied hydroelectric power to farms and small towns, and began to repair the South's damaged forests and soils.[4] Though some New Deal programs were either ineffective or ruled unconstitutional, TVA emerged as one of the most prominent symbols of the successes of New Deal liberalism. In 1933, when TVA was established, per capita income in the Tennessee Valley was a mere 45 percent of the national average. By 1972 the ratio stood at a greatly increased 75 percent, a figure of which TVA was exceedingly proud. The agency attributed much of the difference to its own activities in the region, and it used the irrefutable economic progress of the past decades to push for an expanded mission in the near future.[5]

The agency had a practical reason for wanting to expand the scope of its mission in the Valley. TVA had relied on consistent funding from Congress to pay for the construction of power generation facilities for the first quarter-century of its existence, as the subsidized electric rates offered to impoverished valley residents did not in turn provide sufficient revenue to the authority for its daily operations. During the Eisenhower administration, however, Congress began to withhold dollars, channeling money instead to the task of waging the burgeoning Cold War with the Soviet Union. Aubrey Wagner, TVA board chairman from 1962 to 1978, recognized that TVA's current formula—relying on power generation, navigation, and flood control—was insufficient to financially sustain the agency. It needed to expand its role in the region, as doing so would multiply its sources of revenue. Wagner decided that including more direct local economic development initiatives within TVA's mission could attract additional congressional appropriations, as members of Congress from the Tennessee Valley would be eager to steer federal funds that would generate local jobs. TVA had long used dams to generate electricity for residents of the Valley. The chairman decided that building entirely new communities around the reservoirs created by these dams provided the path forward.[6]

In 1962, the first year of Wagner's chairmanship, TVA began a fierce push for increased riverfront development. It provided reasons to the US Congress why federal support for these projects would be beneficial. First, it would help develop industry in the region. The Tennessee Valley had numerous navigable waterways that, in theory, could provide easy transport of industrial products to other areas of the nation for consumption. The only problem was that the region, focused on maintaining the romantic ideal of the independent rural farmer, had largely failed to develop industrial sites along these promising rivers. TVA could and should rectify this shortsightedness, it said. There was also a more pressing practical reason for this course of action. Due to robust population growth, Tennessee's labor force was increasing more quickly than job opportunities in the state's stagnant farming economy could handle. A failure to diversify the region's economy would soon lead to structural economic disaster.[7] In TVA's estimation, riverfront development would continue to create low-cost hydroelectric power for the Valley, but it would also provide a way to encourage capital investment and industrial development in the resource-rich region.[8] However, as TVA found, the new environmental legislation of the late 1960s and early 1970s created a formidable obstacle to its riverfront development plans.

THE TELLICO PROJECT

TVA's inaugural effort to pursue this new mission centered on constructing a dam on the Little Tennessee River, about twenty-five miles southwest of the TVA headquarters in Knoxville, and then building a new industrial community around the hydroelectric structure. The site seemed to be ideal. It was a rural and impoverished area desperately in need of an economic jolt. Following Wagner's lead, in April 1963 the TVA board voted to endorse the project and seek congressional funding, which came quickly. Congressional favor led to executive support as well. The budget proposed by President Lyndon Johnson in January 1965 included nearly $6 million for the project.[9]

Initial stages of the project proceeded with no apparent problem, as a modernization project for an impoverished rural area seemed to have little obvious downside. Tennessee congressional representative Joe Evins got a favorable vote for the prospective Tellico Dam from the Appropriations Committee and then the full House in 1966. Initial construction of the project began soon afterward in March 1967. The main component of the initiative was the dam on the Little Tennessee River, about a quarter mile above its confluence with the Tennessee River. It seemed to be a perfect location on a river whose utility was already proven. In its promotional materials, TVA referred to the Little Tennessee and its tributaries as "a hard-working river system" already impounded sixteen successful times for hydroelectric generation and flood control.[10]

The project also included creating a thousand-foot-long canal to divert the waters of the Little Tennessee into Fort Loudon Reservoir, enabling these waters to pass through the existing hydroelectric units in the Fort Loudon powerhouse. The reservoir created by the dam would prospectively extend over thirty miles upstream, its impressive length allowing its waters to occupy over fifteen thousand acres. In TVA's boosterish words, this would "create an ideal living, working, and recreation environment . . . [in an area] characterized by low incomes and under-utilization of human and natural resources." Recognizing that "the influx of thousands of people requiring homes and services in an essentially rural area" could result in rapid and uncontrolled sprawl, TVA planned to create a focused suburban-style, single-family-home community on the left bank of the reservoir's lower reaches.[11]

TVA emphasized a multiplicity of recreational, disaster-preparedness, and energy-production benefits in promoting the project. First, it would bring money and jobs to an area that sorely needed both. Pointing out that the nearby Great Smoky Mountains National Park received over seven million visits from tourists every year, TVA claimed that the lake would be a "valuable" supplementary recreational asset that would attract dollars from wealthier areas of the Southeast and the nation. TVA also projected that the diversion of the reservoir waters through the turbines at Fort Loudon Dam would provide 200 million kilowatt-hours of inexpensive electricity for valley residents annually. Emphasizing the environmental benefits of hydroelectric power, TVA claimed that producing this same amount of electricity in a coal-fired steam plant would require about ninety thousand tons of coal each year, the pollution from which mitigated the turbines' operation.[12]

Within TVA's more traditional mission, the agency also pointed out that the Tellico Dam and Reservoir would provide over 100,000 acre-feet of storage for flood control. This would provide needed flood protection for Chattanooga (a city about one hundred miles west of Knoxville, on the border with Georgia) as well as myriad communities along the Tennessee River between Chattanooga and the project.[13] To assuage possible concerns about risk to the drinking water, TVA claimed that the project, despite its massive scale, would not adversely affect water quality "to any significant extent." It also downplayed the possible losses of rare and endangered species, claiming that any rare fish or mollusks in the area affected by the construction also existed securely in other locations.[14]

With all of these ostensible benefits, the project received virtually unanimous support from local governments and business interests. The Chamber of Commerce of nearby Lenoir City resolved in 1969 that the dam was "vital to the economy and welfare" of the city's residents and urged that the level of appropriations for the project increase by such amounts to insure "timely completion." In 1970 the Monroe County Quarterly Court deplored the fact that the project was only 30 percent complete and criticized a delay caused by recent budget cutbacks. In 1972 the town of Madisonville exhorted the "economic development and employment opportunities" of the dam, as did the Board of Mayor and Aldermen of Lenoir City. The same year, the president of the Knoxville Chamber of Commerce (KCC) wrote to Governor Winfield Dunn explaining his support, claiming that the dam's creation of a lake with adjacent properties would address concerns of both environmentalists and urban planners by "providing a place for [growing populations] to live, while at the same time enhancing their environment."[15] To the KCC president it seemed that the concept of environmental quality was synonymous with human recreation, providing a glimpse into how boosters unconvincingly tried to square their support for economic growth with the political power of environmentalism in the early 1970s.

Vague definitions of "environmentalism" aside, not all citizens were persuaded. A vocal minority of area residents opposed the project. Local ecologist Edward Clebsch crystallized the environmentalist viewpoint, writing indignantly to the recently created President's Council on Environmental Quality to criticize TVA's process of land acquisition. He criticized the idea that the financial benefits of the project could derive from the development of pollution-generating industrial sites. According to Clebsch, the dam's economic proceeds would flow overwhelmingly to the privileged few who owned the industrial sites, with the negative externalities distributed to the general populace. Pointing out that TVA expected to receive several million dollars in land sales to industry, Clebsch also found it "revolting" that TVA would use eminent domain to acquire land "and then sell it at an unbelievably high profit to itself."[16]

He also questioned TVA's boosterish claims. Clebsch pointed to "the very high number" of artificial lakes already extant within a short distance of the Tellico project to argue against TVA's claims about the necessity for recreational waterways. Lastly, Clebsch claimed that "even though the TVA denies it . . . there will be periods when the polluted waters of Ft. Loudon Reservoir are able to flow into the Tellico Reservoir." Regarding the consequences of such mixing, Clebsch accused TVA of willful ignorance, as "no one knows and no one plans to find out." In 1971 Tennessee's Republican governor, Winfield Dunn, also spoke out against the dam on environmental grounds, which came as a surprise to TVA, which had long counted on state government support for development projects.[17]

To the agency's surprise, even more outspoken against the project were many local residents, again a vocal minority. They allied with environmentalists to oppose the dam. Chairman Wagner had encountered the opposition in person, having traveled to the nearby town of Greenback in 1964 eager to sell the idea to locals and assuming that they would warmly greet an initiative to improve their area's aggregate income and economic standing. Instead, the trip was a disaster. The rural residents loved the idyllic nature of quiet farm life and were loath to give up agricultural land for industrial development and suburban-style home-building, a deeply rooted cultural ideology that Wagner had not considered. Farmers and anglers from the area were not content to voice their protest against visiting TVA officials; they supplemented their localized grumblings by traveling to the nation's capital in 1966 to speak out against the project in congressional hearings, enraging the TVA head.[18]

Even though it included the state governor, the opposition alliance of environmentalists and farmers seemed to matter little. The US Congress generally sided with Wagner and TVA. Importantly, eminent domain powers backed by Congress gave TVA the ability to seize farmland against the locals' wishes. Private companies also joined the controversy on the side of TVA and the US Congress, creating a seemingly unstoppable alliance in favor of the project. As the debate unfolded, TVA had attracted the support of the Boeing Corporation as a partner to help build the prospective new town of Timberlake on the Tellico Reservoir, a project that was never completed. TVA also in 1972 received approval of its environmental impact statement, prepared in response to National Environmental Protection Act requirements that federal projects be evaluated for their environmental consequences. Rumors of budget overruns and exploding costs, while providing fodder to those already against the dam, did little to move the opinions of those who favored it. By 1973 it appeared that the dam would go forward as planned, despite the vehement and diverse opposition.[19] However, dam opponents had one more powerful weapon to use against the project: the Endangered Species Act.

DISCOVERING THE SNAIL DARTER

In August 1973, zoology professor David Etnier, a Tellico Dam opponent, recognized that the Endangered Species Act might be the last chance for dam opponents. Though the ESA was passed with known species threatened by human development in mind, Etnier realized that newly discovered species would fall under the act's provisions too. He went looking for new species in the Little Tennessee River that might require federal protection. Etnier's expedition was indeed fruitful, as he discovered a tiny, previously unidentified fish barely bigger than a paper clip. The find, eventually known as the snail darter, gave new life to opponents of the dam. The snail darter, while a unique species, was one of over a hundred known species of darter fish, each of which had negligible differences from the others. After extended testimony from both TVA and the environmental opposition, the US Fish and Wildlife Service (FWS) decided to side with the environmentalists. The FWS listed the fish as an endangered species and designated a part of the Little Tennessee River as a "critical habitat" for the snail darter. This designation meant that the area could not be altered in a way that might imperil the snail darter's survival. Even though the dam was 90 percent complete by this point, the ESA now protected the fish and its habitat in the Little Tennessee. TVA could not go forward with the project.[20] Litigation by TVA over the subsequent years advanced within the US court system, and a spring 1978 Supreme Court decision—which saw the Carter administration, especially Attorney General Griffin Bell, siding with TVA against dam opponents—ended with the court ruling that the dam could not be completed.[21]

The national coverage of the snail darter drew a variety of responses. In February 1977, the *Los Angeles Times* published a telling and indignant letter from Martin J. Weisman, a resident of the San Fernando Valley. The story of the rural Tennessee dam had reached as far as the West Coast and made enough of an impact to draw strong written responses from residents there. In his letter, Weisman described the ESA as nothing short of "lunacy." "Is a rare little fish more important than providing power and controlled water for the people of Tennessee?" asked Weisman. He claimed to have no problem with allowing endangered species to live, but only "until their proliferation conflicts with the health, comfort, and livelihood of mankind."[22] Weisman's letter was indicative of the visceral feeling that the Tellico Dam saga had generated: that it was important to protect endangered species, but not to the extent that they became a detriment to commonsense human economic needs.

The Tellico Dam saga indeed played a role in reorienting some of the environmentalist legislation passed a few short years before. The month after the publication of Weisman's letter, the *Christian Science Monitor* reported that Congress was considering curbing the power of the act, specifically the FWS's power to safeguard habitats deemed essential to the survival or recovery of an endangered or threatened species. The mere addition of an organism to the endangered species list did not automatically remove the land it lived on from developmental potential. Since the FWS had broad authority to designate land a "critical habitat," each new listing held the corresponding possibility to impede or prevent a developmental project. According to the *Monitor,* the authority of the FWS faced a "water[ing] down" at the hands of Congress in multiple ways. For example, the interior secretary would have unilateral power to exempt a federal project that was otherwise excluded from a designated critical habitat. Furthermore, the kinds of species that might be eligible for critical habitat protection also faced curtailing, with cold-blooded vertebrates and invertebrates possibly losing habitat protections altogether.[23]

The potential stripping of safeguards for these specific categories could not have been accidental. Fish and Wildlife officials reportedly opposed such restraints on their enforcement powers, but one FWS official seemed to concede the inevitability of the cutbacks. Members of Congress deplored the ESA for blocking construction in their districts. Employing a slew of mixed metaphors, the official noted, "Their pork barrels have taken a beating, and they may be out for blood." They were indeed. The catalyst for the congressional onslaught appeared to be the Tellico Dam controversy, and dam supporters thus targeted river-dwelling frogs, lizards, snakes, and fish for exemption from regulation in order to protect future hydroelectric projects. Though the FWS's associate director promised to "fight . . . tooth and toenail" against the measures, it seemed as if some members of Congress had grown exasperated with the ability of the endangered species law to hold up water development projects in their districts. The Tellico controversy served as an ominous harbinger of what might be in store for other projects in other districts.[24] And with the FWS announcing that it planned to soon add another 1,700 species of plant life to the endangered list to supplement the 609 existing listings of fish and other animals, skeptical members of Congress moved swiftly to prevent potential threats to favored local projects before new listings could cut off waterways from development.[25]

Representative John Duncan, the Republican representative for Tennessee's second congressional district, received a number of letters about the Tellico project in the spring of 1977, during this debate about potentially weakening the power of the ESA. Some of the letters offered Duncan reasons that the Tellico project should end before completion. Frank A. Coleman of Friendsville, for example, argued against the idea that the money already spent on the dam justified its completion. "So 100 million plus has already been spent," Coleman commented, but "this is no way justifies finishing the project." That money, far from being wasted, had been "circulated through the economy" in the form of wages and other payments that had created great benefit for the community. "Let's forget about it," he admonished the representative, and focus on the needs of the present, in which Coleman did not include the dam. "I believe enough of East Tennessee is under water," he noted.[26] Perry W. Hembree of Knoxville also opposed finishing the dam, especially because of the thought of "all that fertile land with its homes, communities, and history being inundated and lost forever." He purposely stated that his opposition had nothing to do with the snail darter, since he had "trouble getting too excited about the possible demise of a small minnow that most people" commenting on the dam had never even seen in person. Instead, it revolved around saving "for posterity" the beautiful East Tennessee land that would be flooded by the dam.[27]

S. Russell Manning of Knoxville offered a more abstract case for why the dam should not be finished, focusing more directly on the fish at the center of the controversy. He vehemently denied that the snail darter was "worthless" because it had no economic value to humanity. Instead, he saw the fish as a symbol of humankind's destruction of the environment in which it was living, which would have ultimately deleterious effects on humanity's own survival. Whether any particular individual believed in the theory of evolution or in the story of Biblical creation, Manning said, "the extinction of a form of life through man's actions" could be nothing else "but an indication that our environment is becoming less beneficial to man." In other words, for Manning, the natural world had either evolved or been created to allow different species to exist in harmony, and the human-caused extinction of other species, including the snail darter, could do nothing but upset that balance, to the ultimate detriment of human-kind. "The plight of the snail darter," Manning summarized, "is a warning that we are moving in the wrong direction by damming our rivers and destroying our land." He offered a slippery slope argument to oppose amendments to the ESA that would allow exemption for individual projects, warning that exempting the snail darter would lead to more and more species exempted for the sake of other projects, which would spiral out of control.[28]

Heather L. Houvenagle couched her opposition to the dam in even more mystical terms. She felt "very strongly" that the dam had negatively affected the quality of East Tennessee's "natural ecosystem," drawing a very clear line between humans and the natural world. Even though she was just "one sole human being," she felt "morally responsible" for the planet on which she lived and held "the deepest reverence and respect for all living things." In particular, she held "great pity and compassion" for anyone who had never experienced "a humble moment beneath one of God's trees or beside the Little Tennessee River as it used to be." She mourned for the river, which was now "naked to the elements," with the trees that "had once held fertile soil" now gone.[29] For her, the construction thus far was nothing less than tragic, and allowing the dam to be finished would be even worse.

Most of the letters to Representative Duncan, however, were in favor of the dam's completion. Their tone ranged widely from begrudging acceptance to full-throated passion. In the first category, a Maynardville attorney claimed that he would "reluctantly" vote in favor of finishing the project. He doubted that the dam would bring all of the optimistic economic benefits that TVA had predicted, but the money already spent could not be ignored. "The majority of the public desires to finish this dam," attorney Moore noted, which was enough to justify its completion, but he did not think that further construction after Tellico should be started.[30] Likewise, Troye D. Summitt of Vonore reported that he had spoken with several of his neighbors about the project and had received "the same thoughts from most of them." Namely, they believed that the dam should be completed because "so many home and farms had been disturbed" by construction thus far and the land simply could not "be returned to its former form" by this point. "If this question" had been asked ten years prior, Summitt argued, "then we would have answered with an emphatic NO," he reported, but the point of no return had been reached.[31]

Less ambiguous was Cam Hammontree of Maryville, who decried the fact that failing to complete the dam would represent "another $100 million down the drain." This was, for Hammontree, part of how "environmentalists" were "costing us" an obscene amount of "dollars and jobs each year." It was time for taxpayers to "wake up" to this mess, he said.[32] Likewise, a letter from Charles and

Nell Lunsford of Sweetwater proposed to "petition whoever halted" Tellico to "come to Monroe County and try to earn a living." Doing so would likely cause dam opponents to "change their minds when they find out how hard it is," and the economic benefits of the dam were of the utmost importance.[33]

Tip Parks of Tazewell, a longtime resident, also expressed very strong support. He had been watching the saga of the snail darter unfold on the television news until he could no longer "hold [his] peace." "I'm angry!" he wrote. He informed Duncan that he had grown up in an era in which the only light available was from a kerosene lamp until the Norris Dam was completed in 1936. His loyalty to TVA for bringing modernity to the region lasted into the present day, and he took it as a personal insult that environmentalists were now blocking the agency's activities. He asked the representative to place "these crazy people" blocking the dam "back in the nut house where they belong."[34] Although he must have known that Duncan did not possess this particular power, Parks's letter made clear his extremely strong support for the project.

Although supported by business interests in the fight against the reach of the ESA, legislators did not pass these provisions curbing the Fish and Wildlife Service's power to safeguard habitats. Opposition to the ESA continued to grow in Congress nonetheless. In April 1978, within the Senate Environmental and Public Works Committee's Resource Protection Subcommittee, John C. Culver (D-IA) offered an amendment that would create a review board drawn from seven federal agencies empowered to grant exemptions from the act for some government construction projects. Under certain circumstances, the proposed board could permit construction of a project that would destroy an animal or plant species if the benefits to humans of the project "clearly outweigh[ed]" the value of the species.[35]

The amendment offered no scale or metric to determine how benefits to humans would compare to the existence or nonexistence of a given species (and it seems impossible that any such measure could be reasonably devised), giving the review board wide latitude to make decisions. The board could not override the ESA with a simple majority vote. Instead, it would take five out of seven members to permit a project to proceed in the face of an endangered species objection. The review board would be composed of the secretaries of the interior, agriculture, and the army; the chair of the Council of Economic Advisers; EPA and NOAA administrators; and an individual nominated by the governor of the state of the project in question. Six of these seven members were presidential appointees. Given such criteria, the ideological orientation of the president making these personnel decisions would influence the panel's decision-making.

This proposed amendment, while seemingly byzantine in its bureaucratic orientation, represented a major change in the nature of the law. One of the things that made the ESA different from other federal regulations was its locally enforceable curbs on development. Other areas of federal regulation—antitrust, financial, and others—relied on vigorous efforts from law enforcement officials like the president and attorney general to function properly. Presidents who disfavored regulations often did not need to persuade Congress to roll them back in order to weaken their power. They simply needed to institute lax enforcement. However, the ESA's provisions allowed local groups to petition local courts to stop an action that might harm endangered species. In the case of Tellico, local groups took their opposition all the way to the Supreme Court, where they took on Jimmy Carter's attorney general and won. This amendment, by potentially taking power back from local opposition groups and putting it into the grasp of high-ranking federal officials, represented a major reduction in the enforcement powers of the ESA.

DEBATING THE AMENDMENTS

In the hearings on the amendment, spokespersons for an array of environmental groups joined the director of the Fish and Wildlife Service to urge non-passage of the amendment. An opposing assortment of utility executives and Smithsonian scientists argued that the act was "too inflexible" and cumbersome as written. Senator Jake Garn (R-UT) went even further, offering an amendment that would allow a state governor unilateral power to waive the requirements of the ESA if no "practical" alternative to the destruction of a species was feasible. Making his views on the utility of the ESA clear, he noted, "I frankly don't give a damn if a 14-legged bug or the woundfish minnow live or die." Garn further predicted that if no amendments easing the act passed, an angry public would insist on repeal of the entire ESA "in a revulsion against environmental excesses."[36] It was admittedly unlikely that the public would ever demand full repeal of the still-popular act, and Garn's amendment empowering state governors went nowhere. It was also undeniable that Garn was channeling collective frustrations of those Americans who thought the act, as currently on the books, was too expansive, too powerful, and too predisposed against projects that would benefit human populations.

Though Garn injected his rhetoric with more than a bit of hyperbole in the pursuit of ESA modifications, his Senate colleague Culver concurred with the basic idea that some action to quell public opinion was necessary. Culver told the hostile environmentalists at the hearing that he sympathized with their aims and supported the goals underlying the ESA, but also cautioned that irritation with the act was reaching critical mass, especially among the business community. The ESA had already caused a vast array of projects to be delayed or cancelled, and it would certainly continue to do so with future endeavors as well. "Storm clouds" were forming over other projects whose parameters contained "irresolvable conflicts" with endangered species, Culver said, and constituents already suspicious of the ESA would see their patience running ever thinner. The longer Congress delayed amending the ESA, the more projects would be jeopardized, Culver warned, and the more outraged the public would become. A reasonable amendment to the act, Culver argued, was necessary in order to stave off the prospect of more restrictive amendments in the future.[37]

In June 1978, the Supreme Court ordered a halt to the dam's construction, which was nearly complete, because it violated the ESA's provisions. Congressman Duncan received another slew of letters after the Supreme Court's decision. Some lauded it. For example, Eugene Stratton, a resident of Alcoa, claimed that East Tennessee already had "the bridges, the roads, the recreational possibilities," and all the other benefits of infrastructural modernity. Another dam would thus bring diminishing returns and was not worth the steep cost. In the agency's early days, Stratton argued, "TVA dams used to be a prize." Now, four and a half decades later, they had become "a drag on the market," wasting money to build projects that were not needed. Stratton implored Duncan to realize that the nation needed to "wake up and stop wasting borrowed money which will hasten the end of our country as we have always known it."[38]

Duncan's reply to Stratton, while polite, also noted that his office had recently conducted a poll of his congressional district. The representative explained that 82 percent of respondents favored completing the dam. Indeed, just as before, most of the letters received after the decision favored the project and continued to make a range of primarily economic arguments to support it along the same lines as the previous waves of letters to Duncan's office.[39]

The debate over the amendments played out in the pages of national newspapers. Near the end of June 1978, Alex Radin, the executive director of the American Public Power Association (an advocacy consortium of public utilities from across the nation), published an indignant letter to the editor in the *New York Times*. He largely echoed Culver's warnings about the need for reform, taking issue with an *NYT* editorial from earlier in the month that had deemed the ESA not obstructive. In light of the Supreme Court's decision to halt the completion of Tellico Dam, it was clear to Radin that the act was "deliberately inflexible," since a $119 million project was being blocked by the snail darter—merely one out of 116 similar species of darter fish. Clearly, Radin argued, something was badly askew. In the problem of reconciling adequate energy supply with protecting endangered species, "some compromises have to be made, but the [ESA] apparently allows for none." He was wary of the congressional proposal for an interagency review board, predicting that the board would be weighted in favor of environmental interests. Instead of a simple majority vote, five members out of seven had to agree to bypass ESA requirements, a high threshold to reach. Radin did not make his preferred alternative clear, but urged major, not incremental, reforms to the ESA.[40]

ENVIRONMENTALIST RESPONSES

The environmentalist rejoinder to these critiques found a particularly strong yet confusing voice in a summer 1978 *Los Angeles Times* piece by Peter Steinhart, a naturalist and journalist with a special interest in the biodiversity of his native California.[41] Unlike most local East Tennesseans against the dam, who lacked a national platform for their views, Steinhart set out to explain the environmentalist view to the rest of the nation. The article, which managed to be both well written and dripping with sarcasm, was also self-contradictory. Steinhart started by mocking the Tennessee state legislature, which had recently expressed support for building the Tellico Dam on the grounds that plants and animals were constantly evolving and being discovered by science. Since biologists and taxonomists were constantly identifying small populations of new species, the legislature said, trying to protect every endangered species meant that the biological fact of evolution was a threat to human progress itself, necessitating a change to the ESA.[42]

Steinhart then chided environmentalists for their approach to endangered species. Stories such as that of the snail darter, Steinhart opined, usually extracted one question from the public: "What good are they?" Hastening to respond, Steinhart said, environmentalists "rush to their typewriters and spill out a few thousand words" about some obscure species in danger. Focusing the debate on endangered species themselves, Steinhart warned, circumscribed the argument in a way that ultimately disadvantaged the environmentalist side. In the case of Tellico Dam, for example, environmentalists should have asked, "Was it necessary for TVA to condemn private homes and farmlands for resale to industry at a profit?" and furthermore, "What of the assertion by the General Accounting Office that TVA's cost-benefit analysis was hopelessly faulty?" These questions, for Steinhart, should have replaced environmentalists' laser-like focus on the snail darter.[43]

Yet local environmentalists in East Tennessee had already launched these critiques as the controversy unfolded, with little practical effect to show for the effort expended. As Zygmunt Plater, the lead counsel for the anti-dam coalition in the snail darter case, pointed out in retrospect, the Endangered Species Act was the last resort to stop the dam exactly because the other criticisms of the project had found little resonance in public discourse:

The farmers [displaced by the dam] and their allies, however, found it virtually impossible to get anyone in power to listen [to their complaints about their own fates or the lack of economic sense within TVA's analyses]. They tried, fighting against the land condemnations, carpooling to Washington to testify against the project, writing letters to local newspapers. For a short time they were able to halt the project because TVA initially refused to do a required environmental impact statement. But the federal agency, supported in Washington by the pork barrel . . . ultimately overrode every citizen effort to block the dam. Demoralized by a string of battles lost, the local dam fighters saw their ranks grow thinner and thinner year by year. Then a small fish swam into the controversy, discovered under the swift currents of the Little T River. The fish was clearly endangered, and federal law said any federal agency action jeopardizing an endangered species violated the Endangered Species Act.[44]

Steinhart was thus chastising dam opponents for failing to do something that had clearly not worked. He returned at the end of his article to make a point that he had already criticized. He had begun his article with a critique of environmentalist tendencies to concentrate on "the value of an obscure animal." Since the question was often unanswerable in the present moment and it often took years to realize a hidden benefit obtainable from an endangered plant or animal, this strategy advantaged those who could emphasize immediate, quantifiable economic benefits to humans. Yet at the conclusion of his article, Steinhart returned to this same line of thought as if he had come up with it himself. Deploring a proposed ESA amendment that would allow the Fish and Wildlife Service to decide that two or more subspecies are similar enough to be lumped together under the act, which would likely classify the more than one hundred species of darter fish as one species for purposes of the ESA, Steinhart complained that this might lead to the elimination of populations that were uniquely useful. "For until we can . . . honestly and accurately say that the northern monkshood holds the secret of eternal life or the Santa Catalina bushmallow is no good now and never will be—we must do what we can to save them all."[45] This was precisely the type of argument that Steinhart, at the beginning of his piece, had chided environmentalists for falling back on.

Steinhart's retreat from posing the "what good are they?" question demonstrated the constrained parameters available to environmentalists in the endangered species debate. Endangered species law was clearly impeding projects that would have been of undeniable economic benefit to humans, and environmentalist critiques of development inevitably boiled down to the notion that a species might, at some point in the future, prove of enough benefit to humans to warrant non-development now. In an era of increasing economic pain for many American consumers, such an argument was becoming progressively more difficult to make with much success. The flimsy logic of Steinhart's newspaper contribution reflected the problems that local environmentalists in East Tennessee faced in the unfolding debate. Local environmentalists had faced challenges in persuading pro-dam locals to oppose the project, and Steinhart's exhortations, seemingly intended to advise and encourage local environmentalists in East Tennessee, certainly did little to help.

DECISIVE OUTCOMES IN CONGRESS

Not two weeks after the publication of Steinhart's July 1978 piece, the US Senate voted overwhelmingly to amend the ESA, creating the proposed interagency review board. Three months later, the House voted for its own version of the ESA amendments and soon agreed to adopt the Senate version. The *Washington Post* did not mince words that fall with a 29 September headline declaring simply that the "Endangered Species Act Is Dying." Recognizing the rising unpopularity of the ESA within Congress and the heavy pressure for change, environmentally inclined representative John Dingell (D-MI) had reportedly been working nonstop to maintain a "holding action" of offering compromises in Congress and averting moves to gut the act or kill it outright.[46]

Dingell's mind-set and congressional agenda told the dramatic story of the ESA's rise and fall. In just a few short years, the act transformed from an unstoppable force, one that no politician dared oppose, into a beleaguered and besieged law whose future was quite unsure indeed. Keeping the ESA as originally written was not an option, as Dingell recognized. The choice was between either a significantly amended act or full repeal. In November, in the face of immense congressional support for the amendments, President Carter reluctantly signed the amendments and made them law. Though Carter generally supported environmental protection, continuing economic sluggishness compelled him to do something to remove perceived obstacles to growth.[47] Upon entering office, Carter had pledged to cut back a number of specific pork-barrel water projects, seeing them as both wasting money and damaging local ecologies. The president quickly found himself drawing anger from legislators who had grown accustomed to reliable money for local water projects and, realizing that he needed to repair relationships with Congress to pass other priorities, moved to make amends.[48] When it came to the Tellico case, the president had little choice, given the sentiments in Congress, other than to go along with the snail darter–inspired opposition to the ESA, lest he provoke another backlash.

The prestige of the ESA took another hit in early November 1979, when around 1,700 plants and a hundred animals were dropped from consideration for ESA protection due to Interior Department inaction. The 1978 amendments

"DELIBERATELY INFLEXIBLE"

required that if a species had been proposed for protection and the agency had not acted on it for two years or more, the agency then had one year to place it on the endangered or threatened list, or it would automatically be dropped from consideration. No longer could the proposed rolls of endangered species fill up endlessly; decisions one way or the other had to be made. Environmentalists blamed bureaucratic ineptitude for the dropped listings and claimed that the Fish and Wildlife Service's incompetence would lead to multiple extinctions. However, it's likely that the FWS had simply grown tired of congressional pressure and had consciously sought to avoid any more confrontations.[49]

The categories of dropped listings were telling. Americans had broadly supported the ESA when it protected "charismatic megafauna" like wolves, bears, moose, and eagles.[50] Plants, mollusks, insects, and other animals without backbones had proved far less likely to receive public sympathy. Indeed, out of the approximately one hundred animals dropped, only one—the black toad—was a vertebrate. The rest were invertebrates like the Madison cave isopod, a type of freshwater shrimp. The prospective extinction of these obscure invertebrate species would likely have inspired a collective yawn from the broad American public, and the Interior Department was thus taking little political risk by letting their protections expire. It was simpler and easier for the exhausted Interior Department simply to allow protective statuses for these species to run out and thus draw sporadic environmentalist complaints than to provoke further clashes with irate members of Congress.[51]

The irony of the Endangered Species Act amendments, though, is that although they had largely been spurred to passage by the Tellico Dam saga, they did not resolve the controversy dragging on in East Tennessee. The new exemption committee voted *not* to exempt the Tellico Dam from the Endangered Species Act, claiming that the project's economic and social benefits did not "clearly outweigh" the negative impacts. Also ironically, the snail darter was scarcely a factor in the committee's decision. Instead, looking at the hard numbers, the committee decided that the dam would not generate enough economic benefit in the region to justify its multimillion-dollar cost. In other words, it simply was not worth the money.[52] Though the snail darter was barely a consideration, the committee's refusal to grant an exemption meant that the ESA legally prohibited the dam's completion. Dam proponents had one last idea to try to circumvent the snail darter and finish the project, and it required some congressional maneuvering.[53]

In 1979, on a day when most legislators were absent, Tennessee representative John Duncan attached a rider to the Energy and Water Resources Appropriation exempting Tellico from the ESA, and the appropriation passed with few caring about the exemption. The Senate deleted the amendment in its version, but Duncan—along with Senator Howard Baker, who called in as many favors as possible—ensured its return in conference. After passing both houses, President Carter, who was under pressure to support energy projects while the Iranian Revolution was causing oil prices to spike, signed it. TVA finally finished the dam, the environmentalist opposition defeated by an anticlimactic legislative proceeding. In November 1979, the long saga of Tellico came to a quiet and strange conclusion.[54]

Not all East Tennesseans enjoyed Duncan's legislative maneuvering. Shirley Nicholson of Knoxville wrote his office to tell him how "utterly disappointed" she and her husband found the Congressman's "sneaky" strategy.[55] In a more measured tone, Wayne Christeson, a Knoxville attorney, wrote that even though he was a supporter of the dam, he did not think that the issue should be resolved at the price of "[Duncan's] own integrity." Duncan's recent actions, he said, threatened his reputation for honesty and fairness. "Remember who and what you are," he lectured the Congressman condescendingly.[56] However, the voters in Tennessee's congressional district who supported completing the project by any means necessary must have been pleased at the outcome.

In the end, the dam validated both the optimistic predictions of its boosters and the fears of its detractors. Although the promised industrial development never materialized around the dam—another case of unfulfilled expectations— the dam did catalyze the development of a number of suburban communities around the new lake, which provided ample boating and swimming opportunities. Yet it also dispossessed a number of small farmers of their land, and the project finished severely over budget. Observers who looked upon Tellico as either an exciting opportunity or a tragic boondoggle each found evidence to support their respective claims.

ENDANGERED SPECIES LAW

Although it was overwhelmingly popular in public opinion upon passage, the Endangered Species Act was more controversial in professional circles. Several distinct criticisms, on both scientific and economic grounds, emerged. First, there was the matter of defining exactly what a "species" was, especially in terms of where one began and another ended, itself a tricky epistemological exercise.[57] Second, the broad-reaching and inflexible nature of the law could interfere with other commonsense actions meant to protect the environment. For example, in 1979 a federal judge in Los Angeles barred the EPA from acting to reduce municipal sewage discharges from the city into the Pacific Ocean. Since the EPA's treatment would remove nutrients from the water that supported a fish population around the discharge point, and since the fish provided a vital source of food for both the endangered brown pelican and the endangered gray whale, the judge ruled that the EPA's plan would indirectly jeopardize the two predators. Though an attorney for the National Wildlife Federation called the ruling "absurd on its face," a characterization broadly expressed by other environmental groups, the EPA was nonetheless legally barred from trying to clean up the ocean.[58] As this case demonstrated, the strict terms of the act, which privileged the survival of individual species—sometimes with several degrees of separation from a proposed action—at the expense of the overall health of broader ecosystems, could generate nonsensical outcomes.

By far the most common criticism of the ESA was that it unfairly impeded seemingly reasonable attempts at economic development, halting projects that could create wealth and improve standards of living merely for the sake of the survival of small, useless animals barely worth protecting. The Tellico controversy might have ended, but this underlying unease with the reach of the Endangered Species Act did not end with closing the dam's gates.

Even with the ESA amended in 1978, rare and endangered species continued to confound water development projects. Not only was hydroelectric development further affected by the act, but water-dependent technologies meant that rare fish impinged upon fossil fuel production as well. Near the end of 1980, the Interior Department declared that it had found three endangered fish—the Colorado squawfish, humpback chub, and bonytailed sucker—swimming in the muddy waters of the White River in northeast Utah. The finding jeopardized Utah's plans to construct the White River Dam and a 105,000 acre-foot reservoir, both of which were essential to developing the state's oil shale and tar sands resources. Petroleum is extractable from tar sand, a gooey mixture of sand and heavy crude, and oil shale from petroleum-impregnated rock, but the process requires heat, solvents, and billions of gallons of water.[59]

Utah had planned to start construction of the dam in August 1981 and complete it by early 1984, which would have allowed private energy companies to use the water by 1985. However, the discovery of the fish threatened to delay the dam by a year or more. Utah's governor, Scott Matheson, suggested that Congress give states a larger role in enforcing the ESA. "I think we ought to have a modicum of jurisdiction on our future," said Matheson. Expressing frustration at the conflicting demands of energy and environmental protection, the governor noted, "We're caught between two public policies and trying to meet the objectives of both," both energy development and "the welfare of the Colorado squawfish."[60] Even with the ESA amendments passed in 1978, there would still be conflicts and controversies over the act's implementation and enforcement. The prospective White River dam in Utah was never built. The questionable technological feasibility of processing oil shale in a cost-effective way combined with ESA concerns to stall the project indefinitely.

The lasting effect of the amendments to the ESA was mixed. Despite environmentalist worries, only one time—in the 1990s, with regard to timber sales and the northern spotted owl—has the interagency review board actually granted an exemption from the ESA. That exemption was later overturned by a federal court. The board therefore never became either the anti-environmentalist wrecking ball that environmentalists had dreaded or the check on the ESA's more objectionable provisions that Congress had intended.[61] Yet despite this seemingly empty outcome, there is no doubt that the hydroelectric controversies of the 1970s discussed in this chapter helped turn opinion against the ESA and the idea of regulation in general. In the long term, the ESA amendments were admittedly perhaps of little practical consequence. But in the moment of the late 1970s, a time that saw an intense rhetorical and political assault upon longstanding government regulations in many economic sectors, the ESA amendments, and the sharp opposition to the ESA in Congress, bolstered and amplified the general anti-government sentiment echoing through Washington and the nation.

Speaking in 1979 about proposed deregulation of the trucking industry, President Carter characterized regulation as a bureaucratic nightmare impeding both common sense and economic efficiency:

> Too many trucks are rattling back and forth empty on the road today, burning up precious diesel fuel because the ICC rules prohibit two-way hauling. Some trucking firms can deliver all the ingredients necessary to make soup to a factory, but are forbidden from hauling soup away from the factory. Other rules defy human imagination. Some truckers can haul milk; they can't haul butter. They can haul cream; they can't haul cheese. Others can transport paint in 2-gallon cans; they can't haul paint in 5-gallon cans. Some truckers are allowed to haul bananas; they can't haul pineapple. They can haul pineapple and bananas if they are mixed.[62]

There were, of course, significant differences between trucking (and airline and railroad) regulation on one hand and environmental regulation on the other. The first meant to protect economic systems from abuse by balancing competing business interests and regulating entry barriers, while the latter was meant to protect people from the actions of business entities.[63] However, Carter's characterization of trucking regulation as an anti-commonsense, bureaucratic folly would have been familiar to anyone who had been following the story of the Tellico Dam, in which a forgettable fish protected by the Endangered Species Act threatened the construction of massive development projects. The rhetorical strategies invoked to inveigh against both economic and environmental regulation had become barely distinguishable. In popular perception, Ronald Reagan inaugurated an era of anti-regulatory, anti-government feeling in the United States. However, the process of loosening state control over American economic

"DELIBERATELY INFLEXIBLE"

life was well underway during the Carter administration. The weakening of the ESA fit coherently into Carter's broader program of deregulation, an agenda that reached across the trucking, airline, and railroad industries and into the arena of environmental regulation as well.

In 1983 the *New York* Times marked the tenth anniversary of the Endangered Species Act's passage by noting its role in saving species like the American alligator, the swift peregrine falcon, and the California condor from extinction.[64] However, the ESA never stayed safe from further attack by politicians. In 1995, for example, Senator Slade Gorton (R-WA) introduced an industry-friendly bill that would have severely weakened the ESA, invoking the rhetoric of "balance" in his advocacy for the bill.[65] Although the bill never made it out of the Senate, it demonstrated the lasting antipathy that some American politicians still held for the ESA.

In the 1970s, concerns about energy security helped substantively roll back environmental legislation, with the Endangered Species Act's ability to block TVA's Tellico initiative making the law appear too broad. However, TVA also played a more direct role in Jimmy Carter's energy policy in a way that intersected with environmentalism. Carter believed that TVA could mobilize its massive resources to promote energy conservation, which would both make the United States more secure by reducing its dependence on foreign oil and promote environmental quality by decreasing energy consumption. Again, Carter's policy initiatives took place within a political-economic context that complicated his plans. The next chapter explores how Carter's conservationist ideas conflicted with Southeasterners' ideas about the role TVA should play in the region, and how the backlash against Carter's plans further discredited his energy agenda.

CHAPTER 5

"HIT BY INFLATION LIKE EVERYONE ELSE"

The Tennessee Valley Authority in the Era of the Market

The Tellico Dam saga was one major narrative that drew the Tennessee Valley Authority into the ongoing tensions between energy production and environmental protection in the 1970s. Another story had to do with the underlying mission and character of the agency itself. In the chaotic economic climate of the 1970s, it was unclear how TVA's impressive resources could address the nation's energy problems. Reflecting his expansive energy plans, Jimmy Carter was eager to marshal TVA's regional infrastructure to benefit the national interest. However, members of Congress representing Tennessee and other Tennessee Valley states were wary of any attempt to increase TVA's scope or slate of activities, as the related costs would lead to increased electric rates for valley residents. Carter's conservationist programs also injected confusion into TVA's long-term construction planning, which had relied on predictions of steadily rising demand. The agency had to readjust to different trends in demand as consumption slowed. The imperatives of the 1970s energy economy changed and transformed TVA, but again the complex and unpredictable economic and political context brought further complications to Carter's energy plans. Ultimately, as America entered a political era defined by a deregulatory and anti-government mentality, TVA suffered a crisis of identity.

The 1970s were a time of confusion in the American macroeconomy. Massive, far-reaching institutions like TVA had to adjust to new realities in both economic dynamics and public opinion. As the title of a famous and influential report promulgated by the Club of Rome in 1972 suggested, there were natural "limits to growth" that would constrain possibilities for human economic expansion in the future, limits that humanity was reaching. Increased population, and the increased use of natural resources that went along with it, would inevitably reach a tipping point that would compel human consumption to slow down, lest humanity wipe itself out by depleting resources necessary for life. *The Limits to Growth* helped crystallize environmentalist fears of continued uninhibited growth. It also spurred many activists and politicians to embrace the goals of resource conservation to stave off societal and environmental collapse.[1] Historians later suggested that fears of overpopulation and overconsumption were perhaps exaggerated, but the fears were real at the time. The idea that robust economic growth could continue indefinitely was seriously in doubt.[2]

Perhaps a better metric than the "limits to growth" paradigm for understanding the 1970s is Judith Stein's recent characterization of the decade as the "Age of Inequality." In Stein's telling, the post–World War II period from 1945 to 1973 represented an "Age of Compression" in which progressive tax rates, significant union strength, sturdy social welfare programs, and other factors helped generate robust purchasing power, upward job mobility, and economic security for the working and middle classes. Underlying this "compression" was relatively curtailed economic inequality, with federal policies helping to guarantee that all economic strata in the United States reaped the benefit of wealth creation. By contrast, the "Age of Inequality" saw oil crises, the rise of the financial sector, and the decline of union strength broadening income inequality and eroding the economic and political power of the middle and working classes, to the benefit of the nation's very wealthiest and to the detriment of almost everyone else. Inflation severely affected working- and middle-class purchasing power, with rapidly rising prices across the economy hurting consumers' pocketbooks.[3]

Whether one understands US history in the 1970s as an era of limited growth prospects or as an age of inequality, a similar basic narrative underlies both paradigms. In the 1950s and 1960s, the United States had maintained impressive economic growth by creating a process in which businesses offered Americans reliable and high-paying jobs, which galvanized consumer spending, which increased business revenues, which encouraged businesses to hire more workers and pay them more, which kept a cycle of economic growth going in perpetuity. High taxation kept individuals from becoming too wealthy. It also funded programs like food stamps, Social Security, Medicare, and Medicaid, which allowed low-income individuals to participate in consumer culture. Regulation in industries like banking, airlines, railroads, and trucking guaranteed certain profits to some businesses but also prevented them from exploiting consumers.[4] The federal government worked vigorously to keep supply and demand balanced, preventing either inflation or unemployment from becoming a significant problem.

This seemingly unassailable system unraveled in the early 1970s. The combined spending of the Great Society and the Vietnam War turned moderate inflation into a upward spiral of rising consumer prices, the oil embargo hurt the US economy and consumer confidence, the Vietnam War and Watergate damaged trust in government and other major institutions, and the powerful environmental movement protested the impact of economic activity on air, water, plants, and animals. Keynesianism, the philosophy that government had a role in managing supply and demand in the macroeconomy, seemed unable to explain a situation in which inflation and unemployment were both running out of control.[5] Individuals, institutions, businesses, and agencies that could have previously avoided worries about confronting thorny economic choices now found themselves having to make quite tough decisions indeed. Seeing American businesses under government regulation as adrift and unable to function, some politicians pursued deregulatory policies to open up competition in business, restore profitability to the private sector, and allow the profit motive to figure out the most productive way to use natural resources. Some businesses would fail without the comfort of regulation, but the cleverest and most efficient, policy makers hoped, would survive.[6] The confluence of all these events helped create a general trust in the processes of unhindered market exchange, and a corollary widespread distrust of government institutions, in the United States.

The Tennessee Valley Authority, one of the most recognizable symbols of New Deal liberalism, was one entity that went through unexpected tumult during these uncertain economic times. However, its status as something between a public agency and a private company made coping with the new macroeconomic climate of the late 1970s especially difficult. Reflecting the idea that there were limits to traditional economic growth, President Jimmy Carter came up with an idea to use TVA's existing capabilities to forge what he saw as a more sustainable and environmentally friendly path forward, applying the agency's resources to the task of conducting cutting-edge research and development to secure America's energy future. Carter believed the bleak projections of imminent resource depletion and questioned the sustainability of perpetual economic growth, and he sought to use TVA to develop new technologies and incentives for energy conservation alongside alternative energy sources. Yet changing the agency in the way he imagined involved reconfiguring organizational structures and spending lots of TVA money. The expanded scope of TVA's activities alarmed Tennessee's representatives in Congress, who were concerned primarily with the impact that these supposed diversions would have on electricity rates for valley consumers. They castigated these measures and the Carter-appointed TVA chairman who pursued them.

TVA's ventures into alternative technology development, its adherence to environmental regulations, and its position within the general economic stagnation of the 1970s led to a larger crisis of TVA's essential mission and identity in the

Valley. TVA's perceived failures further amplified the growing anti-government sentiment pervading American culture and politics. Some policy makers sought to change TVA to adjust it to the increasingly deregulatory, anti-statist political climate of the era. Two initiatives meant to make TVA more like contemporary private-sector businesses, a drastic increase in pay for top executives and a restructuring of the agency's board of directors, received consideration in Congress. Opponents were suspicious of these measures, still seeing TVA as a New Deal agency that should be motivated by public service instead of market imperatives. Conflicts over TVA's central nature played out in the press over the course of the early 1980s, bringing insecurity and low morale to the agency's employees. TVA's only partial adaptation to the age of the market created vast problems for the agency, decreased Southeasterners' affinity for it, and contributed to the general perception of government as a bloated, inefficient entity, incapable of the swift delivery of needed services that the deregulated private sector increasingly seemed to be able to do so very well.

THE NEW CHAIRMAN

In the years from the end of World War II to the beginning of the 1960s, TVA—in the estimation of one analyst—had cemented itself as "the" power company for the Tennessee Valley. Over the two decades following World War II, TVA had established and burnished its reputation and position as an essential institution in everyday Valley life. Its hydroelectricity, forest replenishment, and soil rejuvenation programs helped lift much of the rural South out of poverty and brought the region nascent industry. TVA had a virtual monopoly on electricity in the Valley, as private companies could not use TVA's transmission lines to sell electricity. Because TVA did not have to earn a profit—it merely needed to fund the cost of its operations—it sold electricity at very affordable rates to Valley consumers and producers alike. By the 1960s, the right-to-work provisions of the 1947 Taft-Hartley Act were impelling American manufacturing to move southward. TVA officials were eager to hasten the region's industrial development by providing power for new industrial plants and the workers who labored at them.[7] To supplement TVA's existing hydroelectric plants, the agency added steam plants powered by coal, making a large portion of electricity production independent of the region's rivers. To meet the burgeoning projections of future demand, TVA soon expanded into building nuclear power plants as well. Analysts at TVA and other public utilities believed that private utilities in other parts of the country were underestimating future energy demand and unacceptably restricting expansion of generation facilities. TVA therefore took an aggressive stance to expand the production of cheap and abundant energy.[8]

Jimmy Carter's domestic policy staff looked disapprovingly upon TVA's increasing reliance on fossil fuels and nuclear power in the 1960s and 1970s. Coming to power in the late 1970s, they sought to use the agency's vast scope and resources to promote the new president's energy agenda. They were optimistic that TVA's impressive infrastructure could encourage the president's goals of energy conservation and alternative technology development. Some changes in leadership at the agency would be necessary.

A 1977 vacancy on the agency's board of directors, the body responsible for setting TVA's overall direction and mission, seemed to provide the perfect opportunity for Carter. White House Science Adviser Frank Press wrote Carter confidant Hamilton Jordan a preliminary memorandum to explain that the new president should seek a dynamic, creative candidate that would not let TVA continue with business as usual. Someone with "a reputation as an independent thinker" who would not feel constrained by TVA's current obsession with its power program was necessary. With "renewed vigorous leadership," Press proclaimed, TVA could "once again" become an "exciting demonstrational arm of the Federal government." With the proper guidance, TVA could serve as a shining example of successful conservation practices, of the use of a "mixed energy base" of renewable and nonrenewable resources, and of the productive development of cutting-edge alternative energy technologies. For Press, a "new view of regional development," one that could serve as an example to other areas of the country, was possible with the right selection.[9]

President Carter agreed and began searching for a suitable candidate. J. Wiley Bowers, the executive director of the Tennessee Public Power Association (a consortium of 160 municipal electric power systems and rural electric cooperatives), wrote the president urging the appointment of S. David Freeman to the position. TVA needed a director who could play an "active role" in this new era of "innovation and change," Bowers said. Freeman, who had a strong background at TVA and in the energy sector more broadly, was perfect for the role. Freeman began his career as a TVA engineer and lawyer and later worked as an assistant to TVA's chief counsel. He had also been intimately involved in other high-profile energy matters. In the early 1970s, Freeman directed the Ford Foundation's Energy Policy Project, and after Carter took office in 1977, Freeman worked in the White House assisting James Schlesinger's secret effort to conceptualize and organize the federal Department of Energy.[10]

Freeman had a much longer personal association with TVA than simply employment in his adult life. His parents were immigrants from Lithuania who had settled in Tennessee because Freeman's father, an umbrella maker, had apparently been told that it rained a lot there. Freeman himself still vividly remembered the floods that had regularly ravaged Chattanooga before TVA, and how the utility company brought stability to the region's landscape with its flood control work. The importance of rural electrification and its role in regional development were also ingrained in both Freeman's reminiscences and the region's collective memory. Freeman often liked to point out that most people in the area still referred to their electricity bill as a "light bill," TVA so decisively having taken responsibility for illuminating the region's previously dark nights.[11] Freeman clearly held a deep and optimistic view of TVA's potential for positive economic and social development in the Valley.

Freeman's closeness to Carter, along with his affinity for environmental causes, also drew much criticism. During Freeman's confirmation hearings, Senator John Stennis (D-MS) put a hold on his confirmation due to a suspicion that Freeman was "too much of an environmentalist." In his testimony, Freeman depicted TVA as a tool whose wide-ranging scope and influence could popularize and amplify Carter's hopes for increased energy efficiency and decreased personal consumption. In Freeman's view, TVA could serve as an example to spur a nationwide embrace of Carter's energy ethos, which frightened Southeasterners and their congressional representatives, who demanded that TVA focus squarely on its regional mission to provide cheap electricity. Freeman's national focus was drastically different from those in Congress who saw TVA's role as a servant of Valley residents.[12]

THE FREEMAN IDEOLOGY

Those who feared Freeman's plans should he be confirmed need not have guessed at his intentions. He had recently explained his views at great length in a 1974 analysis of American energy politics and policy. He began his book by referring to 17 October 1973, the beginning of the oil embargo, as "energy Pearl Harbor day," like Carter equating the magnitude of the energy challenge with war itself. Guaranteeing energy security and maintaining a clean environment, he said, would not come about easily or cheaply. Instead, instituting better health and safety protections for workers, creating better safeguards to protect against oil spills, and placing power lines safely underground instead of letting them crisscross above suburban neighborhoods would unavoidably cause the cost of energy to rise. Freeman was also wary of nuclear power. He saw its prevalence as not a product of its natural advantages but instead a consequence of "government's single-minded devotion to atomic energy research over the years," which had "stacked the deck for the future in favor of the one energy source it has so lavishly supported." It was now time, Freeman said, for government to put the same amount of enthusiasm and effort into developing cleaner alternative technologies as it had devoted to nuclear power in years past.[13]

Freeman also denied that unleashing the private sector would be sufficient to solve the nation's energy challenges. Maintaining a secure energy future, Freeman argued, was not achievable by simply allowing private companies to harvest and distribute raw fossil fuel materials from the ground, as had worked in decades past. Coal and oil were damaging the quality of the air and water, and besides, they were running out. The energy of the future would instead emerge from incredibly complicated, "tedious and expensive" engineering experiments that might not pay off for years, projects that private companies seeking a quick and reliable profit would be loath to support. Also not sufficient were the "piecemeal" government policies that had emerged over years and decades as problems were tackled "one at a time." The problem with this approach, he said, was that "the government has instigated different regulatory and promotional programs for coal, atomic energy, natural gas, oil, and shale oil without recognizing that federal boosting of one source might discourage industry from investing in the others." Instead, "a massive federally financed research and development effort," one that could afford to sink money into unsuccessful initiatives for years until a productive solution could be discovered, was necessary.[14]

As Carter was determined to see Freeman ascend to the chairmanship, Senator Stennis eventually released the hold on the nomination and Freeman was confirmed to the position. However, questions about his priorities continued. Soon after his swearing-in, Freeman spoke to Save Our Cumberland Mountains, an organization opposed to strip mining. Giving this speech was indeed a curious act for someone heading the largest coal-burning entity in the Western Hemisphere. Freeman was also initially dedicated to pursuing alternative sources. On the celebration of "Sun Day" on 3 May 1978, a day designated by President Carter for solar power advocacy, the "iconoclast" chairman appeared in front of a Memphis crowd wearing a bright yellow T-shirt over a turtleneck sweater. Freeman brought applause by suggesting that expanded use of solar energy could obviate the need for at least one future nuclear plant currently planned by TVA. Later that day, Freeman posed for a photo opportunity by climbing atop the roof of a suburban Memphis home and dutifully inspecting a solar heating panel.[15]

Freeman did not realistically intend for the sprawling and decentralized TVA to undergo revolutionary change overnight, but major parts of his vision came to fruition quite quickly. A mere year after assuming his chairmanship, he had taken significant steps to return the agency to its New Deal roots as a grassroots social and economic experiment rather than an entity solely focused on power production. Freeman had TVA scientists hard at work on solar research, garbage-fired steam plants, and fuel cells, clean coal–powered units that could produce electricity in small downtown installations. Freeman had moved rapidly to reorient TVA's future focus away from large, centralized coal and nuclear plants toward smaller and cleaner options. "And, as in the old days," according to the *New York Times*, the authority had teams examining soil erosion in north Georgia, aiding small farmers in Alabama, and helping commercial fishing in the 650-mile chain of lakes in the Tennessee Valley. "Now, we're beginning to come back to what [David] Lilienthal called the seamless web," proclaimed Freeman proudly, in which power generation was envisioned as merely one aspect of TVA's overall mission to cultivate the economic and social development of the Valley.[16]

Not long after assuming his new chairmanship, though, Freeman faced sporadic citizen questions about what this new emphasis would mean for TVA's overall identity. Kentucky attorney Granville Clark, for example, was "disturbed" by Freeman's "apparent great interest in areas other than the generation of electrical power." The era of sociological government programs meant for "planning people's lives" seemed to be over, the attorney claimed, and besides, it seemed like a tall order for any government agency to make itself an expert in more than any one given field. "Thus, it would appear reasonable that TVA would be better to devote its time to matters concerning the generation of electricity" and leave other decisions about daily life to people and their communities. Referring to the recent snail darter controversy that had embroiled TVA in controversy, he reiterated that TVA should "leave the decision as to whether the people in the Tellico Project want to live in an industrial area or a rural area up to them."[17]

Freeman's reply attempted to assuage Clark's concerns. "These programs [fertilizers, forests, water quality, wildlife management] are, of course, financed by appropriated money and do not inhibit our ability to operate the power system in a frugal manner." In fact, given that 90 percent of TVA employees were involved in some way with power generation, one could even argue that TVA had "permitted the power program to take up too much of its time" at the expense of other priorities.[18] Freeman may have thought that he had successfully parried Clark's concern, but his agenda soon drew scrutiny. The persistent inquiry into Freeman's plans came not just from Valley residents, but also from members of Congress.

ENVIRONMENTALISM AND TVA

Freeman's ambitious initiatives were indeed not without consequences. For a variety of reasons, they resulted in higher electricity rates for Valley residents. The TVA Act of 1933 required that TVA pay for all electricity generation with current income. As costs of generating electricity went up, electricity rates for consumers had to rise as well. Increases in TVA utility rates had virtually always elicited ire from ratepayers in the Valley, as citizens had become accustomed to low electric rates as a regional birthright. The increases that occurred during

Freeman's tenure were unprecedented and shocking to the Valley population. In the view of one political scientist, public opinion in the Valley simply "was not prepared" for the high rate increases during Freeman's chairmanship. Edward Hopper, an attorney in Huntsville, Alabama, wrote Freeman in late 1978 to warn that the "mood of the region's people is angry, hostile, and resolute. They do not intend to tolerate a continued utility bill that is higher than house payments."[19] Hopper spoke for a much wider swath of public opinion. As TVA sponsored public meetings across the Valley concerning possible rate increases in the late 1970s, the response from citizens was reportedly "uniformly one of anger."[20]

There were several significant reasons for rising rates in the late 1970s and 1980s. One, given that TVA was still burning massive amounts of coal, was the cost of cooperating with environmental and safety regulations, including the black lung and strip mining regulations discussed in chapter 2. TVA seemed to accept these regulations, claiming that its purpose in accounting for the full costs of harvesting and burning coal was "fair and equitable."[21] But the demands for TVA to take adequate steps to ensure environmental safeguards in the course of its operations indeed created burdens on the agency's quest for low rates, and the requirement caused upper-level management to complain. TVA General Manager William F. Willis remarked in 1981 that "our responsibilities, whether they conflict or not, have the force of legal obligation." Willis noted that TVA was simultaneously required to generate power at the lowest possible cost and to "be vigilant in protecting the environment and conserving resources." "Unfortunately," Willis lamented, "the [TVA] Act doesn't tell us how to do any one of those things without hampering our ability to do the others."[22] Though Freeman's TVA may have been trying to internalize the full costs of using certain types of energy, this was not an argument that went over well with irate ratepayer-taxpayers.

A 1977 incident is a case in point. A coalition of ten health and environmental groups, along with the states of Alabama and Kentucky, sued TVA in June for continuing to violate Environmental Protection Agency (EPA) clean air standards. Ten of TVA's twelve giant coal-fired power plants in Tennessee, Kentucky, and Alabama were emitting toxic sulfur dioxide in excess of environmental regulations; together the twelve were emitting over two million tons of sulfur dioxide a year, more than 10 percent of all sulfur oxide emissions from all American utility plants. Two months later, the EPA itself joined the suit. TVA's violations were clear, and TVA and the EPA agreed to a quarter-billion dollar fine for the Authority. However, this punishment paled in comparison to TVA's cost going forward. In order to prevent future pollution, the entire settlement also required that TVA spend $1 billion in capital investment and $550 million for the installation of sulfur dioxide scrubbers, as well as purchase more expensive low-sulfur coal for burning. Scrubbers are metal boxes into whose bottoms coal-fired gases rise. As the gases rise, they are enveloped with a solution of magnesium oxide or limestone, whose acid eats up sulfur and precipitates it out in solid form rather than releasing it into the air.[23]

Periodicals noticed problems with the settlement. As the pro-business *Wall Street Journal* noted, forcing scrubbers on utilities as a broad policy prescription might even have an "effect opposite" to that intended, since if utilities knew that they must install scrubbers regardless of the type of coal burned, they might opt for cheaper, high-sulfur coal instead of more expensive, low-sulfur coal. Since the high-sulfur variety subject to scrubbing might in fact emit *more* carbon dioxide than the low-sulfur alternative, even without the scrubber, the scrubbing requirement was likely a counterproductive policy.[24] Though the settlement required TVA to purchase low-sulfur coal, private utilities elsewhere faced no such burden, and they were free to use the high-sulfur variety if they wished.

In 1978, one TVA board member—Tellico Dam mastermind Aubrey Wagner—resigned rather than vote in favor of the settlement. Another member retired with a "public blast" at the settlement and warned against interference by the EPA in TVA's activities. Since the New Deal, TVA had the charge of providing the cheapest possible electricity to Valley residents, a mission its caretakers took very seriously. These particular TVA members resented the perceived meddling by the relatively new EPA in the affairs of the decades-old Authority and reacted accordingly. The environmentalist sympathizer David Freeman was the only one of the three board members who was amenable to the agreement. The agreement was indeed not signed until a year later, when Richard Freeman (no relation to David) joined the board and voted in favor of the settlement.[25]

The settlement had a stark impact on TVA's operations. In 1981 TVA predicted that the costs associated with the cleanup would increase residential consumers' rates by nearly 10 percent over the course of the next two years. Discussing the settlement, David Freeman claimed that TVA had "no choice" but to comply with regulatory stipulations: "We have 10 coal-fired steam plants that are in violation of the law." For Freeman, nothing was more "distasteful" than being required to raise electric rates. However, he said, "TVA is being hit by inflation like everyone else. We don't make a profit, but we must pay our bills."[26]

This incident indicated the difficulty of TVA's precarious balancing act of cooperating with environmental requirements while complying with congressional demands for low utility rates for Valley customers. A shocked Senator Baker, certainly fearing the political fallout of increased rates, wrote to Environment and Public Works Chairman Jennings Randolph (D-WV) to ask for Senate hearings on the matter "because of the extraordinary importance of the decision." Although Baker couched his request for a national hearing in the fact that the use—and potential mandate—of scrubbers was a topic relevant to other power plants across the country, he also expressed immense concern about the possibility of an increased financial burden on TVA ratepayers, his constituents and voters.[27]

The rising cost of coal was one reason for rising electric rates, but the cost of paying for TVA's new diverse set of programs also affected consumers' pocketbooks. Freeman defended TVA's expenditures before the Senate Committee on Environment and Public Works in March 1981. Though congressional appropriations funded recreation, forestry, and flood control programs, research money for alternative energy sources came mainly from power revenues, and members of Congress were thus concerned that TVA might be both wasting taxpayer money on some programs and unjustly increasing electric rates for Valley residents to pay for others. In his Senate testimony, Freeman attempted to justify the agency's costs by highlighting the fact that many programs incubated by TVA were appropriated for broader national use upon their maturation. Alternative energy research programs that "benefit and are funded by the nation's taxpayers as well as Valley ratepayers," for example, had promising implications for nationwide use. Likewise, recent initiatives in agricultural and fertilizer development that TVA funded were in productive use across the nation. "It is not just a utility and that fact should be kept in mind in considering its performance." Tax revenues, he said, must continue flowing to TVA.[28]

Freeman also declared that the TVA board should not and would not resist modest increases in rates to compensate for increased expenditures on alternative energy, as a drop-off in revenue would damage TVA's ability to finance investments that would pay off handsomely in the longer term. He also believed that curtailing industrial capacity in the present would damage the region's long-term development prospects. If TVA reduced its construction in anticipation of slower economic growth in the future, then those very predictions of reduced economic activity would become a self-fulfilling prophecy. In Freeman's view, a short-term political overreaction to rising power rates would thus only lead to long-term damage. Representatives in Congress, thinking in short timeframes of political campaigns and elections, were reluctant to accept such an argument.[29] For them, TVA needed to get to focusing on power generation by the most efficient means possible, and it needed to do so quickly.[30]

Indeed, constituent outcry about rising TVA rates reached a fever pitch in the Valley. Mr. and Mrs. George E. Latham of Friendsville wrote Representative John Duncan of Tennessee's second congressional district in April to ask that he, Tennessee's governor, and "all concerned" work together on an issue of great importance, namely utility rates. The previous winter, the Lathams had been "shocked out of [their] pants" by the price of heating their home. Indeed, they found themselves in a quandary. Since they were paying more for home heating costs, they decided to trade in their 1968 Ford automobile for a smaller model that would use less gasoline to try to make up the difference. Unfortunately, the huge electric bills meant that they could not make the payment on a smaller car. "There has to be an end to this some where," they wrote. George Latham was working for "every dime" but had "nothing left" for pleasure after the utility bills were paid. In a reference to Stephen King's 1977 novel *The Shining*, the Lathams noted that "all work and no play makes Jack a dull boy." They charged TVA with making exorbitant profits at the expense of hardworking Valley residents. Beneath their signatures, they noted that they were "Registered Voters" as a reminder that Duncan should take their complaints seriously.[31]

Duncan forwarded the Lathams' letter to TVA Chairman Aubrey Wagner and asked for comment. In reply, Wagner denied that his agency was gouging ratepayers and stated that the high electricity rates were unavoidable in the current inflationary economic climate. He noted that of every dollar taken in by TVA, fifty-one cents went toward paying for the cost of fuel, mainly coal. Nineteen cents went to pay interest obligations, eleven cents went to labor, nine cents funded other operating expenses, and four cents paid taxes. Another four cents went toward TVA's payments to the federal treasury for the government's past investment in the agency. As Wagner noted, this left two cents to finance construction of new power generating stations. As Wagner argued, "TVA charges only what is necessary to cover its costs," and government reports showed that Tennessee enjoyed the lowest electric rates of any state east of the Rocky Mountains.[32] Though Wagner seemed to sympathize with the suffering of Valley ratepayers, there seemed to be little in the present moment that could ease their burden.

TVA AND ENERGY CONSERVATION

The 1979 selection of Illinois railway lawyer Richard M. Freeman to the TVA board of directors, which solved the impasse over the 1978 EPA settlement, also brought David Freeman a like-minded individual to help him pursue his audacious goals. Richard, like David, had a deep TVA background, having served as an attorney for the agency from 1948 to 1957. In terms of their vision for TVA, the two Freemans were often hard to tell apart. Richard spoke of wanting "to see TVA come closer to achieving its goal of the integrated development of the Tennessee Valley Region," putting together the region's resources "into a pattern of quality growth." He also talked about how TVA's conservation initiatives could be "a potential demonstration of how a part of the nation's energy problem can be addressed."[33] Such statements were virtually indistinguishable from how David Freeman had already been speaking about TVA for many months. Together, the two made energy conservation a keystone of the agency's activities. However, in addition to the rising cost of coal and the expenditures related to TVA's alternative technology programs, there was also conflict between TVA's extant plans and the conservationist priorities of the Freemans and the incumbent Carter administration.

TVA was initially proud to spread the word about its conservation programs. A boosterish document that declared TVA "ready for the 80's" spoke in glowing terms about TVA's recent conservation initiatives in the Valley. For example, TVA's home insulation program, which provided free home energy surveys to residential customers and no-interest loans for weatherization, had been a rousing success, resulting in over a quarter million home surveys and over a hundred thousand loans.[34] In a talk to the annual meeting of the Tennessee Valley Public Power Association, David Freeman stressed the importance of these home insulation loans, solar hot-water heaters, and other conservation measures. He also called for the Valley to pursue a one-million-kilowatt reduction of commercial and industrial load over the next ten years by pursuing more efficient industrial methods.[35]

However, TVA's turn to conservation in the Valley also had consequences for the agency's existing economic structure. Drawing on the Carter administration's conservation emphasis, David Freeman's TVA encouraged Valley ratepayers to take steps to decrease their individual energy use. Then, as a direct consequence, TVA raised electricity rates on consumers, claiming that a higher price per kilowatt-hour was necessary because less aggregate electricity was selling. TVA had current construction projects to fund and could not afford the dropoff in revenues. Critical periodicals indignantly pointed out this contradiction and castigated TVA for it. Though the *Chattanooga Times* blasted the "mismanagement, poor judgment, bad public relations, [and] general incompetence and inefficiency" of TVA, this was also a clear example of the conflict between the long-term conservationist agenda and the immediate demands of the existing systems of energy distribution.[36]

Furthermore, given the economic upheaval of the mid-1970s, TVA's earlier projections of future energy use turned out to be flawed, which exacerbated the structural planning problems caused by conservation. In the 1960s and early 1970s, the federal government had projected "huge demand" in the future for electric power in the Tennessee Valley, an area to which many Midwesterners and Northeasterners were flocking to seek employment as industrial production in the United States moved southward. In response to this growing population and economic affluence, TVA had built a network of seven nuclear power plants and seventeen reactors, the cost of which reached over $30 billion. The government's projection turned out to be far too high, as the stagflation of the early 1970s stalled the American economy for years and invalidated these optimistic projections. The agency halted further nuclear construction. In May 1979, for example, the agency announced an indefinite halt in the construction of four nuclear reactors already underway at three sites in Tennessee and Mississippi. As a Mississippi newspaper complained, "America's taxpayers are covering the cost of the [government's] mistake and TVA's 2.8 million customers are footing that agency's bill." Already costing millions of dollars, it was reported that "it may reach the billions in the next 10 years."[37]

Incorrect past predictions were a problem, and conservation incentives further exacerbated the problem by making current predictions of future energy use nearly impossible too. A 1979 General Accounting Office (GAO) report criticized TVA for making inaccurate estimates of future demand and recommended canceling planned future projects. Though the GAO blamed TVA incompetence, the diverse conservation measures promoted by Carter's Department of Energy and TVA itself, combined with general economic stagnation, certainly also influenced the agency's troubles in estimating future demand figures. Nonetheless, an experienced TVA worker complained that TVA's current path of constructing generating capacity in excess of anticipated system requirements while spending "substantial" amounts of money to promote conservation "appears to put the ratepayer in a no-win situation." TVA had already seen current construction plans become more complicated because of conservationism and economic slowdown, and now it had to alter projections far into the future as well. At the beginning of May 1979, Freeman's TVA delayed for six months a decision to accept bids, which it already had in hand, for prospective new nuclear power plants.[38]

Though Carter's conservationist ethos may have provided the basis of a more sustainable energy policy in some respects, there were clear complications as it collided with existing systems of energy production. As aggregate energy demand in the Valley slowed after the implementation of Carter's conservation programs, the economics of electricity necessitated that TVA raise rates to compensate for its existing construction programs. This was a politically unacceptable course of action, especially to the Valley's representatives in Congress. Projecting future energy use became a serious challenge, with economic stagnation and conservationist measures each starkly affecting consumer demand. The two Freemans soon found themselves under assault by angry members of the legislative branch, and they subsequently fired off apologetic and defensive responses to alarmed questions about TVA's uneasy financial position.[39]

STAFFING THE AGENCY

David Freeman's tenure as chairman witnessed another complication for the Authority, one that had to do with the staffing necessities that would accompany these new programs and research projects. The agency's organizational structure had become more and more complicated over the previous decades as it grew. In 1978 TVA began a review of its management practices and created a corporate planning process to prioritize and direct the organization's activities. TVA thought that doing so could help handle the challenge of pursuing various and perhaps divergent objectives like coal-fired power, nuclear construction, fertilizer research, conservation awareness, and environmental protection, as well as successfully coordinate and manage the diverse sets of employees necessary to develop and implement these programs.[40]

TVA quickly found that its preparations had been quite inadequate. In 1980, with the Authority in bad financial shape, TVA board of directors member Bob Clement solicited suggestions for cutting costs at the agency, which revealed a long list of complaints from veteran workers. Most of the new administrative staff members, workers complained, had taken minimal steps to acquaint themselves with and fit into the agency's deep-rooted culture, and had instead sought only their own personal advancement. The problem was compounded by the fact that this new staff had been hired at the managerial level and, although incredibly unfamiliar with the day-to-day operations of an electrical utility, now had supervisory authority over workers with years of experience.[41]

One veteran worker, for example, pointed to a management structure that had become top-heavy with inexperienced people, which, as this worker saw it, was hampering production. Another felt that "everyone in management is trying to build a kingdom." In this worker's eyes, the fact that "the more personnel they have, the higher they are placed up the ladder" was a distraction, as managers were more concerned with collecting subordinates than improving work operation. One stated simply that TVA should "stop hiring people with little or no utility experience" for high-level jobs. Others pointed to "too many nontechnical people releasing conflicting statements" that confused the public, as well as all the assistants who were generating piles of work just answering mail and phone calls among their superiors.[42] TVA had long pointed to its decentralized structure as a benefit that would allow it to pursue many activities at once. It now seemed that the decentralization was causing more problems than it was solving.

Veteran workers complained overwhelmingly to Clement about a stunning lack of morale, and they uniformly called for changes that would allow workers to recapture a sense of initiative, productivity, and community in the workplace. In March 1981, Minnesota economist and former TVA official Vernon Ruttan came to the unfortunate conclusion that, in the absence of market exchange, TVA was weakened in its ability to discern which of its services to communities, firms, and individuals were most needed and wanted.[43] TVA was spending money on a diverse set of alternative energy sources that seemed to have no apparent immediate market for sale, the research and development costs of which were increasing the electric rates paid by Valley residents. It was undertaking intense forestry and flood control operations, the concrete benefits of which it could neither measure nor understand. TVA employees then saw their organization pilloried in both the press and in public opinion for wasting resources on quixotic initiatives. Again, TVA's attempts to develop nationally relevant programs and to align its mission with the incumbent president's priorities interfered with its regional goal of efficient electricity production.

TVA chairman David Freeman's inability to reconcile TVA's two manifestations— national technological incubator on one hand and regional utility on the other—along with the pressure put on members of Congress to rein in Freeman's TVA, ultimately led to his demotion. In April 1981, Senator Howard Baker asked President Ronald Reagan to remove David Freeman from the chairmanship while allowing him to remain a member of the board of directors. The senator asked that Charles "Chili" Dean, the manager of the Knoxville Utility Board, replace Freeman as chair. Baker preferred Dean because he was acutely familiar with the problems of the Valley and had fewer grand ideas about national concerns than Freeman. As Erwin Hargrove has noted, "the decision to appoint [Dean] suggests that Baker saw TVA as an institution of the valley and nothing more."[44] Carter's bold experiment with TVA had largely ended, done in by the contradiction between the vision for its influential future and the realities of the political status quo.[45]

EXPANDING THE BOARD

With all of these apparent administrative and managerial problems, clamors arose inside Congress to change the composition of the agency's board of directors, namely by adding more members. The two Freemans in particular had been working in virtual lockstep. Some legislators began to believe that adding more members to create a more decentralized board might help address many of the agency's lingering problems. More voices on the board, proponents of the idea argued, meant that there would naturally be a broader set of ideas on the table to consider with regard to any given issue, which would undoubtedly benefit the agency. A more democratic board would naturally be a more thoughtful and imaginative one. Following this logic, a bill under consideration in the US Senate in 1979 proposed expanding the TVA board from three members to five. The bill also included a residency provision requiring that all members of the board hail from the Tennessee Valley, thus trying to ensure that the board would consider the interests of the people of the Valley first.[46]

Richard Freeman, an Indiana native whose employment status would be in jeopardy, was vocally opposed to the proposal. He inverted its proponents' argument about the impact that more voices would have on the board's functionality. "The board of three," he said in Senate testimony, was the optimal size, big enough to "[provide] for diverse points of view when resolving policy issues," yet also small enough "to maintain the closeness and cohesiveness so essential for effective and timely decisionmaking." Instead of an asset, the existence of more viewpoints on the board would actually be a detriment to the agency's well-being, as it would prevent the board from speaking with a clear, coherent voice. The hypothetical larger board, he said, would generate "a hopelessly chaotic administrative condition" at the upper levels of decision-making, with the stale, institutional bureaucracy of the entrenched executive class taking over instead. Richard Freeman warned that the decisive leadership capabilities of the board would dissipate, with creativity and imagination eliminated. The board would then, tragically, "lose touch with what is happening and what should happen in TVA" amid its own internal squabbling. Though proponents of adding members argued that their idea would make the board more flexible, it was a smaller board, Freeman claimed, that was truly the more adaptable model.[47]

In the short term, Richard Freeman got his wish, as the five-member idea fizzled out in Congress. Howard Baker had introduced the idea of a seven-member board in the Senate in 1981, but the idea faded away when Baker expressed uncertainty in committee hearings.[48] As the agency continued into the 1980s, its underlying problems did not dissipate. Some within the agency itself, especially those serving in TVA's office in the nation's capital, saw TVA's schizophrenic identity as emerging from the fact that it was still acting like a centralized, New Deal–era government bureaucracy, even as American private sector practices had been evolving, adapting, and decentralizing over the past two decades. In order to compete and function in an era of receding government control over the economy, these observers said, TVA needed to emulate recent productive developments in American business itself. In particular, the board—whether it had three, four, five, or whatever number of members—consisted of full-time employees with lengthy terms of service. This arrangement, critics said, rendered TVA unequipped to deal with rapid changes in the macroeconomic, macropolitical climate. More flexibility in TVA's decision-making processes, these critics claimed, was essential in the new information-driven economy of the 1980s.[49]

The Tennessee Valley Industrial Committee, a loosely organized group of large industries in the Valley, was a prominent voice in favor of some sort of change. It relied on huge amounts of TVA electricity and had seen utility bills skyrocket in the past few years. It conceded that a small, hands-on board had been appropriate in TVA's early days, as in the early 1930s the board had faced the daunting task of "getting a fledgling New Deal agency off the ground. It was a board up to its elbows in operations." Decades later, the situation was markedly different. A very involved board "is not, however, the best way to manage an organization with $16 billion in assets . . . and the largest power system in the United States." The board should figure out some way, the committee said, to back away from daily operations and put itself at "almost arm's length" from management to assure an "objective, diverse, expert outside point of view." The committee warned that if TVA did not figure out some better, more cost-effective way of providing power, it might soon lead to employee layoffs in the Valley. "Because of their high cost of operation due principally to electric rates," the companies composing the committee would be "first to be cut back in production" if the economy fell into recession.[50]

TVA's office in the nation's capital, more closely attuned to some of the broader trends playing out in corporate and government practices, was also a strong proponent of reforming the agency's board composition. It echoed some of the same ideas that the Valley's private industries had recently outlined. The Washington office sent its analysis and recommendations in November 1983 to John Stewart, head of TVA's Office of Policy, Planning, and Budget. TVA lagged badly behind current practices in American business, it said. In past decades, businesses had relied on "inside" members with extensive in-company experience to sit on the board of directors and make top-level decisions. More recently, reflecting the new economic realities of more rapid, diverse, and voluminous flows of information and knowledge as a component of daily economic life, companies had increasingly begun to bring in "outside" directors with expertise in law, government, and different fields of business. For example, an executive from a financial services company would serve on the board of a retail company, and vice versa. In addition to tapping different fields of expertise, this practice also allowed more open-mindedness and attention to broader economic context than might be possessed by a group of directors who had spent their entire careers with one company. While corporate boards had once been dominated by "inside" directors, the Washington office pointed out, the situation by 1983 was one in which the average corporate board had nine "outside" directors for every four "inside" directors. This "more open and more democratic" form of corporate governance, the Washington office claimed, had made companies much more flexible and adaptable in a constantly changing world, and it was an example that TVA should seek to imitate.[51]

Concurrent with the memorandum from the Washington office was Representative Ronnie Flippo's (D-AL) introduction of a bill in the House that would triple the size of the TVA board, turning it into a nine-member entity. Seven of the nine would be part-time "citizen directors" from the Tennessee Valley, with another part-time director who could be from anywhere in the nation. In order to smooth the communication process between long-term planning and everyday operations, the ninth member of the board would be TVA's general manager, its top administrative figure. Except for the general manager, the board members would receive $5,000 per year for their part-time service and be paid an additional $250 per day for attendance at official TVA meetings. Flippo claimed that these changes would both "open the TVA policy-making process to fresh insights" and "make the TVA more representative of, and more accountable to, the people of the region."[52] Whether or not these claims were necessarily true— all directors would still be appointed by the president of the United States—it was surely true that this structure would result in a different decision-making process than a three-member board on which two like-minded members could dominate.

The centrality of presidential appointments was key. Given David Freeman's perceived closeness to President Carter's environmentalist and conservationist agenda, one of the main arguments in favor of the restructuring was that it would make the board less politically charged by making it more democratic. However, if the selection process remained the same, a drastic shift in the board's ideological orientation was certainly less likely than proponents claimed. For the same reason, there was no particular reason that a changed board composition would make the utility run more efficiently, especially if the structure of top day-to-day management did not change. Even though David Freeman had happily complied with EPA regulations, they still had the force of law regardless of whether the TVA chairman liked them or not. Therefore, a chairman who unhappily complied with them under the law would have almost certainly presided over the same rate increases that Freeman had.[53] For these reasons, this restructuring plan also ultimately stalled in Congress, and the three-member model remained. Though Representative Flippo was still talking nearly three years later of the "tragedy, the culmination of years of blunders, of operating without any kind of accountability," three full-time directors would continue to guide the agency nonetheless.[54]

EXECUTIVE PAY

The most controversial public issue related to staff had to do with TVA's non-board top executives. In the early 1980s, TVA was having immense trouble retaining expert administrators in light of their relatively low pay. By 1981, for example, TVA had lost over a quarter of its power executives, and just under a quarter of the executives in the Office of Engineering Design and Construction, to private utility companies offering significantly higher salaries. Under the TVA

Act of 1933—passed, of course, in the very different historical context of the Great Depression and New Deal—TVA employees could not draw a salary in excess of that received by members of the board, which in 1980 stood at $55,387 for the chairman and $52,750 for the two other members. Americans had broadly seen the Great Depression as caused by the greed and irresponsibility of private interests, with self-centeredness very nearly destroying the nation's economy. TVA's employees, as instruments of the federal government's New Deal recovery efforts, were viewed properly as in service to the public interest, not their own bank accounts.[55]

Nearly fifty years later, this requirement was drastically impeding the Authority's ability to keep outstanding senior leadership. With the Great Depression now merely a distant historical memory, the nation's cultural antipathy to self-interest and private profit had largely dissipated. Expert TVA executives were often eager to apply their talents elsewhere in pursuit of higher incomes if the opportunity arose. TVA itself, along with members of Congress who noticed the management exodus and worried about its effects on the agency's operations, jumped into action. In order to compete with private utilities for top talent, TVA decided that it had to start thinking less like a government organization and more like a private company. Based on the recommendations of the Senate's Committee on Environment and Public Works, the TVA board instructed its general counsel to explore methods of strengthening the compensation programs for power system employees.[56]

The resulting proposal attempted to get around the salary restriction in the TVA Act and suggested that, as an alternative to direct salary increases, TVA should instead enter into "retention agreements" with approximately seventy-five of its top executives. At an approximate cost of a mere $1 million per year, the bonus program would be contingent upon its recipients agreeing to stay at TVA for a three-year period, and the retention amount could reach as high as $36,800 per individual. For an employee making $52,750 annually, this represented an astronomical bonus of about 70 percent. TVA also proposed that the money for the bonuses come from power revenues and not from federally appropriated funds, which it hoped would mitigate accusations that taxpayer money was going to pay exorbitant executive bonuses. As TVA pointed out, its power-operating budget for fiscal year 1982 was $3.8 billion, and the prospective $1 million increase would, according to the GAO, add about 0.026 percent—in other words, virtually nothing—to rates. The agency strongly asserted that it was cutting costs wherever possible to keep rates low, and that it viewed the bonuses as an investment that would yield greater savings in the end, as it would stop top executives from departing the agency. All three directors—Dean and the two Freemans—emphatically voiced their support.[57]

TVA expressed other reasons for the necessity of the plan to Senator Baker. Citing high turnover in key positions and an inability to recruit needed talent, TVA warned of the risk of nuclear danger. "Nuclear safety is as much a function of experienced managers and operators as fail-safe equipment," TVA claimed, and it would be foolish to operate TVA's network of nuclear plants without the managers essential to ensure prudent operation. Baker strongly agreed. Concluding that a nominal increase in pay was necessary to preserve the safety standards, as well as the low utility rates that he deemed so politically important, he spoke on the floor of the Senate in November to defend the plan. Baker's staff conceded privately that in a time of federal budget cutbacks, the optics of the plan might prove unfavorable. The senator himself calculated that the hard figures on a power bill would prove more important than public consternation about the bonuses.[58]

Several newspapers in the region also lined up behind the plan. One in Knoxville, for example, asked rhetorically how a bonus program could possibly be worth $1 million a year. It then answered its own query by noting that one perceptive coal buyer could save TVA $1 million a *month*. "Or, more correctly, a dumb one could lose the agency that much," the newspaper said. "TVA has already lost what it considered its two top coal buyers to private industry." Another in Kingsport noted that, for executives of other regional utilities, a $70,000 salary was near the bottom; the chairman of Florida Power and Light Co., a smaller entity than TVA, was making over *three-and-a-half times* as much annually. The newspaper conceded that, from a public relations standpoint, the time was inopportune to be asking for more money for management. In the total TVA budget, the periodical proclaimed, "upgrading top salaries is a small investment toward insuring the best people continue to manage such an important and complex agency."[59]

Despite the straightforward and seemingly unimpeachable fiscal analysis, this argument nonetheless proved to be a hard sell to some, who thought that TVA was drifting too far toward market-based thinking and should return to a public-service-based orientation focused on serving consumers, not enriching executives. Not all newspaper commentaries favored the plan; a newspaper from Bristol, Virginia (near the Tennessee border), spoke of the "monumental arrogance" of TVA's management, which was ignoring its "captive customers" with impunity.[60] One individual who agreed with the Bristol paper's point of view was Senator Jim Sasser (D-TN), who had defeated Bill Brock's 1976 reelection bid.

JAMES SASSER AND THE GAO

James Sasser, like Howard Baker, saw TVA as primarily a servant of Valley residents, but the two differed drastically in their respective approaches to the agency. Baker was, of course, not shy in criticizing David Freeman when Freeman took actions that Baker thought might raise Valley electric rates, but in general, the senator was a fierce defender of TVA in Congress and in the press. He worked constantly throughout his career to shield TVA's autonomy and to advocate for its interests with whoever sat in the White House and in the chambers of Congress at any given moment. Sasser, though, used a different tactic, mobilizing various instruments of government oversight to keep constant pressure on TVA's administrators and to weaken TVA's power and autonomy, as Sasser viewed TVA as a self-interested entity focused primarily on increasing its own power at the expense of Valley residents. Where Baker saw the interests of TVA and Valley citizens as generally convergent, Sasser viewed the agency as an insulated, greedy bureaucracy that required significant attention and often chastisement, lest it veer off course from its citizen-focused mission.[61]

An incident in 1982 demonstrated Sasser's antagonistic orientation toward TVA. The senator commissioned the GAO to complete three reports on TVA's activities and financial sustainability. Taken together, the reports were highly critical of the agency, arguing that TVA was misstating the disjuncture between planned future construction costs and likely future revenues. Sasser had specifically asked that TVA not have a chance to comment on the reports before their public release, a request that the GAO honored when it released them in March.[62] The reports embarrassed TVA badly, and the agency's general counsel tasked his staff with investigating whether the GAO had a legal obligation to allow an agency under review to comment on reports before their public release. In response, his staff reported that there was no clear requirement either way. There was no statutory requirement that GAO comply with these types of directives from members of Congress, but neither was there a requirement that the GAO allow agency comment before release. The decision to allow comment instead lay entirely at the discretion of the GAO, so if a member of Congress requested that reports be released without agency comment, legally the GAO could decide whether to honor the request. There was, however, as one staff attorney noticed, a significant difference between legal obligation and practice: "As a practical political matter . . . GAO's self-perceived role of being a servant of Congress appears to have led it to follow a policy of complying with such directives."[63]

The subtext of the memorandum was clear. Sasser embarrassed TVA with the public release of the reports, and there was little TVA could do to stop the senator from taking similar action in the future. TVA booster Howard Baker almost certainly would not have done anything close to that which Sasser felt was acceptable. Sasser, unlike Baker, was clearly unafraid of creating hostile relationships with top officials at the agency. Baker's method of addressing TVA problems was to hold Senate hearings and to warn the agency in the press to keep electricity rates low, but rarely did he take actions that seemed calculated to deliberately antagonize the agency and threaten its reputation. Where Baker generally treated the agency as an ally of Valley ratepayers and issued chiding criticism if TVA seemed to be making mistakes, Sasser treated the agency as if it simply could not be trusted.

Sasser's skepticism for and frequent antagonism toward the agency extended to the compensation plan. Usually seeing TVA as primarily self-interested, he became enraged by the bonus proposal, viewing it as another manifestation of the agency's underhanded tendency to enrich itself at the expense of Valley residents. Skeptical of the idea that a 70 percent salary increase could legally be considered a "bonus," the senator expressed strong public opposition to the compensation plan, and he launched a multipronged attack. Attempting to leverage the GAO against TVA again, Sasser asked the office to provide an opinion on the plan's legality under the TVA Act. He also drafted a concurrent resolution expressing congressional disapproval of the bonuses, then introduced an amendment to TVA's $124 million appropriations bill that would deny the bonuses to managers whose salaries included tax funds. Though TVA was required to pay for power generation solely out of current revenues, federal money helped subsidize some of TVA's more experimental research programs.[64]

Responding to Sasser's actions, the *Chattanooga Times* argued that those who were "going to (loudly) denounce" the plan for retaining top-level managers then had the responsibility to offer an alternative plan; yet "they don't and they won't." Sasser's loud criticism also brought him into conflict with Senator Baker, who was reportedly "increasingly annoyed" by Sasser's use of TVA as a "political football" against Robin Beard, Sasser's opponent for senatorial reelection in 1982. In Baker's view, though it was a government agency partially funded by taxpayer dollars, TVA should have existed outside the bounds of the rough-and-tumble of electoral politics in order to ensure efficient operation uninhibited by partisan distractions and accusations. Sasser refused to be convinced by such exhortations and continued his vocal campaign, which only ended in November 1983 when the GAO analysis commissioned by Sasser ruled that the bonus plan was an illegal circumvention of the TVA Act. TVA would continue to be constrained, for better or for worse, by the salary limits on top executives.[65]

TVA'S SPLIT IDENTITY

In 1980, with TVA in the midst of the cost-cutting measures that had drawn such incensed replies from longtime employees, Richard Freeman received an indignant letter from Valley ratepayer Howard Carver. Carver deplored the idea that, even with "a cost of power that threatens the lives of some"—presumably low-income ratepayers who could not pay summer cooling bills—the "in" thing at the agency was to hire former employees as high-paid consultants who found a "gold mine" giving advice to their former employer. With more than a hint of sarcasm, Carver advised that if TVA insisted on throwing money at untold numbers of former employees as a favor to them, then the agency should probably think about hiring at least one real consultant "to come in and tell you how to reduce costs" for real. "I appreciate the magnitude of your job," Carver told Freeman, "but really 'hard-nosed' business direction begins at the top of any organization." Freeman, as a TVA director, needed to step up his efforts to make the organization more efficient, Carver claimed.[66]

Carver wrote Richard Freeman again about a year and a half later, just as the agency was in the midst of the bonuses controversy. There was no reason to consider higher pay for high-echelon staff, he said. In fact, it seemed surprising that they still had jobs at all. TVA's record, Carver complained, was still "far below the acme of perfection," and in most instances operated with "just plain ineptness and unconcern." He referred to Freeman, again with sarcasm, as a "hard-nosed" businessperson who, given his experience, must have been acutely aware of the "billions spent" to correct the errors made by the TVA board and by its top cadre of "irreplaceable managers." "Do you honestly think," Carver opined, "that TVA could survive in the private world of business with the 'leadership' we have now." To complaints that TVA was losing too many employees, Carver claimed that low pay—the TVA board's preferred explanation—was not primarily to blame. "Nowhere yet," he wrote, "has any mention been made . . . of disillusionment," with the agency and its leadership.[67]

The tragedy of TVA's problems, Carver wrote, was that it left Valley ratepayers adrift with few alternative options. If TVA were hypothetically a private business, then the mechanisms of the market would take care of its inefficiency and waste by forcing it to either adapt or go out of business. However, since TVA had quasi-government status, it was not forced to compete in the same manner as other firms were. Stagnation and ineptitude within its top leadership thrived. A problem of comparable scope, though, was that TVA was not truly a government agency. The TVA Act and its self-financing power program insulated it from many of the political whims that other agencies and bureaus had to endure on a daily basis. Ratepayers feeling wronged could petition Congress for redress. Since Congress did not possess thorough oversight powers over the agency, however, doing so was "sort of grasping at any straw in the wind."[68]

The sheltered and protected state that TVA found itself in was unacceptable to Carver. He outlined two potential identities for TVA to embrace, claiming that the agency had to pick either one or the other. If TVA was a private business, then it needed to petition the Public Service Commission for rate increases, as private utilities were compelled to do, rather than declare them unilaterally. He also commanded TVA to "remove the government-financed pension benefits you enjoy" and find a management class "qualified to operate . . . in a profit-oriented society" instead of employing "political appointees who hold their positions through favoritism." If, on the other hand, TVA was an arm of the federal government, "then some system must be devised to provide checks and balances to protect the people" from agency abuses. Such a system must be sounder than the current, inadequate methods of congressional oversight. "Mr. Freeman," Carver implored, "this is not just my opinion: as you know better, this view is shared by people in all walks of life."[69]

Carver may have been only one ratepayer in the vast Tennessee Valley, but his words indeed reflected the widespread discontent with TVA that emerged in the late 1970s and 1980s. In Richard Freeman's reply to Carver's second letter, the TVA board member conceded, "Historically, the Board and TVA managers have made both good and bad decisions." On balance, though, "I think their performance is far above the average. It is our objective to see," Freeman informed Carver, "that the balance is more plus than minus."[70] Freeman's technocratic reassurances were little comfort to Valley ratepayers, who had spent years reading about TVA's many troubles in the newspapers on a daily basis. Despite numerous attempts at restructuring, securing the loyalties of top executives, and shoring up TVA's lasting financial viability, every attempt to fix TVA's problems seemed to generate more discontent.

Part of the problem had to do with the Carter administration's continued insularity. Reflected in David Freeman's appointment to the TVA board, Carter believed that TVA's massive scope could amplify his expansive energy agenda, promoting both environmental protection and energy conservation. These priorities conflicted with TVA's nearly sacred mission in the Valley to provide the lowest-cost electricity to Valley residents. The cost of environmental protection increased the cost of coal, which necessitated increased utility rates for Valley citizens. Compounding the problem, successful energy conservation measures decreased aggregate demand for power in the Valley, which meant that TVA had to increase rates to make up the budget shortfall.

Carver's irritated letters to Richard Freeman pointed to a larger challenge faced by TVA. In the 1970s, in the phrasing of one historian, the US economy moved from one based on manufacturing physical things to one rooted in more abstract banking transactions (or "from factories to finance").[71] This shift had many broad implications, but the most important were the rise of an economy based on knowledge instead of material goods along with the decentralization of power from traditional institutions, which moved flows of information to economic centrality.[72] Transactions were quicker, indeed almost instantaneous, and companies had to meet nearly immediate changes daily based on new information. Instant adaptability in this new era was of paramount importance; the firms and institutions that could change and adapt to meet constantly shifting realities were most successful. This new reality allowed companies to make massive profits quite quickly, but it also exposed them to the possibility of instant ruin if they navigated poorly.

In this era, TVA was stuck between integration into this new economic reality on one hand and adherence to its traditional, New Deal–era, public-focused identity on the other. TVA had to simultaneously compete for customer loyalties, rather than take them as assumed based on TVA's longstanding Valley mission, and answer promptly to congressional prodding and criticism. As Carver pointed out, TVA was neither wholly a government organization nor an institution of the private sector. While this liminal state held some advantages for the agency, it also damaged TVA's ability to function coherently in this transitional era. Buffeted by multiple constituencies, the public-private tension was a contradiction that TVA was unable to resolve.

In this new market-oriented world, TVA tried to grant its top executives more competitive pay to stop them from moving on to more lucrative opportunities, but the nearly fifty-year-old TVA Act precluded this possibility. Members of Congress who sought to make TVA more like modern corporations also tried to turn the TVA board into a larger panel with part-time commitments instead of full-time. Advocates of the traditional TVA structure defeated them. The battles that played out over seemingly obscure issues like executive pay and board composition in fact revealed larger divisions about the role of TVA going forward. Some observers, like Senator Howard Baker, who supported higher executive pay, and Representative Ronnie Flippo, who wanted a larger and more diverse board, wanted TVA to become more like a private company in some aspects. They believed TVA should be more directly answerable to ratepayers, but also with employees better compensated for their work and more flexible in making decisions. Others, like Senator Jim Sasser, who staunchly opposed executive pay increases, saw TVA as a government bureaucracy that required constant oversight if it was to adhere to its public service mission, and these observers sought to exert persistent and significant congressional control over TVA's perceived excesses. The board of directors split these issues, favoring higher pay for executives but opposing the board restructuring.

TVA was caught in between these different visions of its future as either a private company or a public organization. Given the failure of both the executive pay increase and the board reconfiguration, advocates of retaining the agency's New Deal roots generally won the battle for TVA's identity by preserving the status quo. Though losing major battles, these opponents brought a fresh skepticism of government to their oversight of the agency. Senator Sasser in particular, while wanting TVA to adhere to its New Deal configuration, did not trust the agency to monitor itself nearly to the extent that Franklin Roosevelt had trusted the original board. The public nature of these battles brought turmoil to TVA and its mission in the Tennessee Valley. Whether the defeated reforms would truly have made TVA more efficient and effective is impossible to say. However, the intense controversy about them demonstrates the limits and implications of the anti-government rhetoric of the early 1980s. In the abstract, many Americans turned against the idea of government itself, seeing it as Reagan did—as an inefficient, unresponsive entity. Yet, more concretely, many Valley ratepayers feared that making TVA more like a private business might actually make it *less* responsive to public concerns. The contradictions embedded within these competing viewpoints, and congressional attempts to impose various manifestations of them upon TVA, generated much trouble for the Authority's mission in the Tennessee Valley. With TVA's pullback from its energy conservation mission, another of Carter's energy policies amounted to little of consequence.

TVA's identity problems continued for years after the fights of the late 1970s and early 1980s. Its public reputation slowly recovered over the course of the 1980s, especially as the agency worked through the skewed economics of its nuclear program.[73] However, every attempt in the 1980s and 1990s to make TVA more like a private company was again met by opposition that sought to maintain the agency as a servant of Valley residents, keeping the agency's underlying mission in a state of perpetual confusion. It was not until 2004, after many more years of trying to adapt TVA to the market era, that Senators Lamar Alexander and Bill Frist finally succeeded in inserting a restructuring provision into an omnibus spending bill, which converted the board to a nine-member, part-time model.[74] Most of the part-time directors since that date have already established lucrative careers in business or law, finally resolving the executive pay issue. More sweeping calls to privatize TVA entirely—calls casting the agency as an outdated relic of the New Deal years—have persisted to little effect, with Tennessee legislators of both parties fiercely resisting.[75]

CONCLUSION

In early May of 1982, Ronald Reagan stood beside a giant globe called the Sunsphere to open the World's Fair in Knoxville, Tennessee, an event that doubled as an international energy exposition. He used the opportunity to reinforce his anti-regulation and anti-government political ideology. The president's remarks, characteristically, emphasized market solutions to energy problems: "In the past, we tried to manage a shortage by interfering with the market process. The results were gas lines, bottlenecks, and bureaucracy. . . . Instead of managing scarcity, we'll help ensure continued supplies from a strategic stockpile, alleviating shortages while permitting the private market to work." He continued, "The ultimate solution to our energy problems" would be "the decontrol of all [of] our energy sources."[1]

Along with the president and the secretary of energy, former president Carter and former vice president Walter Mondale created a visible presence at the fair, but Reagan's ethos dominated it. One newspaper spoke of the "warm" reception with which Reagan's words extolling private enterprise were met in the "heavily Republican" region of East Tennessee, with Carter and Mondale forced to be content with a mere touristic visit.[2] However, in addition to highlighting local political trends, the contrasting image of the two leaders was also a fitting metaphor for the preceding few years of American energy politics. Carter had been heavily involved in promoting the World's Fair while serving as president, and he had initiated some of the policies, such as oil decontrol, for which Reagan now claimed credit. Yet it was Reagan who earned accolades and national press attention at the fair. Carter's initial agenda of conservation and sacrifice was eclipsed by an approach that emphasized the ability of the private sector to address energy challenges, which would ostensibly create a new era of abundance.

Such a scene would have been inconceivable just a few years earlier. The 1973 oil crisis had seemed to validate the idea that systems of energy supply were far from secure, a theme that Jimmy Carter echoed and amplified upon becoming president. Carter passed into law a comprehensive energy plan—a task that his two predecessors failed to achieve—which encouraged Americans to use less energy in their daily lives. Initial public opinion expressed favor for Carter's attempts, as Americans were loath to repeat the experience of 1973 and trusted in Carter's leadership. For a time, it appeared that government would successfully address energy problems, as it had already done for the economic collapse of the 1930s, the fight against Fascism in the 1940s, and various civil rights issues of the 1950s and 1960s.

However, the late 1970s were a time of dynamic change in American thinking about energy issues. Events in that period especially seemed to discredit the idea that government had a constructive role to play in energy issues. Assuming office in 1977, Carter had admonished the nation about the need to reconsider its energy use, saying that Americans had to curtail wasteful habits in order to allow time for more sustainable resources and technologies to be discovered and developed. He implemented a number of government programs meant to encourage Americans to use less energy in their daily lives. Yet the Iranian Revolution and resulting oil price spike in 1979 seemed to prove Carter wrong, as the government reorganization creating the Energy Department failed to prevent energy crises from reoccurring. Stopgap measures like encouraging greater domestic coal production fell apart when Carter and his staff proved unable to align the diverse and conflicting interests embedded within the extant political economy. Though Carter scrambled to increase domestic production of energy by proposing ideas such as the Synthetic Fuels Corporation and the Energy Mobilization Board, the window for convincing the nation that better days were in sight had closed.

These energy crises helped make conservative ideas intelligible and palatable to the American electorate. In the late 1970s, a number of pro-capitalist writings—Jude Wanniski's *The Way the World Works,* Irving Kristol's *Two Cheers for Capitalism,* and Arthur Laffer's musings on the benefits of cutting taxes, for example—made the case that unleashing the private sector was the best way to solve economic challenges and improve quality of life.[3] With government trying and failing to solve the energy problem, the crises of 1973 and 1979 made these intellectual ideas about the advantages of capitalism viscerally understandable to American consumers. Consumers who again sat in long lines at gasoline stations concluded that Carter's energy agenda had failed. Promises of future abundance through the power of market processes seemed a more reliable alternative.

Also important was the fact that the second oil crisis of 1979 affected the fate of diverse public energy projects. After 1973 the need to foster new domestic sources of energy seemed self-evident, and the government, better able to absorb costs and take bigger risks than private companies, seemed primed to lead the way. Resources and effort flowed to existing government projects like the Tellico Dam and the Clinch River breeder reactor. Yet the return of gas lines after the Iranian Revolution slowed consumer demand and eventually obviated the need for these projects. Congressional proponents of these projects had successfully been making the argument that new sources of energy were necessary to make US energy supplies secure, but the subsequent decline of energy demand due to consumer fear—and the accompanying collapse of global oil prices in the early 1980s—made these claims much less powerful. Carter's conservationist initiatives caused the need for energy to contract further over the course of the late 1970s, making these projects seem even less necessary. Furthermore, budgets rising far over initial projections contributed to the perception that government itself was wasteful and inefficient.

The new era of a free-market, anti-government approach to the issue spelled the end of some of these public projects, including Clinch River. Though the Tellico Dam survived this age of anti-government politics, the Endangered Species Act review committee established by Carter refused to grant an exemption for the snail darter because the dam was wasteful and over budget. It was only through a legislative sleight of hand that the project continued to completion. Furthermore, with respect to the Tennessee Valley Authority, its top leaders became frustrated and confused about what exactly its mission and identity should be, weakening the agency's reputation and effectiveness. Government energy projects and government programs to encourage conservation both gave way to a new era characterized by a deregulated, market-oriented approach. The era of the market extended to labor politics, too, with deregulated railroads speeding the rise of non-union coal and weakening the long-standing United Mine Workers of America union.

Along with the collapse of local projects, the political power of environmentalism itself suffered in the course of the 1970s. Common narratives tend to pinpoint the Reagan inauguration as the moment when the potency of environmentalism began to decline. Samuel Hays's landmark work on environmental politics, for example, states that Reagan "set out to undo the environmental work of the preceding two decades of Republican and Democratic leadership."[4] However, Reagan was not quite the "anti-environmental revolutionary" of Hays's depiction. If anything, he amplified rhetoric about the perceived overreach of environmentalism already circulating in public discourse in the 1970s.

Environmentalism has thrived in the United States when economic opportunity and comfort are at a relatively high level, as citizens are most willing to give up economic benefits to preserve natural resources when all other needs are met. Environmentalism indeed achieved many successes in the early 1970s as Americans exhorted the need to protect shared resources and living spaces. But the shock of the 1973 oil crisis impacted environmentalism's political power by bringing economic concerns back to the forefront of public policy issues, a trend that continued for several years afterward. Specific laws that had recently passed, like the Endangered Species Act, saw their power scaled back. General political support for environmentalism did not necessarily lead to concrete political successes, as in the case of the Clinch River reactor, which lingered in Congress until fiscal conservatives concerned about rising costs finally killed it. Indeed, another major target for environmentalists in the 1970s, the 234-mile Tennessee-Tombigbee Waterway winding through eastern Mississippi and western Alabama, was completed despite the combined opposition of environmentalists and fiscal conservatives.[5]

In an electoral landslide, Ronald Reagan came into office ignoring and sometimes mocking environmentalist concerns. Though Reagan provoked his own backlash with controversial cabinet appointments, environmentalism never again achieved the heights it had reached with the inaugural Earth Day in 1970. Environmentalism remained a powerful special interest, but it was never without its detractors and skeptics. Although Americans broadly continued to profess reverence for the environment, the seriousness of this commitment was less clear. A 2003 scholarly analysis of public opinion found that, although the vast majority (83 percent) of Americans agreed with the "broadest goals of the environmental movement," they also ranked environmentalism's comparative importance behind an array of other issues, including crime, homelessness, and health care.[6]

Ultimately, this book argues that energy is a historical concept rooted in specific times and specific places, and that the history of energy has therefore intersected with a number of other economic, political, and intellectual histories. Many of Jimmy Carter's energy policies stalled or failed because of these intersections. Attempts to increase domestic production of coal slowed due to labor unrest as well as conflicts between railroad operators and carriers. Desires to reduce funding to outdated nuclear technologies, like the Clinch River breeder, failed. Legislators were determined to keep money flowing to support local engineering and construction jobs near intended construction sites. Carter's desires to use TVA's existing resources to promote conservation and alternative technologies ran squarely into the demands of Valley residents that their subsidized electricity flow without interruption.

The price of oil has risen and fallen several times since the Iranian Revolution, including a spike in 2007 and 2008 that rivaled that of 1979. Every moment of crisis has brought renewed warnings about the need to release the nation from energy dependence, yet no comprehensive solution has been achieved or even seems to be in sight. One of the reasons for this constant tension is that conflicts between energy and environmental priorities have also not dissipated, as ongoing debates about issues like the Keystone XL pipeline and fracking—injecting fluid into the ground to release natural gas from shale rocks—have recently evidenced.[7] The challenge of aligning and satisfying the diverse interest groups embedded within the political economy of energy—corporations, small producers, labor, consumers, environmentalists, and the localities where energy is produced and consumed—goes a long way to explain why.

NOTES

INTRODUCTION: A JOKE TOLD TOO MANY TIMES

1. On the Deepwater Horizon disaster and its environmental consequences, see Antonia Juhasz, *Black Tide: The Devastating Impact of the Gulf Oil Spill* (Hoboken: John Wiley & Sons, 2011).

2. Some of the members of OPEC, including Venezuela and Iran, actually increased production during the embargo, but it was not enough to offset the decline in OAPEC oil.

3. See Natasha Zaretsky, *No Direction Home: The American Family and the Fear of National Decline, 1968–1980* (Chapel Hill: University of North Carolina Press, 1997), 79–80.

4. On Reagan's perceived extremism see, for example, Matthew Dallek, *The Right Moment: Ronald Reagan's First Victory and the Decisive Turn in American Politics* (New York: Oxford University Press, 2004), 39.

5. William H. Chafe, *The Rise and Fall of the American Century: The United States from 1890–2009* (New York: Oxford University Press, 2009), 235. See also Burton I. Kaufman, *The Presidency of James Earl Carter, Jr.* (Lawrence: University Press of Kansas, 1993), 1–3, for a similar argument about Carter's ill-fated bypassing of Congress based on an arrogant notion of himself as a "public trustee" who knew better than the legislature. Carter's legislative troubles likewise frame John C. Barrow, "An Age of Limits: Jimmy Carter and the Quest for a National Energy Policy," in Gary M. Fink and Hugh Davis Graham, eds., *The Carter Presidency: Policy Choices in the Post-New Deal Era* (Lawrence: University Press of Kansas, 1998), 158–78.

6. Garland A. Haas, *Jimmy Carter and the Politics of Frustration* (Jefferson, NC: McFarland & Company, 1992), 2. Haas makes a similar argument as Chafe about the problems created by the secretive nature of the energy bill's creation on 63–71.

7. John Dumbrell, *The Carter Presidency: A Re-evaluation* (New York: Manchester University Press, 1993), 44–45.

8. On national oil policy see, for example, David S. Painter, *Oil and the American Century: The Political Economy of U.S. Foreign Oil Policy, 1941–1954* (Baltimore: The Johns Hopkins University Press, 1986); Ethan B. Kapstein, *The Insecure Alliance: Energy Crises and Western Politics Since 1945* (New York: Oxford University Press, 1990); Ahmed Mahdi, *Energy and US Foreign Policy: The Quest for Resource Security after the Cold War* (New York: I. B. Tauris & Co., 2012). On nuclear power see, for example, Brian Balogh, *Chain Reaction: Expert Debate and Public Participation in American Commercial Nuclear Power, 1945–1975* (New York: Cambridge University Press, 1991); Joseph A. Camilleri, *The State and Nuclear Power: Conflict and Control in the Western World* (Seattle: University of Washington Press, 1984). On hydroelectricity see, for example, Jessica B. Teisch, *Engineering Nature: Water, Development, and the Global Spread of American Environmental Expertise* (Chapel Hill: University of North Carolina Press, 2011); Sarah T. Phillips, *This Land, This Nation: Conservation, Rural America, and the New Deal* (New York: Cambridge University Press, 2007).

9. On local nuclear politics see, for example, Kate Brown, *Plutopia: Nuclear Families, Atomic Cities, and the Great Soviet and American Nuclear Disasters* (New York: Oxford University Press, 2013); John Wills, *Conservation Fallout: Nuclear Protest at Diablo Canyon* (Reno and Las Vegas: University of Nevada Press, 2006); Henry F. Bedford, *Seabrook Station: Citizen Politics and Nuclear Power* (Amherst: University of Massachusetts Press, 1990).

10. Some other recent works examining the local impact of energy production include Robert Lifset, *Power on the Hudson: Storm King Mountain and the Emergence of Modern American Environmentalism* (Pittsburgh: University of Pittsburgh Press, 2014); Christopher F. Jones, *Routes of Power: Energy and Modern America* (Cambridge: Harvard University Press, 2014); Andrew Needham, *Power Lines: Phoenix and the Making of the Modern Southwest* (Princeton: Princeton University Press, 2014).

11. See Samuel P. Hays, *Beauty, Health, and Permanence: Environmental Politics in the United States, 1955–1985* (New York: Cambridge University Press, 1987), 480–81.

12. Meg Jacobs, "The Conservative Struggle and the Energy Crisis," in Bruce J. Schulman and Julian E. Zelizer, eds., *Rightward Bound: Making America Conservative in the 1970s* (Cambridge: Oxford University Press, 2008), 193–94. Jacobs offers a fuller political history of the oil crisis in *Panic at the Pump: The Energy Crisis and the Transformation of American Politics in the 1970s* (New York: Hill and Wang, 2016).

13. For a summary of Carter's energy program, see Russell D. Motter, "Seeking Limits: The Passage of the National Energy Act as a Microcosm of the Carter Presidency," in Herbert D. Rosenbaum and Alexej Ugrinsky, eds., *The Presidency and Domestic Policies of Jimmy Carter* (Westport, CT: Greenwood Press, 1994), 571–93.

14. Jacobs, "Conservative Struggle and the Energy Crisis," 193–94.

15. On the deregulation of various US economic sectors, see Kenneth Button and Dennis Swann, eds., *The Age of Regulatory Reform* (Oxford: Clarendon Press, 1989).

16. Patrick Allitt, *A Climate of Crisis: America in the Age of Environmentalism* (New York: Penguin, 2014).

17. Though some analysts at the time pointed to a stagnating economy in the late 1970s as the main driver of improved air and water quality, many Americans in both parties ascribed the improvements to the implementation of these environmental regulations and supported them strongly. See Eliot Marshall, "Cleaning up the Clean Air Act," *Science*, New Series 214, no. 4527 (18 December 1981): 1328–29.

18. See "Politics Clouds Clean Air Act Debate," *New York Times*, 3 November 1981.

CHAPTER 1: "LITTLE BITTY CARS"

1. I draw here on the analysis of historian David Nye, who identifies five distinct stages of energy crisis lasting through the first term of Ronald Reagan. This slowly rising demand of 1970–1971 represents the first stage, and the OPEC price hikes and embargo of 1972–1973 constitute the second. See *Consuming Power: A Social History of American Energies* (Cambridge: The MIT Press, 2001), 218.

2. Nye, *Consuming Power*, 218; "Environment: Energy Crisis: Are We Running Out?," *Time*, 12 June 1972; *Washington Post*, 11 April 1972.

3. "Energy: And Now, the Chillout," *Time*, 22 January 1973.

4. Daniel Yergin, *The Prize: The Epic Quest for Oil, Money, and Power* (New York: Simon and Schuster, 1991), 600–17.

5. Yergin, *Prize*, 600–17.

6. Richard H. K. Vietor, *Energy Policy in America since 1945: A Study of Business-Government Relations* (New York: Cambridge University Press, 1984), 244–45. The Federal Energy Agency was later renamed the Federal Energy Administration.

7. Price controls affected "old" oil, or oil pumped from areas already discovered at the time, but not newly discovered oil. Old oil withdrew from the market, leading to price increases as new oil dominated domestic supply.

8. See "Oil Profits Soar, Senate Informed," *Milwaukee Journal*, 23 January 1974.

9. Yergin, *Prize*, 600–17; Michael Egan, *Barry Commoner and the Science of Survival: The Remaking of American Environmentalism* (Cambridge: The MIT Press, 2007), 150–51. On the oil crisis' demoralizing impact on American households forced to cut back on energy use, see Natasha Zaretsky, *No Direction Home: The American Family and the Fear of National Decline, 1968–1980* (Chapel Hill: University of North Carolina Press, 1997), 71–104.

10. Vietor, *Energy Policy in America since 1945*, 244.

11. J. Brooks Flippen, *Nixon and the Environment* (Albuquerque: University of New Mexico Press, 2000), 207–08.

12. Yergin, *Prize*, 630–38. Having to handle the Watergate scandal concurrently greatly weakened the Nixon administration's ability to deal with the crisis; see Yergin, 609–19; Martin Melosi, *Coping with Abundance* (Philadelphia: Temple University Press, 1985), 285.

13. "Conservation: Pondering the Tasks Ahead," *Time*, 27 May 1974; Nye, *Consuming Power*, 222–23.

14. "Conservation: Pondering the Tasks Ahead," *Time*, 27 May 1974.

15. Melosi, *Coping with Abundance*, 287.

16. Douglas Brinkley, *Gerald R. Ford* (New York: Times Books, 2007), 77.

17. Nye, *Consuming Power*, 231.

18. See Yanek Mieczkowski, *Gerald Ford and the Challenges of the 1970s* (Lexington: University Press of Kentucky, 2005), 269, which credits Ford mainly with starting a national discussion about energy but concedes that few substantive achievements occurred.

19. The literature on the American environmental movement is vast. Most generally, the years after World War II had witnessed a consumer culture that, according to one historian, was characterized by the belief that "energy and resources were limitless," thus the shocking nature of these disasters. See Egan, *Barry Commoner and the Science of Survival*, 16. On the "dangerous environment" that Americans saw after these catastrophes, see 79–87. Roughly concurrent with the emergence of this new environmental consciousness was the establishment of ecology as an academic discipline. In contrast to scientific fields that focused on economic growth as a narrative of unbounded advancement, ecology examined technological development as a phenomenon "that might lead to progress in one area only to create greater harm somewhere else." See Brian Balogh, *Chain Reaction: Expert Debate and Public Participation in American Commercial Nuclear Power, 1945–1975* (New York: Cambridge University Press, 1991), 259. Before these disasters, the suburbanization of America had forced homeowners to confront environmental dangers on a smaller scale, including overflowing septic tanks and detergents in their drinking water. See Adam Rome, *The Bulldozer in the Countryside: Suburban Sprawl and the Rise of American Environmentalism* (New York: Cambridge University Press, 2001).

20. Peter Z. Grossman, *U.S. Energy Policy and the Pursuit of Failure* (New York: Cambridge University Press, 2013), 169, 172.

21. Grossman, 167–68.

22. See Grossman, 173; Patrick Allitt, *A Climate of Crisis: America in the Age of Environmentalism* (New York: Penguin, 2014), 67–69.

23. John Dumbrell, *The Carter Presidency: A Re-evaluation* (New York: Manchester University Press, 1993), 29.

24. Natural Gas Legislation: Remarks at a News Briefing on the Legislation, 26 January 1977, 21–22; West Chester, Pennsylvania, Students: Question-and-Answer Session with Students from Stetson Junior High School, 27 January 1977, 29; Report to the American People: Remarks from the White House Library, 2 February 1977, 71, all in

Public Papers of the Presidents of the United States: Jimmy Carter: 1977, Book 1 (Washington, DC: Government Printing Office, 1977).

25. On Carter's persistent pessimism see especially Robert M. Collins, *Transforming America: Politics and Culture in the Reagan Years* (New York: Columbia University Press, 2007), 22–25.

26. James Schlesinger Interview, Jimmy Carter Presidential Oral History Project (hereafter JPOH), Miller Center of the University of Virginia, 19–20 July 1984, 2–15.

27. Dumbrell, *Carter Presidency*, 30–31.

28. Stuart Eizenstat Oral History, JPOH, 29–30 January 1982, 25–26.

29. Stuart Eizenstat Oral History, 25–26.

30. See Burton I. Kaufman, *The Presidency of James Earl Carter, Jr.* (Lawrence: University Press of Kansas, 1993), 3.

31. Sean Wilentz, *The Age of Reagan: A History, 1974–2008* (New York: Harper, 2008), 79–80. On Carter and divestiture see Vietor, *Energy Policy in America since 1945*, 223–24. Chapter 2 of this book discusses the coal conversion component of the National Energy Plan at greater length.

32. The Gallup Poll, "Americans Divided over Carter Energy Leadership," 8 September 1977, box 42, folder 10, Howard H. Baker Jr. Papers (hereafter HBJ), Howard H. Baker Jr. Center for Public Policy, University of Tennessee; The Gallup Poll, "2 in 3 Express Approval of Carter Job Performance," 11 September 1977, box 42, folder 10, HBJ.

33. Vietor, *Energy Policy in America since 1945*, 260.

34. Memorandum for Jerry Rafshoon from Greg Schneiders, n.d., box 98, folder Energy, 5/8/78—8/2/78 [O/A 6148], Office of the Chief of Staff Files (hereafter CSC), Jimmy Carter Presidential Library; Wilentz, *Age of Reagan*, 81–83.

35. As Geoffrey Kabaservice argues, the period from Nixon's reelection campaign in 1971 to Ronald Reagan's election in 1980 represented an era in which the influence of moderates in the Republican Party declined precipitously in favor of the party's conservative wing, an outcome that Kabaservice sees as unfortunate. See *Rule and Ruin: The Downfall of Moderation and the Destruction of the Republican Party* (New York: Oxford University Press, 2012), 326–62.

36. "Republican Report: Preface to the Senate Republican Energy Initiative," n.d., box 10, folder 10, HBJ; "Minority Members Unveil Substitute Energy Bill," press release, 25 July 1977, box 9, folder 38, HBJ.

37. "Republican Report: Preface to the Senate Republican Energy Initiative"; "Minority Members Unveil Substitute Energy Bill."

38. "Energy: Another View—A Transcript of the NBC News Special Broadcast," 2 June 1977, box 54, folder 11, Bill Brock Papers (hereafter BB), Howard H. Baker Jr. Center for Public Policy, University of Tennessee.

39. "Energy: Another View."

40. Brock faced public criticism in 1976 when it became known that he had paid only $2,026 in federal income taxes on an income of $51,670 the year before; see "Tax Matter Plagues Brock in Tennessee Senate Race," *New York Times*, 28 October 1976. On Watergate's role in the 1976 congressional elections, see "Long Shadow: GOP Outlook in South for 1976 and Beyond Is Darkened by Carter," *Wall Street Journal*, 11 October 1976.

41. "Energy: Another View—A Transcript of the NBC News Special Broadcast"; Press release, 25 March 1972, box 10, folder 7, BB; Press release, 24 May 1973, box 10, folder 7, BB.

42. Press release, 27 February 1974, box 10, folder 5, BB; Excerpt from *Congressional Record—Senate*, 1 August 1975, box 10, folder 5, BB.

43. Press release, 18 December 1974, box 10, folder 5, BB.

44. Agnes Anderson to Bill Brock, 3 February 1977, box 54, folder 11, BB.

45. Marie C. Artale to Bill Brock, 26 May 1977, box 54, folder 11, BB.

46. On the relationship of suburban expansion and the rise of environmentalism after World War II, see especially Christopher C. Sellers, *Crabgrass Crucible: Suburban Nature and the Rise of Environmentalism in Twentieth-Century America* (Chapel Hill: University of North Carolina Press, 2012).

47. Robert J. Russell to Bill Brock, 28 April 1977, box 54, folder 13, BB; Cynthia Slack to Bill Brock, 9 March 1977, box 54, folder 13, BB.

48. On the relationship of liberalism to individualized consumption, see Kathleen G. Donohue, *Freedom from Want: American Liberalism and the Idea of the Consumer* (Baltimore: The Johns Hopkins University Press, 2003).

49. Bill Brock to Frank A. Sieverman, 16 September 1977, box 54, folder 13, BB. Adam Rome's analysis of the wasteful economy of air conditioning and electric heat, on which much of postwar suburbia was constructed, suggests why an ethic of energy conservation was so difficult to achieve in the suburban setting; see *Bulldozer in the Countryside*, 45–86.

50. Donald E. Dorn to Bill Brock, 15 May 1977, box 54, folder 11, BB; Bill Brock to Donald E. Dorn, 6 June 1977, box 54, folder 11, BB.

51. Joseph S. Larson to Bill Brock, 26 May 1977, box 54, folder 12, BB; Bill Brock to Joseph S. Larson, 15 July 1977, box 54, folder 12, BB.

52. "The Energy Crisis: Remarks by Senator Bill Brock," 18 June 1973, box 17, folder 97, BB.

53. In the late 1970s, business interests including the Business Roundtable and the American Enterprise Institute aggressively pushed a cost-benefit argument about environmental regulations purporting to show that they were undue burdens on economic growth. Such reasoning found wide and warm reception among Republicans, especially Reagan, and helped move the party away from its Nixon-era affinity for environmental protection. See Meg Jacobs, "The Politics of Environmental Regulation: Business-Government Regulations in the 1970s and Beyond," in Kim Phillips-Fein and Julian

Zelizer, eds., *What's Good for Business: Business in American Politics since World War II* (New York: Oxford University Press, 2012), 212–32.

54. Yergin, *Prize*, 674–78.

55. Yergin, 674–78.

56. "Restoring Competition to Energy"—an Address by Senator Edward M. Kennedy before the New England Broadcasters Association, box 98, folder 6, CSC.

57. "Restoring Competition to Energy."

58. The Office of the Chief of Staff files at the Jimmy Carter Presidential Library contain compiled newspaper articles about Kennedy's stances on various issues prior to and during his primary campaign against Carter, which Carter's staff used to formulate campaign strategy.

59. Yergin, *Prize*, 693; Note from Eliot Cutler to Secretary Duncan, Secretary Miller, Ham Jordan, Frank Moore, Jerry Rafshoon, and Jody Powell, n.d., box 45, folder 3, CSC; Memorandum for the President from Stu Eizenstat, 12 July 1979, box 259, folder Oil Company Mergers [CF, O/A 729], Domestic Policy Staff—Stuart Eizenstat's Subject Files, Jimmy Carter Presidential Library.

60. "Ecology Groups to Ask Decontrol of Oil Prices," *Wall Street Journal*, 21 March 1979.

61. "Consumers Take Carter to Task on Oil Decontrol," *Los Angeles Times*, 3 June 1979.

62. "Foes of Oil Decontrol Fail to Budge Carter," *Washington Post*, 2 June 1979; "Consumers Take Carter to Task on Oil Decontrol"; "Oil Decontrol: 'The President Is Wrong,'" *Christian Science Monitor*, 16 May 1979. The CBO report in question estimated that decontrol would spur production of an additional 405,000 barrels of oil per day, while the administration's estimates put the figure much higher, at 950,000 to 1.1 million barrels per day. See "Decontrol Hurts Poor; Enriches Big Oil: Study," *Chicago Tribune*, 24 May 1979. In May, the House Democratic Caucus voted 138 to 69 in favor of a resolution opposing the decontrol plan. Press Secretary Jody Powell responded by claiming that Carter had been forced into supporting decontrol because of congressional inaction on Carter's other energy proposals. See "House Democrats Formally Oppose Oil Decontrol," *Washington Post*, 25 May 1979.

63. "Carter Gets Ally, Foe for Plan to Decontrol Oil Prices, Tax Profits," *Wall Street Journal*, 9 April 1979; "President Warns Oil Industry on Excess Profits," *Washington Post*, 11 April 1979.

64. On the uneasy relationship between the Carter administration and organized labor, see Taylor Dark, "Organized Labor and the Carter Administration: The Origins of Conflict," in Herbert D. Rosenbaum and Alexej Ugrinsky, eds., *The Presidency and Domestic Policies of Jimmy Carter* (Westport, CT: Greenwood Press, 1994), 761–82.

65. "AFL-CIO Favors Thrust of Carter's Plan on Energy, Faults Oil-Decontrol Plank," *Wall Street Journal*, 7 August 1979.

66. Memorandum for John Shenefield from Stuart E. Eizenstat, 8 August 1979; Memorandum for the President from Jim Schlesinger, 23 August 1979, both in box FG-143, folder 7/1/79–8/31/79, White House Central Files, Jimmy Carter Presidential Library; "Energy: Embarrassment of Riches," *Time*, 5 November 1979. In contrast to Schlesinger, Alfred Kahn, Carter's chief adviser on inflation, backed the gradual decontrol plan so that price levels would not drastically increase immediately; see "Kahn Backs Carter's Oil Price Decontrol Plan, Discounts Its Inflationary Effects," *Los Angeles Times*, 7 April 1979.

67. Judith Stein, *Pivotal Decade: How the United States Traded Factories for Finance in the 1970s* (New Haven, CT: Yale University Press, 2010), 207; Energy Briefing Book 8/79—Transportation Energy Initiative, box 44, folder 36, CSC, 8–10; Samuel P. Hays, *Beauty, Health, and Permanence: Environmental Politics in the United States, 1955–1985* (New York: Cambridge University Press, 1987), 447. The Synthetic Fuels Corporation lasted until 1985, when plummeting world oil prices obviated the need for federal incentives for alternatives to oil.

68. Testimony before the Senate Finance Committee on H.R. 3919, W. T. Slick Jr., 12 July 1979, box 527, folder 7, Mike Gravel Papers (hereafter MG), Alaska and Polar Regions Collections, Elmer E. Rasmuson Library, University of Alaska Fairbanks.

69. One of the oil companies' most fervent defenders in Congress, Senator Russell Long of Louisiana, accused Carter of "calculat[ing] to stir up . . . hatred and resentment" of the oil companies for political gain, when the most important goal should have been to incentivize increased production. See "Sen. Long Forecasts Windfall Oil Tax Might Be Passed," *Wall Street Journal*, 16 April 1979. According to one biographer, Long denounced the windfall tax in "apocalyptic terms" and assailed the "hapless" administration officials who had the misfortune of appearing in front of the Finance Committee. See Robert Mann, *Legacy to Power: Senator Russell Long of Louisiana* (New York: Paragon House, 1992), 364.

70. Testimony before the Senate Finance Committee on H.R. 3919, W. T. Slick, Jr., 12 July 1979. On the engineering and logistical challenges presented by the Alaska pipeline construction, see Peter A. Coates, *The Trans-Alaska Pipeline Controversy: Technology, Conservation, and the Frontier* (Bethlehem, PA: Lehigh University Press, 1991). Marathon Oil Company's CEO and president, Harold D. Hoopman, concurred with Slick's analysis in his own testimony to Congress. While the oil industry's expenditures in exploration and production had averaged about $20 billion per year in recent years, Hoopman said, the decreasing availability of easy oil reserves meant that expenditures would have to climb to $40 billion annually over the next several years to maintain production. (Hoopman was using constant 1978 dollar figures for both calculations, meaning that necessary expenditures per year would, according to him, quickly double.) See Statement of Harold D. Hoopman before the Senate Finance Committee, box 528, folder 1, MG.

71. Wilentz, *Age of Reagan*, 96–98; "Nation: Still Looking for a Leader," *Time*, 10 September 1979. For a favorable historical assessment of this speech, see Kevin Mattson, *"What the Heck Are You Up To, Mr. President?": Jimmy Carter, America's "Malaise," and the Speech That Should Have Changed the Country* (New York: Bloomsbury, 2009). For a more dismissive view, see Bruce Schulman, *The Seventies: The Great Shift in American Culture, Society, and Politics* (New York: The Free Press, 2001), 140–43.

72. Wilentz, *Age of Reagan*, 96–98.

73. Though the hostage crisis generated an initial groundswell of renewed support for Carter, it quickly dissipated as the crisis wore on with no solution in sight. Melani McAlister argues that the unrelenting nightly coverage of the hostage crisis made it seem as if the nation itself was under attack, which Carter seemed powerless to counteract. See *Epic Encounters: Culture, Media, and U.S. Interests in the Middle East, 1945–2000* (Berkeley and Los Angeles: University of California Press, 2001), 202–16.

74. "Questions and Answers Concerning Iranian Oil Imports," 13 November 1979, box 249, folder Oil Import Quota [CF, O/A 729], Domestic Policy Staff—Stuart Eizenstat's Subject Files, Jimmy Carter Presidential Library.

75. On the background of Kennedy's entry into the race, see especially Timothy Stanley, *Kennedy vs. Carter: The 1980 Battle for the Democratic Party's Soul* (Lawrence: University Press of Kansas, 2010), 6–8.

76. "Kennedy Puts Oil Decontrol Tab at $1,000 a Family," *Los Angeles Times*, 22 November 1979.

77. The leaders of Canada and Mexico were firmly against such a plan, arguing that it would disproportionately benefit the United States. Since Canada and Mexico would primarily be providing oil and natural gas, they feared that the plan would compel the two nations to provide the United States with discounted raw materials to subsidize America's own domestic economic development and consumer economy. Mexico's president claimed that a continental common market would "entrench existing economic disparities" and imperil Mexico's "sovereign ability to decide on the application of its economic policies." See "Mexico Surprises Canada—Sells Some Oil, but Not Much," *Christian Science Monitor*, 5 June 1980.

78. On Operation Eagle Claw see Richard H. Immerman, *The Hidden Hand: A Brief History of the CIA* (Chichester, West Sussex, UK and Malden, MA: Wiley Blackwell, 2014), 122–24. Kennedy won primaries in Illinois, New Mexico, Pennsylvania, and California, but these victories were not enough to overcome Carter's early victories. On the chronology of primary contests between Carter and Kennedy, see Stanley, *Kennedy vs. Carter*, 132–57.

79. On Kennedy's convention speech and his awkward encounters with Carter, see Stanley, *Kennedy vs. Carter*, 166–69.

80. Reagan quoted in Elizabeth Drew, *Portrait of an Election: The 1980 Presidential Campaign* (New York: Simon and Schuster, 1981), 114. According to Drew, the American

Petroleum Institute had recently estimated that if all potential oil in the United States (including onshore, offshore, and in Alaska) were recovered, domestic production would increase by a maximum of four million barrels a day. Drew noted that the United States was currently importing eight million barrels a day. The four million barrel per day discrepancy led to her skepticism about Reagan's claims.

81. "Decontrol of Oil Is No Cure," *New York Times*, 9 January 1981.

82. "Oil Firms, IRS Seen as Big Gainers in Early Decontrol," *Los Angeles Times*, 14 January 1981.

83. "Decontrol the Price of Oil—Now," *New York Times*, 18 January 1981; "A 'Yes' to Oil Price Decontrol," *Boston Globe*, 18 January 1981.

84. "Decontrol the Price of Oil—Now"; "'Yes' to Oil Price Decontrol."

85. See Robert Stobaugh and Daniel Yergin, eds., *Energy Future: Report of the Energy Project at the Harvard Business School*, new revised 3rd ed. (New York: Vintage Books, 1983), 288, 302.

86. "Speeded Decontrol of Oil Is Indicated by Administration," *New York Times*, 27 January 1981; "Crude Decontrol by Reagan," *New York Times*, 19 March 1981.

87. "Business: Retreat on the Energy Front," *Time*, 21 January 1980.

88. Seattle, Washington: Remarks at a Rally with Area Residents, *Public Papers of the Presidents of the United States: Jimmy Carter: 1980–81*, Book 3 (Washington, DC: Government Printing Office, 1981), 2681.

89. Acceptance Speech by Governor Ronald Reagan, 17 July 1980, in Richard Harwood, ed., *The Pursuit of the Presidency 1980* (New York: Berkley Books, 1980), 418–19; Drew, *Portrait of an Election*, 219; Robert M. Collins, *More: The Politics of Economic Growth in Postwar America* (New York: Oxford University Press, 2000), 136–46. Discussing opinion polls taken in California in 1977 and 1981, political scientist Eric R. A. N. Smith found that, in both years, his subjects not only lacked substantial factual knowledge about energy issues, but also held positions that were not coherent by any reasonable measure. "Our examination of attitude consistency did not reveal any evidence that many people thought about energy issues from a consistently pro-environmental perspective, nor that many people consistently favored development. Instead," Smith notes, "we saw a public in which most people took an almost random mix of pro-environment and pro-development stands." As Smith makes clear, this unsystematic blend of environmental and developmental philosophies was attributable to poor understanding of the issues involved. He concludes, "Most people apparently value the environment and want to protect it but do not understand what government policies follow from that desire." See *Energy, the Environment, and Public Opinion* (Lanham, MD: Rowman & Littlefield, 2000), 125–26.

90. On environmentalism after the 1973 oil crisis, see Allitt, *Climate of Crisis*, 122–55.

91. Wilentz, *The Age of Reagan*, 140; Benjamin Kline, *First along the River: A Brief History of the U.S. Environmental Movement*, 2nd ed. (Lanham, MD: Rowman & Little-

field, 2000), 102. For a hostile assessment of Reagan's environmental policies, see Hays, *Beauty, Health, and Permanence*, 491–526. On Watt as a "lightning rod" for the environmental movement's opposition to the Reagan administration, see James Morton Turner, "'The Specter of Environmentalism': Wilderness, Environmental Politics, and the Evolution of the New Right," *Journal of American History* 96, no. 1 (2009): 134–36.

92. On the "antiregulatory storyline" gaining traction in the late 1970s, see Judith A. Layzer, *Open for Business: Conservatives' Opposition to Environmental Regulation* (Cambridge: The MIT Press, 2012), 84–90.

93. Nye, *Consuming Power*, 235–36.

94. See "The Politics of Environmental Regulation: Business-Government Relations in the 1970s and Beyond," in Phillips-Fein and Zelizer, eds., *What's Good for Business*, 212–32.

95. A number of opinion polls indicated that by 1980 environmentalism's influence was waning. The percentage of Americans who believed that government had gone "too far" with environmental protection increased from 13 percent to 25 percent from 1973 to 1980. While 50 percent in 1978 would accept a slower rate of economic growth for the sake of the environment, only two years later the figure was at 27 percent. See Layzer, *Open for Business*, 80–81.

CHAPTER 2: "RICH, BLACK VEINS OF THE FUTURE"

1. See Robert Lifset, "Environmentalism and the Electrical Energy Crisis," in Robert Lifset, ed., *American Energy Policy in the 1970s* (Norman: University of Oklahoma Press, 2014), 284–85. As Lifset notes, utility companies turned from coal to oil in the late 1960s and early 1970s to help comply with environmental legislation, as oil burns cleaner than coal. At the very moment of the shift, however, the 1973 oil embargo encouraged a shift back to coal.

2. "Carter to Urge Financial, Other Incentives for Industry to Produce Own Electricity," *Wall Street Journal*, 15 April 1977.

3. On the origins of the 1969 act, see Barbara Ellen Smith, *Digging Our Own Graves: Coal Miners and the Struggle over Black Lung Disease* (Philadelphia: Temple University Press, 1987), 128–39; Alan Derickson, *Black Lung: Anatomy of a Public Health Disaster* (Ithaca, NY: Cornell University Press, 1998), 142–82. On the 1972 act (sometimes denoted as an amendment to the 1969 act), see Smith, 169–74. On the 1978 act, see Smith, 199.

4. For a representative national press account criticizing strip-mining, see "Environment: Energy Crisis: Are We Running Out?" *Time*, 12 June 1972.

5. On the passage of this act see Chad Montrie, *To Save the Land and People: A History of Opposition to Surface Coal Mining in Appalachia* (Chapel Hill: University of North Carolina Press, 2003), 173–80. Montrie sees the act as flawed, because it relies on the

oversight of citizens who cannot match coal operators' resources, and because its application has been inconsistent and ineffective. Nonetheless, the cleanup costs increased the price of coal in the short term.

6. "Carter to Urge Financial, Other Incentives for Industry to Produce Own Electricity"; "Environmentalists and Utilities Edge Toward a Clash on Coal Use," *Christian Science Monitor*, 22 April 1977; Meg Jacobs, "The Politics of Environmental Regulation: Business-Government Relations in the 1970s and Beyond," in Kim Phillips-Fein and Julian Zelizer, eds., *What's Good for Business: Business and American Politics since World War II* (New York: Oxford University Press, 2012), 224.

7. "Carter's Coal-Production Plan: Not Off to a Burning Start," *Chicago Tribune*, 9 May 1977. In the early 1970s, the soft coal industry had taken an active role in the shaping of the Clean Air Act, pushing for federal standards requiring emission-control technology in order to avoid municipal regulations that would require switching from high- to low-sulfur coal, regulations they saw as especially onerous. See Richard N. L. Andrews, *Managing the Environment, Managing Ourselves: A History of American Environmental Policy*, 2nd ed. (New Haven: Yale University Press, 2006), 209. Pushing legislative policies to require polluters to install improved technology ("technology forcing") was a common environmentalist tactic. See Samuel P. Hays, *Beauty, Health, and Permanence: Environmental Politics in the United States, 1955–1985* (New York: Cambridge University Press, 1987), 251.

8. "Carter's Industrial Oil, Gas 'User' Tax Rejected in Senate," *Chicago Tribune*, 7 October 1977; "Carter Scores Energy Victory," *Los Angeles Times*, 28 October 1977. On Long's support for Louisiana's oil and gas industries, see Robert Mann, *Legacy to Power: Senator Russell Long of Louisiana* (New York: Paragon House, 1992), 398.

9. "Carter's Industrial Oil, Gas 'User' Tax Rejected in Senate"; "Carter Scores Energy Victory."

10. "Coal Miners Threaten Carter Energy Plans," *Christian Science Monitor*, 3 May 1977.

11. See Elizabeth Levy and Tad Richards, *Struggle and Lose, Struggle and Win: The United Mine Workers* (New York: Four Winds Press, 1977), 44–68.

12. See "Arnold Miller, Once Reform President of UMW, Dies at 62," *Washington Post*, 13 July 1985.

13. "Coal Miners Threaten Carter Energy Plans"; Paul A. Clark, *The Miners' Fight for Democracy: Arnold Miller and the Reform of the United Mine Workers* (Ithaca: New York State School of Industrial and Labor Relations, 1981), 57–74.

14. See the newspaper clippings in box 42, folder 15, M. H. Ross Papers, Special Collections, Georgia State University.

15. "Coal-Labor Accord Being Hammered Out Could Put Dent in Carter's Inflation Drive," *Wall Street Journal*, 31 January 1978. Black lung protections were a top target of coal companies, but since the president was a strong supporter of black lung legislation, it is unsurprising that the BCOA declined to make it a major issue in these negotiations.

16. "Coal-Labor Accord Being Hammered Out Could Put Dent in Carter's Inflation Drive"; "Carter Prepares Plan to Cut Back Coal Use," *Chicago Tribune*, 12 February 1978. According to Council of Economic Advisers Chairman Charles Schultze, Energy Secretary James Schlesinger was the catalyst for Carter's intervention in the strike, walking into a cabinet meeting and proclaiming that the strike would produce an unemployment disaster if not addressed quickly. In Schultze's telling, he tried to argue against intervention, but pro-intervention voices soon drowned him out. See Charles Schultze Interview, 8–9 January 1982, Jimmy Carter Presidential Oral History Project, Miller Center of the University of Virginia, 58.

17. "Carter Warns of 'Stronger Measures' in Asking Talks to Resume in Coal Strike," *Wall Street Journal*, 15 February 1978.

18. One industrial labor analyst later estimated that the strike put approximately 25,500 manufacturing workers out of work in an eleven-state "coal dependent" region stretching from the Midwest to the Southeast. See John Ackermann, "The Impact of the Coal Strike of 1977–78," *Industrial and Labor Relations Review* 32, no. 2 (1979): 181–83.

19. "Weakened UMW Clings to Lewis' Militant Legacy," *Los Angeles Times*, 12 March 1978; "Unions Drag Feet on Way to Altar of Shotgun Wedding," *Chicago Tribune*, 2 April 1980. UAW President Douglas Fraser cast the $2 million contribution as repayment for UMWA assistance to the UAW in the autoworkers union's formative years. "The United Mine Workers stood with the UAW during some of our most difficult struggles," said Fraser. "The miners under John L. Lewis supplied money and organizing help that was crucial to the survival and growth of the UAW in the 1930s. We haven't forgotten that."

20. "Carter Urges Striking Coal Miners and Industry to Resume Bargaining," *New York Times*, 15 February 1978; "Coal Talks Resume at Carter's Bidding," *Los Angeles Times*, 15 February 1978; Gary Fink, "Labor Law Revision and the End of the Postwar Labor Accord," in Kevin Boyle, ed., *Organized Labor and American Politics, 1894–1994: The Labor-Liberal Alliance* (Albany: State University of New York Press, 1998), 243–44. On Marshall's pro-labor background, and his clashes with Carter advisers who preferred to fight inflation rather than stimulate job growth, see Melvyn Dubofsky, "Jimmy Carter and the Politics of Productivity," in Gary M. Fink and Hugh Davis Graham, eds., *The Carter Presidency: Policy Choices in the Post-New Deal Era* (Lawrence: University Press of Kansas, 1998), 98–99. Although Schultze and Marshall had running disagreements on the competing priorities of fighting inflation and addressing unemployment, Schultze somewhat condescendingly sympathized with Marshall's position in the coal strike and blamed Energy Secretary Schlesinger for getting the administration involved in an impossible position. "Poor Ray Marshall—it wasn't his fault. He was given instructions [by Carter] to go out and do all this. They got the miners into the White House and then the miners rejected the pact and everything else." See Charles Schultze Interview, 58.

21. Within a few weeks of taking office, Carter had set a target for a minimum wage increase that was too low for labor's preferences, and his insistence on budgetary restraint dismayed workers who had anticipated large-scale social spending to stimulate unem-

ployment reduction. See William E. Leuchtenberg, "Jimmy Carter and the Post-New Deal Presidency," in Fink and Graham, eds., *Carter Presidency*, 12–15.

22. "Carter's Coal Strike Quandary," *Christian Science Monitor*, 15 February 1978; "Seizure of Mines Still Possible," *Washington Post*, 8 March 1978.

23. Memorandum from Larry S. Gibson to Douglas B. Huron, Coal Strike Situation Reports, box 9, folder Coal Strike: Key Memos, 3/10/78–10/78 [O/A 7751], White House Counsel's Files (hereafter CO), Jimmy Carter Presidential Library.

24. Memorandum from Larry S. Gibson to Douglas B. Huron.

25. "Coal Owners Renew Talk with Miners on Carter Warning," *New York Times*, 16 February 1978; "Carter Seeking Congress Support on Procedure to End Coal Strike," *New York Times*, 20 February 1978.

26. "Seizure of Mines Still Possible"; Memorandum to Honorable F. Ray Marshall from Mary C. Lawton, "Re: Analysis of possibilities for seizure of coal mines," 17 February 1978; Memorandum to the Honorable Robert J. Lipshutz and the Honorable Stuart F. Eizenstat from John M. Harmon, "Seizure Pursuant to New Legislation," 24 February 1978, both in box 9, folder Coal Strike: Key Memos, 2/78 [O/A 7751], CO.

27. "Pact to End Coal Strike Is Announced by Carter; Miners Urged to Back It," *New York Times*, 25 February 1978.

28. "Carter Push Led to Coal Accord—Aides," *Chicago Tribune*, 25 February 1978; "Nation: Entering the Doomsday Arena," *Time*, 27 February 1978.

29. "Coal Strike and Its Impact on Carter's Energy Plan," *New York Times*, 1 March 1978; "Coal Pact Is Viewed as Spur to Inflation," *New York Times*, 5 March 1978.

30. "Coal Pact Is Viewed as Spur to Inflation." Inflation czar Alfred Kahn, according to one historian, believed that powerful trade unionists exercised monopoly power to keep their own wages high and exploited nonunion workers, and he insisted that "Carter had to put labor in its place." See Dubofsky, "Jimmy Carter and the End of the Politics of Productivity," in Fink and Graham, eds., *Carter Presidency*, 99.

31. Gary M. Fink, "Labor Law Revision and the End of the Postwar Labor Accord," in Boyle, ed., *Organized Labor and American Politics, 1894–1994*, 245.

32. Memorandum from Wayne L. Horvitz to Honorable F. Ray Marshall and Honorable Landon Butler, Subject: Coal Negotiations, 1 March 1978; Memo for the President from Stu Eizenstat, "Actions in the Coal Strike," 3 March 1978, both in box 9, folder Coal Strike: Key Memos, 3/1–9/78 [O/A 7751], CO.

33. Memorandum from Wayne L. Horvitz to Honorable F. Ray Marshall and Honorable Landon Butler, Subject: Coal Negotiations, 1 March 1978; Memo for the President from Stu Eizenstat, "Actions in the Coal Strike," 3 March 1978.

34. "Carter Expected to Start Action Today to End Coal Strike," *Los Angeles Times*, 6 March 1978.

35. "Carter Expected to Start Action Today to End Coal Strike"; "Nation: Entering the Doomsday Arena," *Time*, 27 February 1978. The Forms quotation comes from an un-

dated *Time* article in box 9, folder Coal Strike 1978: Coal Operators—Correspondence, etc., 2/78 [CF, O/A 97], CO.

36. "Carter Expected to Start Action Today to End Coal Strike"; "Nation: Entering the Doomsday Arena"; Jimmy Carter to Attorney General Griffin Bell, 9 March 1978, box 9, folder Coal Strike: Key Memos, 3/1–9/78 [O/A 7751], CO; Temporary Restraining Order, box 9, folder Coal Strike: Pleadings, 3–4/78 [O/A 7751], CO.

37. Memorandum for Bob Lipshutz and Stu Eizenstat from Doug Huron, Re: Seizure, 8 March 1978, box 9, folder Coal Strike: Key Memos, 3/1–9-78 [O/A 7751], CO; *Washington Post*, 12 March 1978. To bolster the administration's case for invoking Taft-Hartley, several cabinet officials submitted affidavits outlining the broader economic damage that the strike was causing. Agriculture Secretary Bob Berglund, for example, predicted food shortages and sharply higher prices for consumers, since a disruption in electric power would affect dairy, poultry, beef, and hog producers. Other cabinet officials testified to similar problems caused by the strike. See Affidavit of Bob Berglund, Secretary of Agriculture, 8 March 1978, box 9, folder Coal Strike: Pleadings, 3–4/78 [O/A 7751], CO.

38. "Miners 'Caught in Middle' of Dispute," *Christian Science Monitor*, 13 March 1978; "'Some Progress' Reported in Talk on 96-Day Coal Strike," *Washington Post*, 12 March 1978.

39. "Most of Miners Defy Work Edict," *Chicago Tribune*, 14 March 1978; "Miners Defy Work Order," *Los Angeles Times*, 14 March 1978; "UMW Council's Close Vote on Coal Pact Casts Shadow over Rank-and-File Ballot," *Wall Street Journal*, 17 March 1978. The UMWA had been an independent union since being forced out of the American Federation of Labor in 1948. Meany's conspicuous support for the UMWA against the administration thus highlighted the AFL-CIO's stark dissatisfaction with Carter.

40. "Tentative Coal Pact Gives UMW Better Deal," *Chicago Tribune*, 15 March 1978; "U.S. Delaying 80-Day Coal Injunction," *Washington Post*, 17 March 1978; "Coal Strike Incident Highlights for March 14, 1978," box 9, folder Coal Strike: Key Memos, 3/10/78–10/78 [O/A 7751], CO.

41. "Relieved Carter Hails Coal Settlement," *Washington Post*, 26 March 1978; "Coal Miners OK Three-Year Pact by Wide Margin," *Los Angeles Times*, 25 March 1978; "Coal Mined for First Time in 112 Days as Strike Ends," *Los Angeles Times*, 28 March 1978; "U.S. Reliance on Coal: Doubts Remain," *Christian Science Monitor*, 27 March 1978.

42. John Dumbrell, *The Carter Presidency: A Re-evaluation* (New York: Manchester University Press, 1993), 17. Dumbrell's analysis draws extensively upon interviews with former presidential aides. On Carter's reticence to take sides in labor disputes, see also Taylor Dark, "Organized Labor and the Carter Administration: The Origins of Conflict," in Herbert D. Rosenbaum and Alexej Ugrinsky, eds., *The Presidency and Domestic Policies of Jimmy Carter* (Westport, CT: Greenwood Press, 1994), 774–79.

43. Burton I. Kaufman argues that Carter's "primary [labor] concern was with the unorganized, bottom rung of the labor market rather than with more highly paid union

members." See *The Presidency of James Earl Carter, Jr.* (Lawrence: University Press of Kansas, 1993), 29.

44. Kaufman, *Presidency of James Earl Carter, Jr.*, 78.

45. On the Ford administration's UMWA policy, see, for example, Memorandum from Mike Duval to W. J. Usery Jr., Fall Coal Strike, 29 May 1974; Memorandum from Warren Hendriks to Ken Cole, Meany Meeting with the President, 13 August 1974; Memorandum from Mike Duval to Ken Buchen, Coal Dispute, 15 August 1974; Memorandum of Telephone Conversation with Meyer Bernstein, 14 August 1974, all in box 4, folder Coal Strike Fall 1974 (1), Michael Raoul-Duval Files, Gerald R. Ford Presidential Library.

46. See, for example, Paul J. Nyden, "Rank-and-File Movements in the United Mine Workers of America," in Aaron Brenner, Robert Brenner, and Cal Winslow, eds., *Rebel Rank and File: Labor Militancy and Revolt from Below during the Long 1970s* (New York: Verso, 2010), 173–97.

47. See Ackermann, "Impact of the Coal Strike of 1977–78," 187–88.

48. An internal memorandum outlined the administration's perception of the dire situation that the strike was creating. Cyrus Vance, Carter's secretary of state, noted that the strike was reducing domestic energy production by the equivalent of about three million barrels of oil per day, or roughly the entire daily production of Kuwait. As domestic reserves of coal dwindled, Vance said, more oil imports were needed to replace the lost production. Vance feared that "because the cushion of excess supply in the world market is small, any significant increase in demand," such as would be created by a continued coal strike, "would lead to increased pressures within OPEC to raise world prices," perhaps permanently. See Memorandum for the President from Cyrus Vance, 20 February 1978, RAC Project, NLC-128 [Plains File]-13-5-12-7, Jimmy Carter Presidential Library.

49. Judith Stein, *Pivotal Decade: How the United States Traded Factories for Finance in the 1970s* (New Haven: Yale University Press, 2010), xii. See also W. Carl Biven, *Jimmy Carter's Economy: Policy in an Age of Limits* (Chapel Hill: University of North Carolina Press, 2002), x.

50. The story of the Yablonski murders helps frame Jefferson Cowie, *Stayin' Alive: The 1970s and the Last Days of the Working Class* (New York: The New Press, 2010), 23. On the broader declining public image of organized labor, see Lawrence Richards, *Union-Free America: Workers and Antiunion Culture* (Urbana and Chicago: University of Illinois Press, 2008); David Witwer, *Shadow of the Racketeer: Scandal in Organized Labor* (Urbana and Chicago: University of Illinois Press, 2009); James B. Jacobs, *Mobsters, Unions, and Feds: The Mafia and the American Labor Movement* (New York: New York University Press, 2006).

51. See, for example, Gary M. Fink, "Fragile Alliance: Jimmy Carter and the American Labor Movement," 783–803, and Russell D. Motter, "Seeking Limits: The Passage

of the National Energy Act as a Microcosm of the Carter Presidency," 572, in Rosenbaum and Ugrinsky, eds., *Presidency and Domestic Policies of Jimmy Carter.*

52. See Levy and Richards, *Struggle and Lose, Struggle and Win*, 108–12.

53. "Coal Strike and Its Impact on Carter's Energy Plan."

54. On the creation of the ICC, see Thomas K. McCraw, *Prophets of Regulation: Charles Francis Adams, Louis D. Brandeis, James M. Landis, Alfred M. Kahn* (Cambridge: Harvard University Press, 1984), 62. On the macroeconomic climate creating political space for a deregulatory agenda, see Thomas Borstelmann, *The 1970s: A New Global History from Civil Rights to Economic Inequality* (Princeton: Princeton University Press, 2012), 148–49.

55. "New Railroad-Aid Law: A Giant Step," *New York Times*, 5 February 1976.

56. "Coal Shipping Controversy: Rail vs. Pipeline," *Christian Science Monitor*, 15 March 1978.

57. "ICC Approves $660 Million Rail Freight Rate Boost," *Washington Post*, 8 June 1978; "3.7% Rail-Rate Rises Cleared," *New York Times*, 8 June 1978; "ICC Fines L&N Road $1 Million," *Washington Post*, 18 August 1978.

58. "L&N Seeks 22% Boost in Coal Freight Rates to Pay for Equipment," *Wall Street Journal*, 4 October 1978; "Rail Rates Increase of 6.5% Approved, Effective Friday," *Wall Street Journal*, 12 December 1978.

59. "ICC Allows Rails to Give Priority to Certain Items," *Wall Street Journal*, 27 June 1979; "TVA's Coal Procurement Program," box 37, folder 14, Chili Dean Papers (hereafter CD), Special Collections, University of Tennessee, 8–12. The report on the coal procurement program noted, for example, that the rates for rail transportation at L&N's Gallatin station had increased 154 percent from fiscal year 1978 to fiscal year 1979; the rates for the Widows Creek station rose 120 percent in the same period.

60. "Coal-Hauling Rate Increases Attacked," *Washington Post*, 22 November 1979; "U.S. Seeks Cut in Railroad Rate for Hauling Coal," 28 November 1979.

61. "Coal-Hauling Rate Increases Attacked"; "U.S. Seeks Cut in Railroad Rate for Hauling Coal"; "ICC Proposes to Alter Its Method of Setting Coal-Hauling Rates," *Wall Street Journal*, 19 November 1980.

62. "Coal Rates Too High, 2 Rails Must Refund $2.8 Million to Utility," *Wall Street Journal*, 21 May 1980.

63. Memorandum for the Vice President from Steve Simmons, Meeting with Texas Delegation on Rail Bill, 1 July 1980, box 78, folder Rail Deregulation—Memorandums/Internal, 4/80–7/80, Domestic Policy Staff—Steven Simmons' Subject Files (hereafter DPSSS), Jimmy Carter Presidential Library.

64. National Coal Association Staff Analysis, Railroad Deregulation: Implications and Alternatives for Coal Producers and Users, 23 May 1979, box 81, folder Rail Deregulation—William Johnson File, 5/79—7/79 (CF O/A 10,681), DPSSS; "Compromise Gets Rail Deregulation through Senate," *Washington Post*, 2 April 1980; "Bid to Curb

Rail Bill Defeated," *New York Times*, 3 July 1980. On Eckhardt's role in the 1980 rail deregulation, see Gary A. Keith, *Eckhardt: There Once Was a Congressman from Texas* (Austin: University of Texas Press, 2007), 289–90.

65. "Rail Deregulation Foes Win in House on Rates," *New York Times*, 25 July 1980; "Compromise Is Reached on Rail Deregulation Bill," *Chicago Tribune*, 6 September 1980. As it turned out, later in the 1980s shippers charged that the ICC had become *too* passive in the face of deregulation and Reagan's prevailing anti-government rhetoric, and they claimed that the ICC was shirking this duty to protect shippers "captive" to a single railroad. These shippers called for reregulation of the railroads, an effort that went nowhere. See "It's 'Captive Shippers vs. Railroads—Again," *Richmond Times-Dispatch*, 21 September 1986; "Don't Reregulate the Nation's Rails," *Chicago Tribune*, 13 June 1987.

66. For the best analysis of the exceptional dangers of coal mining and the effects on worker militancy, see Thomas G. Andrews, *Killing for Coal: America's Deadliest Labor War* (Cambridge: Harvard University Press, 2008), 147–48.

67. On declining corporate profits and the effect on labor markets in the 1970s, see Norman Caulfield, *NAFTA and Labor in North America* (Urbana and Chicago: University of Illinois Press, 2010), 1–7.

68. Coal companies' opposition to deregulation appears to have been shortsighted, as the increased efficiency of railroads under deregulation resulted in coal freight rates actually dropping by 6 percent (adjusted for inflation) from the end of 1981 to the end of 1986. See "Don't reregulate the nation's rails," *Chicago Tribune*, 13 June 1987.

69. "UMW Threatens Strike over Reagan Budget Cuts," *Wall Street Journal*, 20 February 1981.

70. "UMW Begins Coal Strike," *Chicago Tribune*, 27 March 1981; Ronald Garay, *U.S. Steel and Gary, West Virginia: Corporate Paternalism in Appalachia* (Knoxville: University of Tennessee Press, 2011), 143–44.

71. "Coal Miners Returning to Jobs but Strike Leaves Problems for UMW and Industry," *Wall Street Journal*, 8 June 1981.

72. "Coal Miners Returning to Jobs but Strike Leaves Problems for UMW and Industry."

73. "'New Coal' Is Building Steam as American Energy Export," *Christian Science Monitor*, 18 January 1982.

74. See Barbara Freese, *Coal: A Human History* (New York: Penguin Books, 2003), 137–38; John H. M. Laslett, "'A Model of Industrial Solidarity?': Interpreting the UMWA's First Hundred Years, 1890–1990," in John H. M. Laslett, ed., *The United Mine Workers of America: A Model of Industrial Solidarity?* (University Park: Pennsylvania State University Press, 1996), 11–12.

75. In the early 1980s, with its bargaining power decreased in the face of the rise of non-union coal, the UMWA shifted its strike strategy from a general national strike approach to a "selective strike strategy" that sought to turn private companies against each other. Under this approach, coal miners would strike against only a few companies,

which would quickly fall behind companies whose workers were not striking, and it would force targeted companies to come to a quick agreement with the miners to stay viable. Rather than relying on the weakened power of the UMWA itself, this strategy instead leveraged the competitive forces of the coal market. See Paul F. Clark, "Legacy of Democratic Reform: The Trumka Administration and the Challenge of the Eighties," in Laslett, ed., *United Mine Workers of America*, 469–72.

76. In 1970, 93 percent of the nation's bituminous and lignite coal came from mines east of the Mississippi; by 1990, it was a mere 61 percent. In the intervening years, the western states had greatly increased shipments of coal to electrical utilities. See Gregory A. Elmes and Trevor M. Harris, "Industrial Restructuring and the United States Coal-Energy System, 1972–1990: Regulatory Change, Technological Fixes, and Corporate Control," *Annals of the Association of American Geographers* 86, no. 3 (1996): 507–29.

77. "Carter Helps UMW Get Its Way," *Chicago Tribune*, 27 February 1978.

CHAPTER 3: "THE MODEL-T OF REACTORS"

1. A brief history of the early breeder program from its 1955 inception is in Glenn T. Seaborg, *The Atomic Energy Commission under Nixon: Adjusting to Troubled Times* (New York: St. Martin's Press, 1993), 151–89.

2. See, for example, Richard Epstein, *Takings: Private Property and the Power of Eminent Domain* (Cambridge: Harvard University Press, 1985).

3. See, for example, Terry L. Anderson and Donald R. Leal, *Free Market Environmentalism* (San Francisco: Pacific Research Institute for Public Policy, 1991). See also Brian Allen Drake, *Loving Nature, Fearing the State: Environmentalism and Antigovernment Politics before Reagan* (Seattle: University of Washington Press, 2013), 114–38.

4. Brian Balogh, *Chain Reaction: Expert Debate and Public Participation in American Commercial Nuclear Power, 1945–1975* (New York: Cambridge University Press, 1991), 302–11.

5. Balogh, *Chain Reaction*, 302–11.

6. The period from 1970 to 1979 in the US Congress witnessed a number of reform measures, the side effects of which included a shift in power from individual committee chairs to centralized party leadership. This shift allowed Tennessee's powerful senator Howard Baker to exert a measure of control over the fate of the Clinch River reactor in a way that would have been nearly impossible a few years before. On the changing structures of power in the US Congress in these years, see Julian Zelizer, *On Capitol Hill: The Struggle to Reform Congress and Its Consequences, 1948–2000* (New York: Cambridge University Press, 2004), 2–11.

7. Frederick V. Maick to Howard H. Baker Jr., 28 February 1973; Press release, 14 March 1973, both in box 10, folder 4, Bill Brock Papers (hereafter BB), Howard H. Baker Jr. Center for Public Policy, University of Tennessee.

8. "Controversial Clinch River Reactor Plan Is Poised to Proceed," *New York Times*, 10 March 1981.

9. "Controversial Clinch River Reactor Plan Is Poised to Proceed."

10. Maick to Baker, 28 February 1973; Press release, 14 March 1973, both in box 10, folder 4, BB. See also "Tennesseans Fear Loss of Jobs If Carter Cancels Breeder Project," *New York Times*, 6 June 1977.

11. "Nader on 'Breeders,'" *Chicago Tribune*, 5 June 1975. On Nader's broader anti-nuclear stance, see especially "Nader Claims Public Is Misled on Nuclear Peril," *Los Angeles Times*, 29 April 1975, in which he criticized the perceived "secrecy and censorship" of the Atomic Energy Commission and Nuclear Regulatory Commission and accused them of colluding with private industry to cover up the risks of nuclear power. Nader's criticisms appear at length in Ralph Nader and John Abbotts, *The Menace of Atomic Energy* (New York: W. W. Norton & Company, 1977).

12. Barry Commoner, *The Poverty of Power: Energy and the Economic Crisis* (New York: Alfred A. Knopf, 1976), 94–95.

13. Sheldon Novick, *The Electric War: The Fight Over Nuclear Power* (San Francisco: Sierra Club Books, 1976), 281.

14. On the congressional debate about the breeder during the Ford years, see Nader and Abbotts, *Menace of Atomic Energy*, 284–85.

15. Robert J. Duffy, *Nuclear Politics in America: A History and Theory of Government Regulation* (Lawrence: University Press of Kansas, 1997), 160.

16. For the same reason, Carter announced the same month that the United States would "delay indefinitely" the construction of the prospective Barnwell reprocessing plant in South Carolina, which would have separated fissionable plutonium from spent nuclear fuel. See James Mahaffey, *Atomic Accidents: A History of Nuclear Meltdowns and Disasters: From the Ozark Mountains to Fukushima* (New York: Pegasus Books, 2014), 419–20, for an account critical of this decision.

17. Sean Wilentz, *The Age of Reagan: A History, 1974–2008* (New York: Harper, 2008), 79–80; Samuel P. Hays, *Beauty, Health, and Permanence: Environmental Politics in the United States, 1955–1985* (New York: Cambridge University Press, 1987), 182.

18. "Clinch River Symbol of Split in Nation on Nuclear Power," *New York Times*, 25 February 1978.

19. Decision Analysis Report, Case Study: Breeder Reactor Program, RAC Project, NLC-126 [Office of the Staff Secretary]-7-25-3-4, Jimmy Carter Presidential Library, 118. A gaseous diffusion plant creates enriched uranium by forcing uranium hexafluoride, a gas, through semipermeable membranes.

20. Decision Analysis Report, Case Study: Breeder Reactor Program, 113.

21. "The Clinch River Votes," *Washington Post*, 22 June 1977.

22. "Support Growing for Clinch River Breeder Reactor," *Washington Post*, 11 June 1977.

23. "Church: Liberal Champion of Clinch River Facility," *Washington Post*, 15 June 1977; "Sen. Church Embraces Atom," *Chicago Tribune*, 18 July 1977. With obvious hyperbole, Church also accused Carter of leading the country toward "nuclear isolationism" and "nuclear anarchy." Church gave an extended speech supporting the breeder in England on 18 June 1977, excerpts of which were printed in "Like It or Not, It's the Plutonium Age," *Washington Post*, 1 July 1977. Church's liberal past was well documented; according to former Senate staffer Ira Shapiro, Church made his name as one of the most vocal critics of the Vietnam War and had also "always distrusted large corporations, which he equated with the lumber and mining companies that came into Idaho to extract its natural resources." See *The Last Great Senate: Courage and Conviction in Times of Crisis* (New York: PublicAffairs, 2012), 122–24.

24. "Time Out at Clinch River," *Washington Post*, 24 July 1977.

25. Deborah Shapley, "Engineer's Memo Stirs Doubts on Clinch River Breeder," *Science*, New Series 197, no. 4301 (22 July 1977): 350–52.

26. Summary of Statement of W. H. Young, Vice President Burns and Roe, Inc., to Subcommittee on Nuclear Regulation of Committee on Public Works, United States Senate, 11 July 1979, box 145, folder Clinch River Breeder Reactor (2), 1977, Marilyn Lloyd Papers (hereafter ML), Special Collections, University of Tennessee at Chattanooga.

27. "House, in Rebuff to Carter, Votes Funds for Clinch River Reactor," *New York Times*, 21 September 1977.

28. "Clinch River and the World," *Los Angeles Times*, 22 September 1977; "The Right Reaction to Clinch River: Veto," *New York Times*, 6 October 1977. On Teller's vehement support for nuclear power, see Patrick Allitt, *A Climate of Crisis: America in the Age of Environmentalism* (New York: Penguin, 2014), 109–10.

29. "Senate Panel Votes Clinch River Funds," *Washington Post*, 29 October 1977.

30. "Clinch River Symbol of Split in Nation on Nuclear Power," *New York Times*, 25 February 1978. In a classified memorandum, Carter's national security adviser expressed similar warnings about the effects of Congress's actions on relations with Europe. See Memorandum for the President from Zbigniew Brzezinski, "NSC Report for 1977: A Critical Appraisal," 12 January 1978, RAC Project, NLC-128 [Plains File]-9-13-5-1, Jimmy Carter Presidential Library, 23.

31. "Clinch River Symbol of Split in Nation on Nuclear Power."

32. "Compromise at Clinch River," *Los Angeles Times*, 19 March 1978; "Proposal to Replace Clinch River Reactor with Safer Plant Faces Battle in Congress," 22 March 1978. One way to account for potential variability in the estimated benefit of a technology like a jet engine is to build a demonstration model and see how it functions in practice, but in the case of a massive technology like a giant power plant, building a full-scale breeder is impossible. The smaller demonstration model was meant to begin initial tests on effectiveness. See Alvin M. Weinberg, *Nuclear Reactions: Science and Trans-science* (New York: American Institute of Physics, 1992), 6.

33. "Compromise at Clinch River"; "Proposal to Replace Clinch River Reactor with Safer Plant Faces Battle in Congress."

34. Lloyd sent a strongly worded letter to her colleagues on the House's Science and Technology Committee calling Carter's breeder policy "mis-directed" and asking them to vote for the amendment. See Marilyn Lloyd to Colleague, box 146, folder Clinch River Breeder Reactor (5), 1977–1978, ML.

35. "Unit Votes Continued Aid for Clinch River," *Washington Post*, 13 April 1978.

36. John W. Wydler to the President, 4 April 1978, box 145, folder Clinch River Breeder Reactor (3), 1978, ML. On the history of the Soviet breeder program, see Paul R. Josephson, *Red Atom: Russia's Nuclear Power Program from Stalin to Today* (Pittsburgh: University of Pittsburgh Press, 2005), 47–80.

37. John W. Wydler to the President, 4 April 1978, box 145, folder Clinch River Breeder Reactor (3), 1978, ML.

38. See "Dream Machine," *Atlantic Monthly*, April 1983, 85.

39. See David E. Hoffman, *The Dead Hand: The Untold Story of the Cold War Arms Race and Its Dangerous Legacy* (New York: Random House, 2009), 13–26.

40. David Norcutt to John J. Duncan, 24 October 1977, box 89, folder 3, John Duncan Sr. Papers (hereafter JD), Howard H. Baker Jr. Center for Public Policy, University of Tennessee.

41. Pietro F. Pasqua and Carl O. Thomas to Ralph W. Millett Jr., 22 March 1978, box 89, folder 4, JD.

42. Dianne S. Turner to Editor, The Knoxville News Sentinel, 24 May 1978, box 89, folder 3, JD.

43. John J. Duncan to Dianne S. Turner, 31 May 1978, box 89, folder 3, JD.

44. "Senate Panel Votes Clinch River Reactor Compromise"; "Plan That Halts Reactor at Clinch River, Sets Study for New One Back by Carter," *Wall Street Journal*, 13 July 1978; "House Won't Cut Funds for Clinch River Reactor," *Chicago Tribune*, 15 July 1978. On the House Science and Technology's skepticism about this compromise plan, see Olin E. Teague to the President, 16 August 1978, box 6, folder 8, Domestic Policy Staff—Kitty Schirmer and Erica Ward's Subject Files, Jimmy Carter Presidential Library. In this letter, committee chairman Olin Teague asked that Carter meet with four or five members of the committee to address their "widespread uncertainty" about his true intentions. The chairman of the engineering firm Burns and Roe had written Teague in June to explain that he had met with Carter at the White House and was disappointed to find that Carter possessed "no flexibility" on the breeder. He urged Teague and the committee to continue funding for the original project. See Kenneth A. Roe to Olin E. Teague, 26 June 1978, box 6, folder 8, Domestic Policy Staff—Kitty Schirmer and Erica Ward's Subject Files, Jimmy Carter Presidential Library.

45. "The Embattled Clinch River Project Is Breeding Nothing but Expenses So Far," *Washington Post*, 9 December 1978.

46. Jimmy Carter to Walter Mondale, 24 April 1979, box 96, folder Clinch River Breeder Reactor, 5/5/79–6/6/79, Office of Congressional Liaison Files (hereafter OCL), Jimmy Carter Presidential Library; James R. Schlesinger to Henry M. Jackson, 24 April 1979, box 249, folder Clinch River Breeder Reactor, 4/24/79–1/29/80, OCL.

47. Press release, 27 April 1979, box 96, folder Clinch River Breeder Reactor, 5/5/79–6/6/79, OCL.

48. See J. Samuel Walker, *Three Mile Island: A Nuclear Crisis in Historical Perspective* (Berkeley and Los Angeles: University of California Press, 2004), 209–44.

49. See Russell B. Olwell, *At Work in the Atomic City: A Labor and Social History of Oak Ridge, Tennessee* (Knoxville, University of Tennessee Press, 2004).

50. This does not mean that TMI had no effect at all on the debate. Later, in the 1980s, when congressional opinion turned against the breeder, nuclear industry defenders like former Manhattan Project scientist Alvin Weinberg would voice their support for the breeder as part of a broader defense of nuclear power against safety concerns. However, in press coverage of the breeder debate in 1979 and in Carter administration documents, references to Three Mile Island simply fail to appear.

51. "Clinch River Nuclear Project Is Supported in Congressional Study," *Wall Street Journal*, 10 May 1979.

52. "Putting an End to Clinch River," *Washington Post*, 25 July 1979; "House Again Rejects Carter's Bid to Kill Clinch River Project," *Wall Street Journal*, 27 July 1979.

53. General Accounting Office report, "Federal Actions Are Needed to Improve Safety and Security of Nuclear Materials Transportation," box 505, folder 1, Mike Gravel Papers, Alaska and Polar Regions Collections, Elmer E. Rasmuson Library, University of Alaska Fairbanks. On the national security concerns related to transporting plutonium waste, see Gene I. Rochlin, *Plutonium, Power, and Politics: International Arrangements for the Disposition of Spent Nuclear Fuel* (Berkeley and Los Angeles: University of California Press, 1979), 247.

54. Environmental Study Conference Update, 17 July 1979, box 146, folder Clinch River Breeder Reactor (6), 1979–1985, ML. By this point, the administration had also backed away from its attempts to encourage European nations to abandon breeder technology. In May 1980, Carter's national security staff also noted that many other countries (Belgium, Italy, West Germany, the UK, France, and Japan, among others) remained as committed to breeder technology as ever. Because the US had a broader mix of indigenous natural resources (including significant amounts of natural U-235 in Colorado), the US possessed "more flexibility" in choosing a long-term energy strategy. It was for this reason, Carter's staff noted, that Europe and Japan had adopted a "more aggressive" posture on breeders and other advanced reactors, which the US would not necessarily be compelled to follow. See PRC Presidential Decision Paper, Nonproliferation Planning Assumptions, 12 May 1980, RAC Project, NLC-132 [NSC Institutional Files]-79-7-7-4, Jimmy Carter Presidential Library, 2, 20.

55. "Clinch River Project Advances in House," *Washington Post*, 25 April 1980.

56. "Reagan Said to Support Tennessee Nuclear Plant," *New York Times*, 26 February 1981; "Controversial Clinch River Reactor Plan Is Poised to Proceed"; "Controversial Clinch River Reactor Survives Budget Ax," *Christian Science Monitor*, 23 July 1981.

57. See Richard K. Lester, "Backing Off the Back End," in Alvin Weinberg, Marcelo Alonso, and Jack N. Barkenbus, eds., *The Nuclear Connection: A Reassessment of Nuclear Power and Nuclear Proliferation* (New York: Paragon House Publishers, 1985), 105.

58. "Reagan Said to Support Tennessee Nuclear Plant"; "Controversial Clinch River Reactor Plan Is Poised to Proceed"; "Controversial Clinch River Reactor Survives Budget Ax." On NEPA requirements see Lynton Keith Caldwell, *The National Environmental Policy Act: An Agenda for the Future* (Bloomington: Indiana University Press, 1998), 48–72.

59. "Controversial Clinch River Reactor Survives Budget Ax."

60. "Reagan Said to Support Tennessee Nuclear Plant"; "Controversial Clinch River Reactor Plan Is Poised to Proceed"; "A Nuclear D-Day in Congress," *New York Times*, 7 May 1981.

61. "House Panel Opposes Reactor," *New York Times*, 8 May 1981.

62. "The Staying Power of the Clinch River Breeder," *Wall Street Journal*, 17 July 1981.

63. "Three That Deserve to Lose," *Washington Post*, 21 July 1981.

64. "House Approves Funds for Two Controversial Nuclear Projects," *Washington Post*, 25 July 1981.

65. "Senate Narrowly Rejects Fund Cuts for Waterway, Tenn. Reactor," *Washington Post*, 5 November 1981; "Funding Cleared for Clinch River and a Waterway," *Wall Street Journal*, 5 November 1981.

66. "Senate Narrowly Rejects Fund Cuts for Waterway, Tenn. Reactor"; "Funding Cleared for Clinch River and a Waterway"; "Clinch River Project Is Hit by Shake Up of Top Management," 4 November 1981.

67. "U.S. Has to Honor Pact on Clinch River Plant," *New York Times*, 20 March 1982.

68. "Congress Coalition Opens Fight to Kill Clinch River Project," *New York Times*, 17 June 1982; "NRC Again Rejects a Proposed Speedup of Work on Clinch River Breeder Reactor," *Wall Street Journal*, 18 May 1982; "Class Act at the NRC," *Washington Post*, 20 May 1982; "NRC Resurrects Clinch River Nuclear Project," *Washington Post*, 6 August 1982; "Clinch River Breeder Reactor Clears Hurdle," *Wall Street Journal*, 6 August 1982; "NRC to Let Work Start on Breeder Reactor," *Los Angeles Times*, 6 August 1982.

69. "Clinch River Project Is Right at Home in Oak Ridge," *New York Times*, 29 September 1982.

70. Eliot Marshall, "The Perils of Clinch River," *Science*, New Series 218, no. 4568 (8 October 1982) 137–38.

71. "Dump the Clinch Breeder," *Chicago Tribune*, 13 December 1982; "Clinch River by a Thread," *New York Times*, 23 December 1982.

72. "Dump the Clinch breeder"; "Clinch River by a Thread"; "Clinch River Funds Denied," *Boston Globe*, 23 June 1983; *Chicago Tribune*, "Clinch River Ailing, but Work Stays at Fevered Pitch," 24 June 1983. On Weinberg see Allitt, *Climate of Crisis*, 109. Weinberg and Edward Teller usually lined up on the same side of nuclear issues but split on the breeder.

73. Russ Manning, ed., *The Second Nuclear Era: A New Start for Nuclear Power* (New York: Praeger Publishers, 1985). See also Alvin M. Weinberg, *The First Nuclear Era: The Life and Times of a Technological Fixer* (New York: American Institute of Physics, 1994), 129–31.

74. "Ready for Construction," news release, 14 September 1983, box 146, folder Clinch River Breeder Reactor (7), 1983, ML.

75. "Exhibit at Oak Ridge Library to Feature Breeder Reactor Model," news release, 25 August 1983, box 146, folder Clinch River Breeder Reactor (7), 1983, ML.

76. "End Run to Clinch River," *Washington Post*, 26 September 1983; "Subcommittee Witnesses Urge Congress to Approve Clinch River Alternative Financing Plan," news release, 15 September 1983, box 146, folder Clinch River Breeder Reactor (7), 1983, ML; Ronald Reagan to Tom Bevill, 4 October 1983, box 146, folder Clinch River Breeder Reactor (7).

77. "Senate Vote Virtually Kills Clinch River Atom Reactor," *New York Times*, 27 October 1983.

78. Eliot Marshall, "Clinch River Dies," *Science*, New Series, 222, no. 4624 (11 November 1983): 590–92.

79. Marshall, "Clinch River Dies." On the NRDC's extended campaign against the breeder, see Nader and Abbotts, *Menace of Atomic Energy*, 190–95. The story of this centrifuge plant in Portsmouth mirrored some of the aspects of Clinch River, thus it is no surprise that it, too, brought the hostile attention of environmentalists. In the mere six years since Portsmouth had been chosen as the plant's site, for example, the estimated cost of the project had more than doubled, from around $4 billion to $10 billion. Furthermore, while the plant's centrifuge technology was cutting edge in 1977, by 1983 it seemed already on the verge of obsolescence. See "Portsmouth, Ohio, Is Chosen by U.S. for Uranium Plant," *Wall Street Journal*, 12 July 1977.

80. Duffy, *Nuclear Politics in America*, 182–83.

81. The late 1970s and early 1980s represented a period of fierce controversy among experts about whether a growing world population would result in either resource shortages or improved technological capability, and thus whether the future would be characterized by scarcity or growth. Projecting future energy needs was therefore a highly complicated endeavor that lent itself to a wide range of interpretations. For the best analysis of these debates, see Paul Sabin, *The Bet: Paul Ehrlich, Julian Simon, and Our Gamble over Earth's Future* (New Haven: Yale University Press, 2013).

82. S. E. Luria, "The Goals of Science," *Bulletin of the Atomic Scientists* 33, no. 5 (May 1977): 30.

1. "Reclamation Chief Backs Hydro Power," *Los Angeles Times*, 14 December 1976.

2. On the history of endangered species law from the late 1950s to the early 1970s, see Charles C. Mann and Mark L. Plummer, *Noah's Choice: The Future of Endangered Species* (New York: Alfred A. Knopf, 1995), 149–63.

3. Sarah T. Phillips, *This Land, This Nation: Conservation, Rural America, and the New Deal* (New York: Cambridge University Press, 2007), 78–80. On the stagnant agricultural economy of the South in the first half of the twentieth century, see Paul K. Conkin, *A Revolution Down on the Farm: The Transformation of American Agriculture since 1929* (Lexington: University Press of Kentucky, 2008), 50.

4. Phillips, *This Land, This Nation*, 78–80. For more on the New Deal development of the South, see Bruce J. Schulman, *From Cotton Belt to Sunbelt: Federal Policy, Economic Development, and the Transformation of the South, 1938–1980* (New York: Oxford University Press, 1991), 112–34.

5. *Environmental Statement: Tellico Project* (Chattanooga, TN: TVA Office of Health and Environmental Science, 1972), I-1-43.

6. Kenneth M. Murchison, *The Snail Darter Case: TVA Versus the Endangered Species Act* (Lawrence: University Press of Kansas, 2007), 12–13. For more on the community development initiative, see Aelred J. Gray and David A. Johnson, *The TVA Regional Planning and Development Program: The Transformation of an Institution and Its Mission* (Burlington, VT: Ashgate Publishing Company, 2005), 77.

7. "A Program for the Preservation and Development of Industrial Areas along Tennessee's Waterways" (Nashville: State-Local Waterfront Industrial Site Committee, 1962), 1, box 4, TVA Reports, 1933–1973, MS-828, Special Collections, University of Tennessee.

8. For more on Wagner's reasoning see William Bruce Wheeler and Michael McDonald, *TVA and the Tellico Dam, 1936–1979: A Bureaucratic Crisis in Post-industrial America* (Knoxville: University of Tennessee Press, 1986), 31–35.

9. Murchison, *Snail Darter Case*, 7–22.

10. *Environmental Statement: Tellico Project*, I-1-1, I-1-5; Erwin C. Hargrove, *Prisoners of Myth: The Leadership of the Tennessee Valley Authority, 1933–1990* (Princeton: Princeton University Press, 1994), 175; "Upper Little Tennessee River Region: Summary of Resources" (Knoxville: Tennessee Valley Authority, 1968), 5, box 3, TVA Reports.

11. *Environmental Statement: Tellico Project*, I-1-2, I-1-3.

12. *Environmental Statement: Tellico Project*, I-1-2, I-1-3.

13. *Environmental Statement: Tellico Project*, I-1-2, I-1-3.

14. *Environmental Statement: Tellico Project*, I-1-28, I-1-42.

15. Resolution by the Chamber of Commerce—Lenoir City, Tennessee, 1 May 1969; Monroe County Quarterly Court, 20 April 1970; Resolution in Support of the Tellico

Dam and Reservoir, Town of Madisonville, 14 April 1972; Resolution by the Board of Mayor and Aldermen, City of Lenoir City, Tennessee, 10 April 1972; James C. Talley II to Governor Winfield Dunn, 25 January 1972, all in box 10, folder 11, Howard H. Baker Jr. Papers, Howard H. Baker Jr. Center for Public Policy, University of Tennessee.

16. *Environmental Statement: Tellico Project*, I-4-7, I-4-9, I-4-10. For more on Clebsch's relationships with other dam opponents, see Wheeler and McDonald, *TVA and the Tellico Dam*, 136, 144.

17. *Environmental Statement: Tellico Project*, I-4-7, I-4-9, I-4-10; Hargrove, *Prisoners of Myth*, 176.

18. Zygmunt J. B. Plater, *The Snail Darter and the Dam: How Pork-Barrel Politics Endangered a Little Fish and Killed a River* (New Haven: Yale University Press, 2013), 20–22. On TVA's delaying of the announcement that it planned to buy land near the project site and sell it at a profit after the dam's construction, see Wheeler and McDonald, *TVA and the Tellico Dam*, 41–43. On the agricultural tradition and cultural conservatism of the Little Tennessee Valley, see 46–63.

19. Hargrove, *Prisoners of Myth*, 176. On NEPA requirements see Lynton Keith Caldwell, *The National Environmental Policy Act: An Agenda for the Future* (Bloomington: Indiana University Press, 1998), 48–72.

20. Murchison, *Snail Darter Case*, 80–107. Though contemporary accounts claimed that Etnier happened to discover the snail darter in the river by accident, later interviews with participants in the case have revealed that Etnier was purposefully looking for species that would fall under the ESA's provisions.

21. Murchison, *Snail Darter Case*, 108–40; Hargrove, *Prisoners of Myth*, 175–76.

22. "Endangered Species Act Is Lunacy," *Los Angeles Times*, 13 February 1977.

23. "Endangered Species Rules to Be Curbed?" *Christian Science Monitor*, 10 March 1977.

24. "Endangered Species Rules to Be Curbed?"

25. "Endangered Species Endanger Dams," *Washington Post*, 11 February 1977.

26. Frank A. Coleman to John J. Duncan, 8 April 1977, box 106, folder 1, John Duncan Sr. Papers (hereafter JD), Howard H. Baker Jr. Center for Public Policy, University of Tennessee.

27. Perry W. Hembree to John J. Duncan, 9 March 1977, box 106, folder 1, JD.

28. S. Russell Manning to John J. Duncan, 10 March 1977, box 106, folder 1, JD.

29. Heather L. Houvenagle to John J. Duncan, 15 February 1977, box 106, folder 2, JD.

30. Chas. Roy Moore to John J. Duncan, 28 March 1977, box 106, folder 1, JD.

31. Troye D. Summitt to John J. Duncan, 16 February 1977, box 106, folder 2, JD.

32. Cam A. Hammontree to John J. Duncan, 5 February 1977, box 105, folder 5, JD.

33. Charles and Nell Lunsford to John J. Duncan, 10 February 1977, box 106, folder 1, JD.

34. Tip Parks to John J. Duncan, 14 February 1977, box 105, folder 5, JD.

35. "Hearings Open on Amending the Endangered Species Act," *New York Times*, 14 April 1978.

36. "Hearings Open on Amending the Endangered Species Act."

37. "Hearings Open on Amending the Endangered Species Act."

38. Eugene Stratton to John J. Duncan, 20 June 1978, box 105, folder 5, JD.

39. John J. Duncan to Eugene Stratton, 22 June 1978, box 105, folder 5, JD.

40. "Letter: On Endangered Species: The 'Impossible' Criteria," *New York Times*, 24 June 1978.

41. "Those Endangered Species: What Good Are They?" *Los Angeles Times*, 2 July 1978. Steinhart later published a book-length study of endangered species in California. See *California's Wild Heritage: Threatened and Endangered Animals in the Golden State* (Sacramento: California Department of Fish and Game, 1990).

42. "Those Endangered Species: What Good Are They?"

43. "Those Endangered Species: What Good Are They?" Like many large, multiyear federal projects, the Tellico Dam had seen its projected final cost rise steadily over time, which drew more critiques from dam opponents but did not pose a serious threat to the dam's construction.

44. Plater, *Snail Darter and the Dam*, 3.

45. "Those Endangered Species: What Good Are They?" For a response to this argument see Mann and Plummer, *Noah's Choice*, 132–34, who argue that saving *every* species would grind human civilization to a halt. "Biodiversity as a whole has overwhelming utilitarian value," they claim, "but most individual species do not."

46. "Endangered Species Act Is Dying," *Washington Post*, 29 September 1978.

47. "Endangered Species Act Is Dying"; Shannon Petersen, *Acting for Endangered Species: The Statutory Ark* (Lawrence: University Press of Kansas, 2002), 63–64.

48. See Jeffrey K. Stine, "Environmental Policy during the Carter Administration," in Gary M. Fink and Hugh Davis Graham, *The Carter Presidency: Policy Choices in the Post-New Deal Era* (Lawrence: University Press of Kansas, 1998), 185; John Dumbrell, *The Carter Presidency: A Re-evaluation* (New York: Manchester University Press, 1993), 40.

49. "1,700 left off Endangered Species List," *Chicago Tribune*, 7 November 1979.

50. The "charismatic megafauna" phrase comes from Petersen, *Acting for Endangered Species*, 3.

51. Petersen, *Acting for Endangered Species*, 63–64.

52. Petersen, *Acting for Endangered Species*, 65.

53. Patrick Allitt, *A Climate of Crisis: America in the Age of Environmentalism* (New York: Penguin, 2014), 124–27.

54. Allitt, *Climate of Crisis*, 124–27; Hargrove, *Prisoners of Myth*, 177; Mann and Plummer, *Noah's Choice*, 170–73. Almost a year after the dam was completed, David

Etnier, who had originally discovered the snail darter, located another population in a different portion of the Tennessee River, sixty miles downstream from Tellico.

55. Shirley Nicholson to John J. Duncan, 20 July 1979, box 129, folder 1, JD.

56. Wayne Christeson to John J. Duncan, 2 August 1979, box 129, folder 1, JD.

57. Mann and Plummer, *Noah's Choice*, 28–29.

58. "Environmentalists, Like Developers, Find Endangered Species Act Can Delay Plans," *Wall Street Journal*, 21 March 1979.

59. "3 Endangered Fish Delay Utah's Construction of Dam and Reservoir," *New York Times*, 7 December 1980.

60. "3 Endangered Fish Delay Utah's Construction of Dam and Reservoir."

61. See Petersen, *Acting for Endangered Species*, 65.

62. Trucking Industry Regulation Remarks Announcing Proposed Legislation, 21 June 1979, *Public Papers of the Presidents of the United States: Jimmy Carter: 1979*, Book 1 (Washington, DC: Government Printing Office, 1979), 1114.

63. See Benjamin C. Waterhouse, *Lobbying America: The Politics of Business from Nixon to NAFTA* (Princeton: Princeton University Press, 2014), 32.

64. "Endangered Species Act Marks a Decade of Gains," *New York Times*, 28 December 1983.

65. See, for example, "'Balanced' off the Planet," *Atlanta Constitution*, 15 May 1995.

CHAPTER 5: "HIT BY INFLATION LIKE EVERYONE ELSE"

1. On *The Limits to Growth* see David Nye, *Consuming Power: A Social History of American Energies* (Cambridge: MIT Press, 2001), 227.

2. For a historical critique of the idea that resources were running out, see Patrick Allitt, *A Climate of Crisis: America in the Age of Environmentalism* (New York: Penguin, 2014), 79–89.

3. See Judith Stein, *Pivotal Decade: How the United States Traded Factories for Finance in the 1970s* (New Haven, CT: Yale University Press, 2010), x–xiii.

4. On postwar prosperity see Joyce Appleby, *The Relentless Revolution: A History of Capitalism* (New York: W. W. Norton & Company, 2010), 300–7; Michael Lind, *Land of Promise: An Economic History of the United States* (New York: HarperCollins, 2012), 329–62; Robert M. Collins, *More: The Politics of Economic Growth in Postwar America* (New York: Oxford University Press, 2000), 40–67.

5. See Appleby, *Relentless Revolution*, 325–30; Lind, *Land of Promise*, 363–91; Collins, *More*, 68–165.

6. On the deregulatory political climate of the 1970s, see David H. K. Vietor, *Contrived Competition: Regulation and Deregulation in America* (Cambridge: Harvard University Press, 1994); Kenneth Button and Dennis Swann, eds., *The Age of Regulatory Reform* (Oxford: Clarendon Press, 1989); Thomas Borstelmann, *The 1970s: A New Global*

History from Civil Rights to Economic Inequality (Princeton: Princeton University Press, 2012), 148–49.

7. On the decline of the industrial Midwest and Northeast and the rise of the Sunbelt Southeast and Southwest, see especially Bruce J. Schulman, *From Cotton Belt to Sunbelt: Federal Policy, Economic Development, and the Transformation of the South, 1938–1980* (New York: Oxford University Press, 1991); Elizabeth Tandy Shermer, *Sunbelt Capitalism: Phoenix and the Transformation of American Politics* (Philadelphia: University of Pennsylvania Press, 2013); Matthew Lassiter, *Silent Majority: Suburban Politics in the Sunbelt South* (Princeton: Princeton University Press, 2006); Jefferson Cowie, *Capital Moves: RCA's Seventy-Year Quest for Cheap Labor* (New York: The New Press, 2001); Thomas J. Sugrue, *The Origins of the Urban Crisis: Race and Inequality in Postwar Detroit* (Princeton: Princeton University Press, 1996).

8. Erwin C. Hargrove, *Prisoners of Myth: The Leadership of the Tennessee Valley Authority, 1933–1990* (Princeton: Princeton University Press, 1994), 118–28.

9. Memorandum for Hamilton Jordan from Frank Press, "Preliminary Comments on the Tennessee Valley Authority Board of Directors," 23 February 1977, box 23, folder 8, Domestic Policy Staff—Kitty Schirmer and Erica Ward's Subject Files (hereafter DPSSW), Jimmy Carter Presidential Library. In this memorandum, Press recommended three candidates for the TVA vacancy, none of whom eventually got the job; however, the one that Press thought would be most appropriate to take over the chairmanship was Alfred Kahn, who later became Carter's special adviser on inflation. On TVA's diverse experimental initiatives in its early years, see Sarah T. Phillips, *This Land, This Nation: Conservation, Rural America, and the New Deal* (New York: Cambridge University Press, 2007), 80–98.

10. "A New Dynamo for the TVA," *Chicago Tribune*, 28 May 1978; memorandum for Jordan from Press, "Preliminary Comments on the Tennessee Valley Authority Board of Directors," 23 February 1977, box 23, folder 8, DPSSW; J. Wiley Bowers to the President, 8 June 1977, box 286, folder TVA [Tennessee Valley Authority] [O/A 6239], Domestic Policy Staff—Stuart Eizenstat's Subject Files, Jimmy Carter Presidential Library. The 1974 publication resulting from Freeman's time at the Ford Foundation outlined alternatives to big power growth and became an energy primer for candidate Carter.

11. "New Dynamo for the TVA."

12. Hargrove, *Prisoners of Myth*, 197. Freeman drew criticism from nuclear power advocates for skeptically questioning whether the next big step in increasing generating capacity should be nuclear power. Those in the oil sector were also wary of his conservationist impulses; one executive claimed that "Freeman's basic philosophy" was "to drive the growth rate to zero as quickly as possible." See "Energy: A Conservationist Shakes the TVA," *Time*, 29 May 1978.

13. S. David Freeman, *Energy: The New Era* (New York: Walker and Company, 1974), 3, 148, 172.

14. Freeman, *Energy*, 12–13, 159, 228.

15. "New Dynamo for the TVA." On Save Our Cumberland Mountains see Chad Montrie, *To Save the Land and People: A History of Opposition to Surface Coal Mining in Appalachia* (Chapel Hill: University of North Carolina Press, 2003), 182–91.

16. "T.V.A. Chairman after One Year," *New York Times*, 29 May 1979.

17. J. Granville Clark to David Freeman, 8 October 1977, box 3, folder CI-CL, Richard M. Freeman Correspondence Files (hereafter RF), Tennessee Valley Authority Records, RG142, National Archives at Atlanta. In TVA's records, David Freeman's correspondence from 1977 to 1978 is filed together with Richard Freeman's correspondence from 1978 to 1986. David Freeman's correspondence from 1979 to 1984 is filed separately.

18. S. David Freeman to J. Granville Clark, 13 November 1977, box 3, folder CI-CL, RF.

19. Edward L. Hopper to Richard M. Freeman, 19 October 1978, box 5, folder HL-HZ, RF.

20. See Hargrove, *Prisoners of Myth*, 227.

21. "TVA's Coal Procurement Program," box 37, folder 14, Chili Dean Papers (hereafter CD), Special Collections, University of Tennessee, 8–12.

22. Speech by William F. Willis to the Tennessee Municipal League, 10 July 1981, box 17, folder 71, CD.

23. Clipping from *Knoxville Journal*, 19 April 1979, box 1, folder 2, CD; clipping from *Nashville Tennessean*, 13 March 1979, box 1, folder 2, CD; clipping from *Knoxville News-Sentinel*, 27 July 1978, box 12, folder 3, Howard H. Baker Jr. Papers (hereafter HBJ), Howard H. Baker Jr. Center for Public Policy, University of Tennessee.

24. "Carter's Coal-Production Plan: Not off to a Burning Start," *Chicago Tribune*, 9 May 1977; "The Coal Conversion Muddle," *Wall Street Journal*, 28 July 1977. In the early 1970s, the soft coal industry had taken an active role in the shaping of the Clean Air Act, pushing for federal standards requiring emission-control technology in order to avoid municipal regulations that would require switching from high- to low-sulfur coal, a regulation they saw as especially onerous. See Richard N. L. Andrews, *Managing the Environment, Managing Ourselves: A History of American Environmental Policy*, 2nd ed. (New Haven: Yale University Press, 2006), 209. Pushing legislative policies to require polluters to install improved technology ("technology forcing") was a common environmentalist tactic; see Samuel P. Hays, *Beauty, Health, and Permanence: Environmental Politics in the United States, 1955–1985* (New York: Cambridge University Press, 1987), 251.

25. Clipping from *Knoxville Journal*, 19 April 1979, box 1, folder 2, CD; clipping from *Nashville Tennessean*, 13 March 1979, box 1, folder 2, CD; clipping from *Knoxville News-Sentinel*, 27 July 1978, box 12, folder 3, HBJ; Hargrove, *Prisoners of Myth*, 180.

26. Clipping from *Nashville Tennessean*, 13 March 1979, box 1, folder 2, CD.

27. Unidentified newspaper clipping, box 1, folder 1, CD; Howard H. Baker to Jennings Randolph, 25 July 1978, box 12, folder 3, HBJ.

28. Testimony of S. David Freeman before Senate Committee on Environment and Public Works, 16 March 1981, box 36, folder 10, CD.

29. Testimony of S. David Freeman before Senate Committee on Environment and Public Works, 16 March 1981, box 36, folder 10, CD. TVA's general manager agreed with Freeman's analysis, explaining to one complaining ratepayer that "to shut down plants and lay off employees now would cost us the new generating capacity needed for future regional growth." See W. F. Willis to Robert S. Dabney III, 12 May 1980, box 3, folder DA-DD, RF.

30. Ironically, though Freeman faced criticism from members of Congress who thought TVA was not cutting back construction *enough* in order to adapt to reduced growth, some Valley residents blasted TVA for cutting back construction *too much* and causing mass layoffs of Valley workers. See, for example, S. David Freeman to John S. Fandrich, 3 February 1978, box 4, folder FA-FD, RF.

31. Mr. and Mrs. George E. Latham to John J. Duncan, 17 April 1978, box 115, folder 4, John Duncan Sr. Papers (hereafter JD), Howard H. Baker Jr. Center for Public Policy, University of Tennessee.

32. Aubrey Wagner to John J. Duncan, 11 May 1978, box 107, folder 3, JD.

33. Interview with Richard M. Freeman, 9 January 1979, box 39, folder 185 Freeman, Richard M., RF.

34. "TVA: Ready for the 80's," 16 December 1980, box 15, folder 012 Executive Branch, RF.

35. Hargrove, *Prisoners of Myth*, 203.

36. Clipping from *Chattanooga Times*, 16 October 1981, box 36, folder 6, CD.

37. Clipping from *Tupelo Journal*, 17 October 1981, box 36, folder 6.

38. "T.V.A. Chairman after One Year"; Hargrove, *Prisoners of Myth*, 224. For TVA worker comments, see the folder labeled "Cost Cutting Surveys" in box 35, folder 18, CD.

39. For more on utilities building plants to meet demand that failed to materialize in light of conservationist initiatives, see *Wall Street Journal*, 2 September 1980. For the Freemans' shaky position vis-à-vis members of Congress, see, for example, their reply to Jamie L. Whitten, the chair of the House Appropriations Committee, 21 March 1979, in box 19, folder 101 General Program of TVA 1977–1980, RF. In response to Whitten's insinuation that TVA had "lost a sense of cost consciousness," they cited a "thorough study of its construction activities by the highly respected Theodore Barry & Associates," claiming, "TVA is well on its way toward implementing almost all of the recommendations of that report." Despite these insistences, TVA's cost and expenditure problems continued long afterward, as did criticism from Congress.

40. Hargrove, *Prisoners of Myth*, 238. For the top officials replaced during this reorganization, see Aelred J. Gray and David A. Johnson, *The TVA Regional Planning and Development Program: The Transformation of an Institution and Its Mission* (Burlington, VT: Ashgate Publishing Company, 2005), 97–98.

41. See contents of the folder labeled "Cost Cutting Surveys" in box 35, folder 18, CD.

42. "Cost Cutting Surveys" in box 35, folder 18, CD. On the top-heavy management structure that emerged in the early 1980s, see Gray and Johnson, *TVA Regional Planning and Development Program*, 98–101.

43. Hargrove, *Prisoners of Myth*, 216. Ruttan's conclusion came in his introduction to the "Summer Study" report, a group of papers published after eleven academics and policy analysts came together in June 1979 to examine possible TVA regional development missions. See Hargrove, *Prisoners of Myth*, 210–17.

44. See Hargrove, *Prisoners of Myth*, 238.

45. Howard Baker took over as Senate Majority Leader in 1981 and, according to one periodical, "seemed determined to put his personal stamp on TVA." Baker tried to expand the board of directors to seven members, which failed, but he succeeded in getting Reagan to appoint Dean to the chairmanship. See "TVA's New Head Isn't Likely to Spark Big Change at Federally Run Utility," *Wall Street Journal*, 7 July 1981. Although Dean had different priorities than David Freeman and was more conservative in his vision for the agency, the fact that the two like-minded Freemans outnumbered Dean on the three-member board meant that the Freemans still exerted significant influence on some issues. See Hargrove, *Prisoners of Myth*, 242–43.

46. Richard M. Freeman, Testimony re: S. 970, 14 August 1979, box 19, folder 103(1) Board of Directors, DRFR, 6–7. Bob Clement, who had unsuccessfully run for the Democratic Party's Tennessee gubernatorial nomination in 1978, joined the board in fall 1979 and left when Dean was appointed. Like Dean, Clement consistently battled the two Freemans, especially on rate increases, and like Dean, he usually found himself outnumbered by them. See Hargrove, *Prisoners of Myth*, 228.

47. Richard M. Freeman, Testimony re: S. 970, 14 August 1979, box 19, folder 103(1) Board of Directors, DRFR, 6–7. Freeman also argued against the residency requirement, turning to familiar rhetoric to speak of TVA not merely as a regional institution but as "a national demonstration and an asset of the entire Nation" that needed a variety of geographical interests directing it.

48. See "Caution on TVA: This Isn't the Time for a Board Overhaul," *Memphis Commercial Appeal*, 11 October 1997. According to the paper's retrospective on past restructuring attempts, Baker "first favored, then cautioned against, then favored again a board expansion," making his real position hard to discern.

49. In the 1970s, technological developments like the computer chip made business practices quicker, more decentralized, and more efficient, and made rapid, nearly instantaneous exchanges of knowledge and information into a key aspect of daily life; see L. David Hoeveler, *The Postmodernist Turn: American Thought and Culture in the 1970s* (New York: Twayne Publishers, 1996). On the increasingly decentralized and deregulatory political and social climate of the 1980s, see especially Daniel T. Rodgers, *Age of Fracture* (Cambridge: Harvard University Press, 2011).

50. Presentation and background information, Tennessee Valley Industrial Committee, Meeting with Valley Congressional Delegation, 3 March 1982, 5, 7, box 11, folder Tennessee Valley Industrial Committee, RF. The committee self-identified as "a major contributor to the economy of the Tennessee Valley region" that employed approximately 45,000 Valley residents.

51. Memorandum from TVA Washington Office to John Stewart, 4 November 1983, box 19, folder 103(1) Board of Directors, RF.

52. Press release, Office of Ronnie G. Flippo, 4 November 1983, RF.

53. See "Caution on TVA: This Isn't the Time for a Board Overhaul." The idea of a board restructuring reemerged in 1997, spurring the Memphis paper to review past attempts.

54. "T.V.A., Once Model Agency, Now Swamped by Troubles," *New York Times*, 11 June 1986.

55. Memorandum from Jo Cooper to Senator Baker, 5 October 1981, box 12, folder 5, HBJ; clipping from *Knoxville News-Sentinel*, 11 October 1981, box 36, folder 6, CD. On TVA's original public-interest ideology, see David A. Colignon, *Power Plays: Critical Events in the Institutionalization of the Tennessee Valley Authority* (Albany: State University of New York Press, 1997), 88–94.

56. Memorandum from Jo Cooper to Senator Baker, 5 October 1981, box 12, folder 5, HBJ; clipping from *Knoxville News-Sentinel*, 11 October 1981, box 36, folder 6, CD.

57. Memorandum from Jo Cooper to Senator Baker, 5 October 1981, box 12, folder 5, HBJ; memorandum from Jo Cooper to Senator Baker, "Senator Sasser's Response to TVA's Plan for Providing Additional Compensation to Key Power Employees," 13 October 1981, box 12, folder 5, HBJ; "TVA Rescinds Plan for Big Salary Boosts," *Wall Street Journal*, 23 November 1983.

58. TVA to Senator Baker, "Retention of TVA Power System Management: Mitigating the Salary Crisis," 30 September 1981, box 12, folder 5, HBJ; clipping from *Knoxville News-Sentinel*, 11 October 1981, box 36, folder 6, CD.

59. Clipping from *Knoxville Journal*, 8 October 1981, box 36, folder 7, CD; clipping from *Kingsport Times*, 10 September 1981, box 36, folder 7, CD.

60. Clipping from *Bristol Herald Courier*, 13 October 1981, box 36, folder 7, CD.

61. See Hargrove, *Prisoners of Myth*, 235–36.

62. Memorandum from Wayne R. Gildroy to Herbert S. Sanger Jr., "General Accounting Office Requirements Regarding Agency Review of GAO Reports Prior to Their Release," 8 July 1982, box 15, folder 011E General Accounting Office, RF.

63. "General Accounting Office Requirements Regarding Agency Review of GAO Reports Prior to Their Release," 8 July 1982, box 15, folder 011E General Accounting Office, RF.

64. Clipping from *Memphis Commercial Appeal*, 16 October 1981, box 36, folder 6, CD; clipping from *Chattanooga Times*, 24 October 1981, box 1, folder 4, CD.

65. Clipping from *Chattanooga Times*, 24 October 1981 box 1, folder 4, CD; memorandum from Cooper to Baker, 13 October 1981, box 12, folder 5, HBJ; Excerpt from *Congressional Record—Senate*, 5 November 1981 (S. 12990), box 12, folder 5, HBJ; "TVA Rescinds Plan for Big Salary Boosts." Sasser won reelection in 1982 and again in 1988.

66. Howard M. Carver to Richard Freeman, 29 April 1980, box 3, folder CA-CF, RF.

67. Howard M. Carver to Richard Freeman, 27 October 1981, box 3, folder CA-CF, RF.

68. Howard M. Carver to Richard Freeman, 27 October 1981, box 3, folder CA-CF, RF.

69. Howard M. Carver to Richard Freeman, 27 October 1981, box 3, folder CA-CF, RF.

70. Richard M. Freeman to Howard M. Carver, 29 October 1981, box 3, folder CA-CF, RF.

71. See Stein, *Pivotal Decade*.

72. On the emergence of "market" in economics discourse, see Rodgers, *Age of Fracture*, 41–76. On the decentralization of ideas of "power," see 77–110.

73. See Hargrove, *Prisoners of Myth*, 276–79.

74. "TVA Execs Rewarded in Big Year—$11.5 Million in Bonus Offsets Salary Ceiling," *Memphis Commercial Appeal*, 31 December 2004.

75. In 2013, for example, Barack Obama floated the idea of privatizing TVA but drew quick condemnation from Tennessee Republicans.

CONCLUSION

1. *Public Papers of the Presidents of the United States: Ronald Reagan: 1982*, Book 1 (Washington: Government Printing Office, 1983), 544.

2. "Pomp and Festivity Prevail as Knoxville Opens World's Fair," *New York Times*, 2 May 1982.

3. See Patrick Alitt, *The Conservatives: Ideas and Personalities throughout American History* (New Haven: Yale University Press, 2009), 228–31.

4. Samuel P. Hays, *Beauty, Health, and Permanence: Environmental Politics in the United States, 1955–1985* (New York: Cambridge University Press, 1987), 491.

5. The story of the Tennessee-Tombigbee Waterway is in Jeffrey K. Stine, *Mixing the Waters: Environment, Politics, and the Building of the Tennessee-Tombigbee Waterway* (Akron: University of Akron Press, 1993).

6. Deborah Lynn Guber, *The Grassroots of a Green Revolution: Polling America on the Environment* (Cambridge: The MIT Press, 2003), 3.

7. On fracking and Keystone XL, see, for example, Daniel Yergin, *The Quest: Energy, Security, and the Remaking of the Modern World* (New York: Penguin, 2012), 259–63; 329–34. For a critical view of these initiatives, see, for example, Naomi Klein, *This Changes Everything: Capitalism vs. the Climate* (New York: Simon & Schuster, 2014).

INDEX

coal industry; oil; Tellico Dam project
environmentalism and environmental regulations: authority of FWS, 103, 104–5, 107, 113; coal industry impacted by, 43, 47, 126–27, 161n5, 162n7, 181n24; conflict with energy regulations, overview, 3–4, 9–10, 31; and initial opposition to Tellico Dam, 102–3 (*See also* ESA); under Nixon, 7, 13, 16; obscured in deregulatory politics, 23–24, 26, 37–38, 156n53, 160n89; and opposition to Clinch River breeder, 72–73, 86, 95; public opposition to, 38, 161n95; public support for, 10, 15–16, 153n17, 154n19; Reagan's ambiguous view of, 37–38, 147, 148, 156n53
EPA (Environmental Protection Agency), 7, 16, 27, 47, 126–27
ERDA (Energy Research and Development Association), 19, 20, 73
ESA (Endangered Species Act): amendments to, 10, 107–10, 112–13, 116; criticism of, 104–5, 107, 108–9, 114–17; passage of, 7, 16, 97; used against Tellico Dam project, 103–7, 110–12
Etnier, David, 103, 177n20, 178n54
European breeder development, 75, 76, 78, 79–80, 83, 86, 173n54
Evins, Joe, 100
Exxon, 28, 31

farmland dispossession, 102–3, 106, 110–11, 114
FEA (Federal Energy Agency), 12–13, 19, 20
Federal Mediation and Conciliation Service, 46
Federal Power Commission, 20
Flippo, Ronnie, 135–36, 143
Flowers, Walter, 78
Ford, Gerald, 4, 14–15, 22, 56, 58, 75, 154n18
foreign affairs: European breeder development, 75, 76, 78, 79–80, 83, 86, 173n54; impact on energy economy, 4, 12–13, 28, 32–33, 37
Forms, David, 53

Fraser, Douglas, 163n19
Freeman, Richard, 127, 129–30, 134, 137, 140–42, 183n47
Freeman, S. David: conservation initiatives, 129–31; defense of rising rates, 127, 128, 182n29, 182n39; demotion, 133; energy ideology, 123–25, 180n12; nomination as TVA chairman, 122–23; support for executive bonuses, 137
Frist, Bill, 144
Furness, Betty, 30
FWS (Fish and Wildlife Service), 103, 104–5, 107, 113

GAO (General Accounting Office), 83–85, 89, 90, 110, 131, 139–40
Garn, Jake, 108
GM (General Motors), 47–48
Goldwater, Barry M., Jr., 79
GOP. *See* Republican Party
Gore, Al, 70, 88
Gorton, Slade, 117
Greenbaum, Jill, 89
Gulf Oil Corporation, 50

Haas, Garland A., 5–6, 151n6
Hammontree, Cam, 106
Hargrove, Erwin, 133
Harmon, John, 50
Hays, Samuel, 147
Hembree, Perry W., 105
Hoopman, Harold D., 158n70
Hopper, Edward, 126
Horvitz, Wayne, 46, 52
Houvenagle, Heather L., 106
Huron, Doug, 54
hydroelectric power, 96–97. *See also* Tellico Dam project

ICC (Interstate Commerce Commission), 42, 58–62, 64–65, 168n65
Iranian hostage crisis, 32–33, 37, 159n73
Iranian Revolution, 27–28
Irwin, John, II, 11
Israel, conflict with Egypt, 4, 12, 13

Jackson, Henry, 30, 82
Jacobs, Meg, 8, 9, 38
Johnson, Lyndon B., 6, 30, 100
Jordan, Hamilton, 122

Kabaservice, Geoffrey, 155n35
Kahn, Alfred, 51–52, 158n66, 164n30, 180n9
Kaufman, Burton, 56, 165n43
Kemp, Jack, 22–23
Kennedy, Edward, 28–29, 30, 33, 157n58, 159n78
Keynesianism, 120
Khomeini, Ayatollah, 27, 28
Kissinger, Henry, 12, 18
Kristol, Irving, 146

labor unions. *See* UMWA
Laffer, Arthur, 146
Latham, George E., 128–29
Lawton, Mary, 50
Lewis, John L., 45
Lifset, Robert, 161n1
Lloyd, Marilyn, 78, 79, 80, 87, 91–92, 172n34
LMFBR (Liquid Metal Fast Breeder Reactor), 71, 73
L&N (Louisville & Nashville Railroad Company), 59, 60, 167n59
Long, Russell, 21, 44, 158n69
Los Angeles Times, 53, 55, 77, 78, 104, 110
Lunsford, Charles and Nell, 106–7
Luria, Salvador, 94

Manhattan Project, 83
Mann, Charles C., 178n45
Manning, S. Russell, 105–6
Marathon Oil Company, 158n70
market fundamentalism. *See* deregulatory politics
Markey, Edward, 30, 34
Marshall, Ray, 40, 48, 52, 55–56, 163n20
Matheson, Scott, 115
McAlister, Melani, 159n73
McCormick, Mike, 77, 79

Meany, George, 54, 57, 165n39
Mesa Petroleum, 35
Mexican fossil fuel supplies, 33, 159n77
Miller, Arnold, 45–46, 50, 51, 56, 57
Mondale, Walter, 82, 145
Montrie, Chad, 161–62n5
Moore, Roy, 106
Morton, Rogers C. B., 11
Moynihan, Daniel Patrick, 88
MSBR (Molten Salt Breeder Reactor), 71, 72

Nader, Ralph, 72–73, 170n11
National Energy Plan (1977), 31, 44
National Environmental Policy Act, 86, 103
Natural Resources Defense Council, 93
Nelson, Gaylord, 73
New Deal, 25, 98, 137
New York Times, 51, 77–78, 87, 89, 91, 109, 117
Nicholson, Shirley, 114
Nixon, Richard, 4, 7–8, 12–14, 16, 38, 71
non-union coal, 54, 62, 64–66, 169n76
Norcutt, David, 80
Novick, Sheldon, 73
NRC (Nuclear Regulatory Commission), 82, 87, 89–90, 170n11
nuclear arms race, 79–80
nuclear power, 69–70, 123, 180n12. *See also* Clinch River breeder
Nye, David, 153n1

Oak Ridge National Laboratory, 71, 80–81, 83. *See also* Clinch River breeder
OAPEC (the Organization of Arab Petroleum Exporting Countries), 4, 14, 151n2
Occupational Safety and Health Administration, 7, 27, 43
Ohio Edison Company, 47
oil: fear of depleting supply, 17–18, 28; increasing US demand for, 11–12; price controls, 4, 7–8, 16, 38 (*See also* price decontrol); spills, 3, 15–16
oil companies: and divestiture, 20; entrance in coal market, 65; profits during oil crises, 13, 14, 28; view of price decon-